INDIA INVENTED
A Nation-in-the Making

INDIA INVENTED
A Nation-in-the Making

Arvind N. Das

(Second Revised and Enlarged Edition)

MANOHAR
1994

ISBN 81-7304-081-8

First Published 1992
Second Revised and Enlarged Edition 1994

© Arvind N. Das

Published by
Ajay Kumar Jain
Manohar Publishers & Distributors
2/6 Ansari Road, Daryaganj
New Delhi - 110 002

Lasertypeset by
AJ Software Publishing Co. Pvt. Ltd.
305, Durga Chambers
1333, D.B. Gupta Road
New Delhi - 110 005

Printed at
Rajkamal Electric Press
B 35/9 G.T. Karnal Road
Delhi - 110 033

PREFACE

In today's context of techno-economic globalisation and politico-ethnic fragmentation, the very identity of India is becoming indistinct. Indeed, questions have been raised about whether such an identity is at all viable or even desirable.

The irony is that while earlier the concepts of nationalism were questioned by the Left which posited it against working class internationalism, today it is the ideological Right wing that is most vocal in dismissing ideas of nationhood and political-economic sovereignty. Indeed, in the last few years, the Rightists have suddenly discovered sub-national ethnicities as the social fragments most compatible with the ideological hegemony of the market. On the other side, it is the Left that, having suffered severe political blows, is trying to reconstitute ideas, concepts and modes of human existence "beyond the fragments".

In India's case, the picture is even more complex on account not only of the existence of the many pluralities—caste, class, ethnic, linguistic—that make up its identity but also because of its republican Constitution whose ideals have yet to be turned into realities even though its limitations are already apparent.

This book is situated at precisely such a crossroad of possibilities. It seeks to examine the concept of India with all its particularities (with their changing natures) as well as in terms of the general features that create the idea of the nation. Among the latter are civilisational heritage spanning various religions and cultures, different modes of socio-economic existence, varieties of technological stages, constitutional provisions, forces of economic nationalism and, most important of all, the struggle of its people for a sovereign, republican, democratic society. The task of conceptualising India within such a context is obviously too large for the scope of a single book. This publication therefore is in the nature of only an intervention in a wide-ranging debate. The effort will have been worthwhile if it succeeds even in defining some of the parameters of the discourse on India.

In writing this book, I have tried to combine the urgencies of journalism with the methodologies of research. It is for readers to judge how far the attempt has succeeded but for myself I have always felt that it is only when academics address the immediacies around them directly or metaphorically, that their work becomes useful. Similarly, worthwhile journalism may or may not be "literature in a hurry" but in any event it should not have the pretensions of "research at a breakneck speed."

I have drawn on the work of many scholars and benefited from discussions with other colleagues. I have been able to cite only a few of them in the *References*, but if I were to try to thank all of them by name, the acknowledgements would become far too long, longer perhaps than even the text. As such, I have no option but only to record sincere gratitude towards all those with whom I have worked and talked over the last decade and hope that they will accept my thanks when they come across a reflection of their ideas in the text.

I started some of the research which has gone into this book when I was working at the Centre for Social Studies, Surat. Long discussions there with Professor Ghanshaym Shah, Prof. Pradip Bose, Prof. Jaganath Pathy and the cooperation of the entire staff of the Centre became invaluable inputs. The work was carried on when I joined *The Times of India*. The editorial conferences there have provided a great deal of stimulation and I particularly appreciate the effort of Dr. Dileep Padgaonkar for the manner in which he has been admirably conducting often acrimonious debates. His own contributions to the on-going discussions have also been extremely valuable.

This book would never have been produced without the enormous work put in by Mr. Vinay Kumar Sharma, Mr. O.P.Bhasin and Ms. Rimmi Chadha. The cover has been creatively designed by Ms. Brinda Datta. I have no words to express my gratitude towards them.

Mr. Ramesh Jain has not only published the book in record time but is also responsible for its finalisation at all. Had it not been for his initiative in persuading me to limit explorations into various ideas into one book for the time being, my wanderings into areas far afield would have continued. My thanks are due to him for blowing the 'time out' whistle.

I have discussed this book (and much else, of course) with Dr. Manoshi Mitra and have benefited tremendously from her researches into socialist feminism and popular participation in development. Her contribution to this work is immense.

Exploring, discovering, imagining, inventing India, its past, present and future, have been meaningful for me because of the searching questions asked by my daughter Srijana. Some of the apprehensions reflected in this book are on account of her and her generation's future as Indians; much of the hope is also due to faith in her and her generation.

The book, therefore, is dedicated to Srijana and her generation, who will invent India in their own image. I hope it will be possible for them to do so in peace and in accordance with the values of republicanism and equity.

PREFACE TO THE SECOND EDITION

Events have moved fast since this book was first published. Much has changed in the world and even more has changed in India. The disintegration of world powers into nationalities and then into mutually destructive ethnicities is now a definite pattern. At the same time as politics has fragmented the world over, the economy is being globalised. In between, society is seeking the security of communities which are self-defined and seek to be self-regulating. The era of modernity seems to be ending but it is not clear whether it is pre-modernity or post-modernity that humanity is approaching.

In India, the Babri masjid has been destroyed and the securities scam has broken out. The first event represents a major break from India's carefully cultivated secularism which made it incumbent on the State to protect minorities. The second reveals the extent to which the authority of the State has been whittled down and its resources have been privately appropriated under the cover of liberalisation. Both reflect a serious transformation of the Indian State.

This transformation has also been dramatically illustrated by the resuits of the recent elections held in some north Indian states. While the electoral verdict has been variously interpreted, there are some aspects which stand out incontrovertibly. First, it is clear that the attempt by Hindu fundamentalists to seize power through the use of Ram as their electoral mascot has not succeeded. Even as the obsolescence of the "Congress system" of politics, which has prevailed for a long time, is apparent, religion-based sectarianism has not been favoured by the electorate as the alternative. Indeed, even the election results indicate that the attempted homogenisation of the so-called majority community, defined on the basis of religion, has failed on account of the deeper caste- and class-based divisions that exist in Indian society. Thus, caste as the denominator of electoral politics has proved much more powerful than communal calculations.

However, it is also clear that while the subaltern sections have asserted themselves through the discriminating exercise of their franchise, presence on the political stage has been established only for the segments which are upwardly mobile. The upper caste monopoly over power has been broken but there has been no qualitative change in those who wield power. Only a quantitative accretion has occurred in the ranks of the power-brokers. The so-called "backwards" or, to be more precise, the upper segments of the backwards castes — some of which are already among the *noveau riche* classes, agrarian and otherwise—have already been prominent in politics and public affairs in south India. They have now firmly established their presence even in north India and they have been joined also by the upwardly mobile elements of the Dalits who have benefited to an extent from the State policies of job reservations, etc. over half a century. This political phenomenon, however, does not indicate that fundamental changes have taken place in the social hierarchy which obtains and neither exploitation and oppression nor patronage and clientilism have by any means, been ended.

Meanwhile, an important aspect of the recent elections is the determination shown by the minority religious community in protecting the constitutional order through tactical voting. Despite the prevarication by the government in implementing the statutory obligations of the State, the minorities—and the poor and oppressed—have once again affirmed their belief that India can survive only as a secular, pluralistic polity. This assertion represents a stage in the evolution of India in which elements of civil society seem to have overtaken the State as the principal motor of change. It also creates not only a lag but even a situation of potential conflict between the two.

The State is not only at odds with civil society but is in many respects also being overtaken by it. There is a hollow ring to the proclamations the State makes regarding its promises to civil society which are enshrined in the Constitution itself. Consequently, perhaps, social formations—class, caste, communities, ethnicity, linguistic identities—and even anti-social phenomena such as communalism are becoming more important than political citizenship. At the same time, the transnationalisation—globalisation of the economy in the guise of external liberalisation puts enormous strains on social structures.

In these circumstances, the existence of the nation itself is threatened: it faces the twin dangers of endless fragmentation leading to an uncontrollable implosion as well as an outward explosion induced principally by exogenous factors.

The second edition of the book comes in this context. The importance of understanding what constitutes India cannot be overstressed and yet it is not possible to demarcate India in terms of clear, unambiguous, cut-and-dry criteria. It is not even possible to examine comprehensively the bewildering welter of all the facts, or, for that matter, even all the self-evident ones, regarding India in a book which is less than encyclopaedic in scope. Therefore, what has been attempted is a mere imagining of India, as clearly as possible in the light of broad socio-economic processes and general politico-cultural objectives, discerning the wood without losing count of the trees. Thus, additional information and analysis have been added on the experiences of the on-going changes in economic policies as well as on the intensified attempt to communalise India particularly after the destruction of the Babri masjid, but the focus has been kept on imagining India as it is now and as it should be in the future.

CONTENTS

CONTENTS

INTRODUCTION

'ETHNICITY': A LOOK INTO THE INDIAN KALEIDOSCOPE

The cliche about India representing "unity in diversity" has become so well-worn that it has ceased to have any particular meaning. And yet it is not mere truism that India is constituted of bewildering and kaleidoscopic patterns of peoples with different and dynamic identities. They constitute a social and political pluralism which is difficult to describe and almost impossible to define.

A commonsense conclusion about such cultural heterogeneity contained within a 'soft' political system (Myrdal 1968) would be that it just could not last: the fissiparous tendencies, the centrifugal forces, the mutual conflicts among people must rend the society apart and break the country's unity. This conclusion was supported by historical experience which seemed to demonstrate repeatedly that India was only a geographical entity rather than a cultural, social or political unit. Even in very recent times, the traumatic experience of Partition of India on religious grounds in 1947 seemed to substantiate prognostications of political fission.

The commonsense conclusion appears to have been proved wrong at least up to now for that residual political entity which emerged as India after the break-up of 1947. The country has stayed on as a unit in spite of the various levels of social conflict that exist within it. Indeed, the political processes in post-Partition India appeared to be moving towards unification, consolidation, centralisation and homogenisation rather than towards further fragmentation. A balance of forces seemed to have been arrived at and a political system evolved to suit the needs of keeping a pluralist social conglomeration together. Even after great strains and stresses, the system seemed to work.

Nevertheless, the myriads of social conflicts too continue to exist. While economics and politics, by and large, have been geared towards keeping India one, their impact is not only inadequate in terms of solving social and cultural conflicts but in fact tends to exacerbate some of them. The balance was, and is, extremely precarious and a great deal of political acrobatics has been going on merely to maintain the status quo.

There are so many forces pulling and pushing the country and the people in different directions that it is well-nigh impossible to present in any work which is not encyclopaedic in scope a comprehensive or even adequate picture of the social, economic, political and cultural complexity of India. In the following pages we shall therefore, restrict ourselves merely to a part of one significant aspect of the current Indian scene that is related to articulation of its various ethnicities.

At the very outset it is useful to start with the most general observation that in India, *no two Indians are equal.* The stratification of society is so deep that it virtually negates any concept of social egalitarianism. Class, religion, caste, sex and age are only some of the coordinates of the multidimensional social grid on which every individual in India is differentially placed and so many are the variables of hierarchy that no two individuals can be considered to be equal. *Homo hierarchicus* (Dumont 1970) thrives in India. Differentiation of individuals is so intense that although individuals do coalesce in social groups, the groupings themselves are so extremely fragmented, segmented and stratified that the very concepts of 'majority' and 'minority' appear to be illusory. Indeed in parts of Bihar, where social conflicts of various sorts are particularly acute, this phenomenon finds apt illustration in the very linguistic usage: the English word majority has been integrated into different languages and dialects but its usage (pronounced as *maejrity*) does not denote a number more than half of the total but simply group or set (e.g. *sab dakaiton ne apna apna maejrity bana liya hai*: Every dacoit has formed his own group)!

The concept of the 'majority' is obscured in so many other ways too so that it signifies neither numerical superiority nor necessarily social dominance. For instance, the very structure of the political parliamentary democratic system is so designed that the party in power — with even an overwhelming number of seats in the legislature — can get to its position on much less than 50 per cent of the popular vote (even if those who do not, or cannot, vote are ignored in such a calculation). Outside the electoral political sphere too, social power exercised by groups of people — religious, caste-based, economic, etc. — is quite disproportionate to their numbers. And, even if numbers are not taken to be significant, there is considerable dissonance among other factors too so that, for instance, social power exercised on account of position in the religious and caste hierarchies may not be related to economic standing. Any majority–minority classification, therefore, on the basis of a single factor is simplistic and even one on the basis of more than one factor can be quite misleading. In such a situation, definition and identification of 'majority groups' and their counterpart 'minorities' are necessarily, at best, only approximate.

To limit our coverage however, we will refer to some well-known 'minorities', using the term with full appreciation of its inadequacy and even inaccuracy. Further, even among the minorities our reference will be to only some features of what, for lack of a better term, are called 'ethnic minorities', clarifying at this stage itself that ethnic in this context does not, and indeed, given the great historical admixture in India, cannot have any racial connections whatsoever but is used as a description of socio-cultural specificities. Even the cultural content of 'ethnicity' is, in many Indian situations, not exclusive and distinct and, particularly in discussions of caste-based and religious minorities, references to 'ethnicity' are specially inaccurate and unscientific.

Having a *priori* entered this caveat, we must also make it clear that, given the various constraints of the present exercise, we are concerning ourselves with only a fragment of the complexity of the Indian situation and our principal focus in the following pages will be, again using the term as a literal short- hand, on aspects of the 'tribal' situation, the 'caste-class' conundrum and specific contextual references to the federal structure in the light of linguistic and religious/communal questions.

Before coming to the discussion of the specific Indian context, it is also necessary however to note the aspects of the changing situation in the world where 'ethnicity' is increasingly becoming an important determinant of politics. Now, this would be perfectly explicable if 'ethnicity' itself were a defined social concept. However, not only has 'ethnicity' itself changed over time but indeed the social meaning it acquires in different places, even in the same time frame, is also different.

We refer to the range of meanings of 'ethnicity'. From standing for conceptualising a racially-defined social group measurable through anthropometric tools, 'ethnicity' has progressed to a catch-word to describe almost any type of social grouping. The progress from specificity to generality, even vagueness, has both watered down the concept and also given it immense power.

The power of vaguely characterised 'ethnicity' has been demon-strated in recent years all over the world, and most dramatically in eastern Europe, particularly Yugoslavia, and the Soviet Union. As an ideological-political counter-point to the concept of class, 'ethnicity' has emerged as the focus of the destruction of economic systems, of social structures and of political formations. It has also simulta-neously served as a platform on which popular groupings of different sorts have articulated their sentiments. These sentiments have generally gone against other major "umbrella" ideas like "national-ism", "internationalism" and "class organisation". They have also generally focused on the local, the particular, the specific. In one sense, the expression of such sentiments through the medium of 'ethnicity' has taken away from the grandness of grand social theory, with both civil society and state having been insidiously attacked.

At the same time, it is difficult to conclude that 'ethnicity' has always been a 'liberating' idea. Undoubtedly in some situations it has been posited against stultifying statism and other types of oppres-sions and ideological hegemonisms. To the extent that it has brought politics down from rarefied Hegelian heights to the "grass-roots", it has helped to de-mystify processes of how people organise themselves. However, not only in many cases has the grass of 'ethnicity' been demonstrated to be without roots, but also, being an undefined concept, 'ethnicity' has also had a visceral gut-quality, based on raw emotion rather than deliberate cogitation. As such, it has turned in many instances into another oppressive form of social organisation with almost an animal-level quality of immediacy. Only time will tell if this is what *homo sapiens* are all about.

In any event, in the very first instance, 'ethnicity' has been posited against 'class' on the one side and 'nation' on the other. The conceptual cobwebs surrounding these two have helped in the apparent clarity (on account of immediacy) of 'ethnicity' confronting these terms. In the following pages, we shall examine the elements of this confrontation between 'class' and 'nation' and 'ethnicity' in the Indian context. For, it is the outcome of this confrontation that will determine not only India of the future but also the rest of humanity.

INDIA INVENTED, DISINVENTED AND RE-INVENTED

The disintegration of the Soviet Union offers a sobering warning to Indians. After all, that empire was cobbled by centuries of absolutist czardom and was held together for seventy years by the ideals of socialism as well as the power of an overarching State. By contrast, India exists on the basis of a soft State, a weak ideal and fragile institutions. Hence, the dangers to its unity are far greater.

At present, there are two alternative modes of defining India. One is based on a Constitution carefully crafted by an elite which adopted the premises of modernity. The other, which is no less elitist and fortunately up to now not predominant, is supposedly based on the 'primordialism' of *hindutva*. The first has the brittleness of a devised structure; the second has the degenerative character of organic matter. In fact the second is not even totally organic; it too has a synthetic nature such as that of artificial compounds which chemists created in their laboratories.

The first, modernistic view is limited by the idealistic but false Nehruvian assumptions of the existence in India of a 'composite culture'. This well-intentioned myth was propagated by Jawaharlal Nehru through his *Discovery of India*. It has been perpetuated by naive part-time historians who see the symbol of Ustad Bismillah Khan playing the *shehnai* in the Vishwanath temple at Varanasi and close their eyes to the substance of the notice outside the same temple barring entry to "untouchables and *malechhas*". In their undoubtedly laudable attempt to create a wholesome concept of India, many left- nationalist historians too have made the mistake of taking Jawaharlal Nehru's historigraphical exercise as indeed a discovery of the past when it was in fact an invention for the future.

Both Nehru and, much more clearly, B.R. Ambedkar realised that India did not exist as a nation; what they were promoting was a vision of nation-in-the-making, a new formation shaped by republican ideals and cast in the mould of a modernistic Constitution. Ambedkar was explicit on this issue. "In believing that we are a nation, we are chasing a great delusion. We can only attempt to become a nation-in-the-making", he wrote on the eve of drafting the Constitution.

On the other side of the ideological divide, the primordialists who were, and are, opposed to modernist ideals, were much more certain about their conceptualisation of India as an exclusivist Hindu nation. In their view, the monolithic unity was represented, as Golwalkar wrote in 1947, by "one culture, one language, one nation — Hindu, Hindi, Hindustan." He was elaborating the idea put forward by the most articulate theorist of Hindu exclusivism, Savarkar, who held in his *Hindu Rashtra Darshan*, published as late as 1949, that Muslims constituted a separate nation and hence he gladly accepted the partition of India. It is not wrong to see Savarkar and Golwalkar as the flip-side of Jinnah.

Serious history however finds it difficult to accept either the starry-eyed concept of latter-day Nehruvians of an idyllic composite culture or the steely-eyed bigotry of the advocates of *hindutva* whose theory is premised on a perennial conflict between mutually antagonistic religious communities.

Separate communities did exist in India and they met only occasionally. The very absence of civil society, as Dirk Kolff (1990) has shown, allowed at best for a back-to-back existence of communities. There was some intermingling of cultures, and music, art, food and several other elements of life did evolve with a degree of compositeness. The most interesting aspect of this, however, lies in the incorporation of the caste system among Muslims, pointing to the essentially fragmented nature of Hindu society itself rather than inter-community compositeness. Even in medieval times Manu and Mandal were more important than mandirs and masjids.

The redeeming feature was the existence of what has been called "fuzzy communities", indistinct groupings with neither internal cohesion nor well-known externalities, and, as such, the presence of communities without overt communalism. If a group did not know how far it extended and what was its strength in numbers, it was not likely to have an acute and aggressive self-awareness.

Colonialism changed that blissful state of social ignorance. Enumeration and categorisation for reasons of State had a deep social impact. The superintendent of the 1921 Census, Middleton had said, "We pigeonholed everyone by caste and community. We deplore its effect on social and economic problems but we are largely responsible for the system we deplore. Government's passion for labels and pigeonholes has led to crystallisation and fragmentation."

The moving finger of the census-taker wrote and, having writ, moved on. But the subaltern colonised mind, subject to the hegemony of the numerate, accepted the divisions as real and material. Once numbers had been counted and the tally was taken as the truth, it became a political tool. Hindus were told that they constituted a majority and an effort was made to persuade them to act as a uniform community regardless of sect, caste or even class affiliations.

Today's *hindutva* has its ancestry in that synthetic creation of organic entity. And now, within the context of democratic politics, it seeks to turn numerical majority into political majoritarianism, thereby subverting democracy itself. While democracy is based on the majority-minority dichotomy, it is also given strength by the existence of pluralisms which make for a kaleidoscopic shifting of those patterns. A person may think in one context that he belongs to a majority community but he may also be part of a minority in terms of caste, region, language or political persuasion. It is this which moderates majority rule within democracy.

The danger of *hindutva* as the defining principle of Indian nationhood is that it seeks to create and perpetuate a permanent majority, one based on an artificial and homogenised Hinduism. The destruction by the Vishwa Hindu Parishad of the many small temples of the Little Tradition, including shrines dedicated to the monkey-god Bajrangbali, before the destruction of the Babri Masjid itself, in order to build the grand designer temple of Ram diminishes the rich variety of Hinduism itself. It encroaches upon sacred space, disregards sacred time as the Shankaracharya of Dwarakapeeth has asserted, disrupts sacred tradition and destroys, through calendar art, sacred iconography of even the *maryada purshottam saumya* (tranquil) Ram by imposing an invented *raudra* (warrior) Ram.

The juggernaut of such a *hindutva* tries to steam-roller over not only religious minorities but even pluralities within Hinduism. That is why it is scared of the assertion of caste identities through the implementation of the recommendations of the Mandal Commission.

On the other side, the modernists too try to fashion an India on the basis of wishful thinking, a centralising, homogenising, westernised State shaping society. Even that is a half-hearted attempt. Tired proponents of the Nehruvian notion of the State determining the nation, now speak not of the nation-State but of a civilisation-State, a concept which evokes shades of *hindutva*.

Both are fundamentally flawed because they are not premised on a realistic appreciation of the nature of either society or the State. While society is essentially characterised by particularities, specificities, diversities and pluralities, the State today has effectively declared itself as bankrupt. A nation cannot be forged by either those who limit themselves by eager religious ghettoisation of their minds or by mere pragmatists who cut the coat of national pride and policies according to the cloth grudgingly supplied by international bankers.

India has to be invented. But the invention has to be, first and foremost, of an ideal for Indians. The ideal can only be equity, participation, plurality. Otherwise, static instruments with gravitational disequilibrium will crumble and organic unities which do not account for living particularities will putrefy.

India was invented by its Constitution-makers to conform to an ideal of democracy, social change and equity. The ideal has got subverted by "status quo-ism", over-centralisation and sectarianism. The votaries of homogenised *hindutva* are eroding the idealism on the one side. On the other, weak-kneed pragmatists, bending with the prevailing economic wind, are undermining national autonomy and hence the very concept of nationhood. This is a dangerous situation. For, if the ideals around which India has been fashioned are destroyed, India cannot survive.

II

The current controversy on intellectual property rights has highlighted that patents on inventions have a limited validity. They expire after a specified period and the invention becomes free to be used or abused by anyone inclined to do so. Something like this seems to be happening to the very concept of India invented by people like Jawaharlal Nehru and B.R. Ambedkar.

The constitutional scheme putting India together on the basis of a modernist interpretation of a pluralist past is being subverted by various forces. The most obvious of course are those who posit a primordial majoritarianism premised on organic *hindutva* but there are others too who are simplifying, vulgarising and fragmenting India. Among those who are contributing to this process of the disintegration of the concept of India, and therefore of the nation itself, are paradoxically those who claim to stand for unification at the grandest level — for globalisation itself.

It is necessary therefore to debunk a few myths about globalisation. In the first place, it is important to note that although the term has gained currency in recent times, it is by no means a new concept. From times immemorial, humanists and universalists articulated the essential unity of the species homo sapien. In India itself, the sentiment was voiced through the noble concept of *vasudhaiva kutumbakam* (the world itself is one family).

The problem arose because universalist humanism was fragmented over time and *homo hierarchicus* prevailed over *homo sapiens*. While social differentiation, stratification, exploitation and oppression are the realities of everyday existence, globalism can only be an elusive ideal. In the meanwhile, what are real and palpable are castes, classes, groups, nationalities, ethnicities and, at best, "imagined communities."

In this context, two complementary and yet contradictory social processes arose to put body into the concept of globalism once again. One developed as a response to the ever-widening circles of production of goods and services on account of the extension of capitalism. The other, its part and counterpart, was the integration of the producers and consumers of those goods and services. The first and most significant analysis of the global integration brought about by capitalism is in the work of the now unfashionable Karl Marx, just as the first major political statement on globalisation at a popular level is in his affirmation, premised on class analysis, that workers have no nation.

Today's globalisers however do not exhibit a similar integrity of analysis by refusing to acknowledge that globalisation is a process encompassing both the inanimate — produced goods — and the animate — people. Thus, while they promote the globalisation of production, they have little to say on the differentiation in consumption and even less on the fragmentation of the ordinary people. They swear by the market but their market consists of discrete segments.

It is important to note the consequences of such a partial ideology of the market for the concept of India. Simple-minded liberalisers do not tire of talking of the integration of India through the hawking of brands over the length and breadth of its politically determined expanse. Their idea of India is summed up in the market reach of particular soaps and tooth powders. The more sophisticated among them talk of the unity brought about not only by the fetishism of commodities but also by the interpenetration of credit and labour, pointing to the enormous money market and labour migration.

But the rub in defining a socio-political identity, in this case the concept of "Indian-ness", through the use of market categories lies precisely in the double-edged nature of those categories. The very extent of the market segments of brands reveals its limits. First, no brand— not even the secular Constitution—has a universal reach and acceptance, as the actions of the purveyors of the alternative "Ram brand" and "Bajrangbali sub-brand" testify. Secondly, even in terms of the buying and selling of tangible goods, no less than 30 per cent of the Indian population, nearly 300 million people, are cut off from the market by the "Lakshman *rekha*" of the poverty line. Thirdly, although the burgeoning size of commodity-buyers, as brought out by the oft-quoted NCAER survey, has been seized upon by those who argue about the integration of India by the market, they ignore other significant data. They fail to note that an extremely large proportion of items in the consumption basket of even those with household monthly incomes of Rs. 2,000 and above, comprising around 300 million individuals, is of goods produced fairly near their places of residence.

In other words, while the size of the Indian market — and hence its integrative potential — is undoubtedly large, it consists neither of one homogeneous whole nor even of a series of concentric circles but of an intricate pattern of small circles overlapping one another. Such a variegated economy cannot by itself support broad national unity.

Even the modification of the concept of the market by adding credit and labour, in addition to commodities, as its constituents does not provide the basis for assuming that such a market protects and promotes the concept of India. Even a cursory glance at the variety in the credit market — ranging from the 25 per cent per week "Madrasi *sood*" (interest) charged from hapless tribals in Chhatisgarh to the regulated institutional interest rate regimes applicable to the modern sector — shows that money itself has many meanings in India. And even s Margaret Thatcher discovered that sovereignty premised on the coin of the realm in a context of supra-national monetary unification is counterfeit currency. When the index of exchange is illegal *hawala*, the money market respects no national boundaries.

The idea of the labour market bringing about unity is even more unreal. It is true that millions of people travel long distances to search for livelihood and even the Shiv Sena has not been successful in its parochial segmentation of India. However, unlike the commodity market, the labour market is live and creates a logic of its own.

The predominant logic of the labour market today is one of emigration rather than of operation within the national economy. Brawn drain through manpower export is the flip-side of brain drain. And, when eyes are firmly fixed westwards, as one metaphorically stands on the beaches of Bombay searching for ships to take one away, the back is turned on the nation, the imagined community. It should be instructive for those who pin India's hopes on the remittance economy and NRIs to note that no nation in history has been sustained by those whose greatest desire is to get away from it, by those for whom the grass is immeasurably greener on the other side of the green card. If that were not so, the waves of emigrants from Poland and Greece, Yugoslavia and Sicily who left for the New World would have made their native countries immensely prosperous even as they and others ravaged the natives of another continent.

If however, neither the market nor organic, divisive primordialism make the nation, what is there to prevent the disintegration of India?

India is both an idea and a reality. The reality is being fragmented in the name of religious exclusiveness. The idea is being
dismembered by those hard-headed pragmatists who have no use for
civilisations and ideologies.

The pragmatists are of two sorts : those who base their actions
on mere calculations of the day's profit and loss, and others who
premise the definition of their self-identity only on the actions of the
rulers of the day. The first lot have no concern with either society
or State; the second swear by the State but restrict themselves to
merely echoing the government.

Under these circumstances, in an unequal world where
"globalisation" is only an euphemism for subordination by and
integration into one dominant system, it is time to worry about
India. Globalisation, if it is to be meaningful, has to be based on
equity : exploitation and partnership do not go together. In the
meanwhile, the fragmentation of a carefully constructed concept of
India can only lead to primordialist barbarism. Between the Scylla of
subjugation and the Charybdis of disintegration, the idea of India
has to steer a careful course. The waters are turbulent and ideological lifebuoys have been removed.

III

Forty-four years ago, at the stroke of a midnight hour, when the
world was asleep, India woke up to light and freedom. It was a poor
country bled by two centuries of colonialism. It was a civilisation
vivisected by the narrow-mindedness of its politicians. But it was a
people full of hope in the heart : freedom mattered, national pride
was not a dispensable intangible and political and economic sovereignty was worth the struggle and sacrifices.

Barely had the generation of that midnight's children reached
middle-age that the country once again stood on a point of historical
departure with its economy tottering on the brink of the chasm of the
debt-trap and consequent loss of political-economic sovereignty.

The sad part was that the severity of the crisis confronting the
country was not even apparent to a majority of its population. Far
worse, many politicians, who had no excuse of being deprived of
information, acted not only as if it was business as usual but indeed

even as if it was the best situation in the best of all possible worlds. The sheer irresponsibility reflected in the postponement of the budget in February 1991 exhibited a political casualness which in fact arose out of the elite's total lack of concern about India's economic sovereignty.

The country was standing on the edge of bankruptcy. At the end of 1990, India had reached a situation where it almost defaulted on its international economic obligations. It had never defaulted earlier. Undoubtedly, India had borrowed and incurred huge debts but it had always been able to service those debts in time. In December 1990 however, India's foreign exchange reserves dipped so low that there was every likelihood of its joining the ranks of the many Latin American and Afro-Asian countries which have not been able to service their debts.

India was able to just scrape past that ignominious condition because, almost fortuitously, it received a cash compensatory facility (CCF) of US$1.8 billion from the International Monetary Fund (IMF). With this manna from the monetary heaven, India was able to ward off its creditors who were howling at the door of its economic sovereignty and national self-respect. By February 1991 the kitty was again almost empty and the bill-collectors had not stopped knocking.

The managers of India's economic affairs had thought that they would be able to ward off doom once more by obtaining an "upper tranche", a substantial loan from the IMF and use the breathing time thus gained to put the domestic economic house in order. However, the IMF would lend only if there were evidence that Indian policy-makers were serious about making the necessary fiscal adjustments and, more important, structural changes that would prevent it from sliding down the debt-trap. Although the CCF was not accompanied by the spelling out of conditionalities, there was obviously a "gentleman's agreement" that policy steps would be taken through the annual budget. That would have provided a face-saver not only for India but also for the IMF which does not enjoy its Shylock image. The well-laid plans of mice and men however were rendered awry by the most self-serving, short-sighted and partisan considerations which prevented the budget from being presented. The result was that ruin once again stared India in the face.

While imports and debt-servicing consumed the CCF funds, the cumulative current account deficits built up an external debt of more than $ 70 billion and repayments that exceeded 30 per cent of export earnings. Exports could not be pushed up to get out of this jam. In the meanwhile, the government of India continued to carry on its business through further borrowings and through inflation, in other words through borrowing from the future.

While hoarding, profiteering and the Bush fire in West Asia all contributed to inflation and the overall economic down-turn, the most important contributor was the inability of the government to check its own current spending on preening itself, on defence and on subsidising its political and electoral clients. Regardless of the prescriptions of the IMF, India could not possibly have sustained such extravagance for long. In early 1990, before India was subjected to fiscal disciplining by the IMF, a "hard budget" was talked of. However, it was the very "hardness" that scared those who fashion policy and the budgetary horse was put out to grass.

Since India was unable to demonstrate that it was prepared autonomously to take hard decisions, it inevitably slipped into the clutches of the IMF. In April-May 1990, the foreign exchange reserves sank to the bottom of the barrel. And yet, debts had to be serviced and imports had to be made if only to pander to the needs of the economic class that the political elite represents. The managers of the country's finances had to shuffle their feet and try to borrow more to service current debts. In the economic sphere, India almost became Brazil. Or Argentina. Or Peru. Because, in the meantime, it sold off virtually all holdings of long-term foreign securities which help to provide cover to the Indian currency.

But did Indians even notice the change? The loss of economic sovereignty was not as dramatic and cathartic as that midnight hour when India had gained political independence. Life continued. For the one-third of Indians who subsist on the margin between life and death, no change could occur. For the other one-third too, those who are located at the far end of the economic spectrum where all is light and colour, the elite life-style was hardly affected : nothing, not even the national down-slide into the debt-spiral, had affected the Latin American elite and the same could be the case in India.

What was affected is the ability to look the world in the eye and also the competence to take domestic decisions autonomously, a denouement which goes against the current of the freedom movement and post-Independence economic reconstruction. It in turn affected the very concept of economic nationalism. For, there is no half-way house between sovereignty and subjugation. The pipe-dreams of the "liberalisers" that by selling a part of India's real estate or by exporting manpower or by enticing oil-rich sheikhs to invest or, for that matter, dining with the devil, Indian leaders will be able to buy back freedom have no basis in actuality. Neither are investors so flush with funds nor are they likely to choose India as the country on which to shower their largesse. It speaks of the lack of national self-confidence, pathetic in the case of India with its immense economic, political and cultural reserves, that the elite should be able to outline for it only the alternative of a supine Bangkokisation through turning India into one more "rest and recreation" basket case for the affluent philistines of the world.

The way out for India was to wake up before it got too late, retrace the steps that had been taken towards the precipice in a fit of political somnambulance and rebuild the country, painfully if necessary, in the light of the vision that Nehru so stirringly outlined that night in August 1947. Instead, in the middle of the most severe balance of payments crisis which ever confronted the country, the political class of India plunged it into mid-term elections which protracted the administrative uncertainty and deepened the economic agony.

What followed was that India was led by its leaders straight into a debt trap which was disguised under the catchy slogans of "globalisation" and "liberalisation". Clever attempts were made to rationalise the loss of economic and even political sovereignty and a large section of the country's westward-looking elite welcomed the measures. However, they had a significant impact on the very notion of economic nationhood and the ingenious logic of the liberalisers could not disguise the fact for long. Disingenuous accounting and politicking were not sufficient.

A few years ago, when social banking and differential rates of interest were not yet dirty words, some tribals in Srikakulam district of Andhra Pradesh were given cattle under various credit schemes aimed at alleviating poverty. The tribals had no land and as such could not use the animals for draught power. However they had other uses for the cattle. They slaughtered them and ate them up.

This simple supplementation of the tribals' food entitlement should have ended that short-lived exercise in spreading the 'safety net' but for the problem that it caused to the bankers' double-entry accounting system. The matter ultimately reached the deputy governor of the Reserve Bank of India in charge of the rural credit department. That worthy visited Srikakulam to grapple with the accounting problem. It was finally solved when the bankers accepted the advice of a young, unorthodox civil administrator.

The solution was as simple as the tribals' act of temporarily assuaging their hunger. "Why don't you," he suggested, "redesignate the production loan into a consumption loan, treat it as short-term borrowing instead of long-term credit and charge the rate of interest accordingly?"

The moral of the story is that when popular wisdom is substituted by accounting needs, reality is lost in the intricacies of double-entry bookkeeping. When political economy is abbreviated to mere economics, the situation becomes catastrophic.

That is what happened in India in the middle of 1991. The essence of the various measures announced by the minority government to meet the economic crisis revolved round an overwhelming concern to avoid defaulting on repayments due on the ill-considered short-term borrowing indulged in during the preceding years. And the policy-makers' attention was focused on borrowing more from the International Monetary Fund, World Bank and whoever else could lend to repay those short-term debts. In other words, the thrust of the government's economic activism was to replace short-term loans with medium-term loans. The books had to be balanced even if the entries were still made with the reddest of the red inks!

After all, the IMF and World Bank merely advance credit which needs to be repaid. The government's continuing endeavours are aimed therefore at persuading them to let the country increase and restructure its debt burden. Even in that respect, the policy-makers are not content to restrict themselves to merely demanding the amount that is due to India as a member of the IMF but, like Oliver Twist, they are forever asking for more. Quite naturally the IMF is acting like Fagin.

The government's policy aims to alter the trend of the last few years. From the middle of the 1980s there has been a massive increase in India's borrowings from private creditors. The World Bank's *World Debt Tables* 1990-91 show that whereas India's out-standing debt to private creditors in 1970 was only $330 million, it registered a dramatic increase to $8,944 million in 1985 and went up by leaps and bounds thereafter to the staggering sum of $21,405 million in 1989. Against this, while loans from official creditors, including multilateral agencies and other countries, also went up from $7,507 million in 1970 to $31,427 million in 1985 and $54,776 million in 1989, the increase was less precipitate.

However, figures for short-term loans, those for less than a year, are even more alarming. From $926 million in 1980, they spurted to $3,129 million in 1985 and $4,689 million in 1989. Quite obviously, somewhere along the way, the policy of hand-to-mouth existence was adopted. When the moneylenders began knocking on India's door, the country was hard put to pay for its profligacy.

The term profligacy to describe such hand-to-mouth existence is advisedly used. In the same period in which India's short-term liabilities mounted, with net flows on such debts going up from $273 million in 1985 to $917 million in 1989, the import of goods and services rocketed from $21,518 million in 1985 to $32,229 million in 1989. Exports went up more modestly from $15,538 million in 1985 to $24,191 million in 1989 while gross national product (GNP) crept up from $212,969 million in 1985 to $262,089 million in 1989 when it even registered a small decline from $267,208 million in the previous year.

It is legitimate to ask what these enormous short-term and long-term loans were meant for. Quite obviously, their utilisation for productive purpose was limited, to put it mildly. While total external debt liability as a proportion of the GNP shot up from 11.9 per cent in 1980 to 19.2 per cent in 1985 and 23.9 per cent in 1989, it did not have an invigorating impact on the GNP itself. It is not unfair to conclude therefore that while those who ran the country during that period made India live well beyond its means, they also strained the national ways and means position to indulge an unpro-ductive class.

Now, it is important to realise precisely what is being attempted through the "new economic policy", what is being hoped for and what is being achieved.

As India haltingly raises money from foreign banks, in trickles of hundred million dollars against gold, and as it is promised instalments of $200 million by the IMF for proven good behaviour, the emphasis is still on borrowing more and more.

This is not surprising. The *World Debt Tables* make it amply clear that during the last decade while net flows from debts rose and even grants trickled in, net direct foreign investments were a puny six million dollars in 1970 and *zero* in *all* the subsequent years. So much for the opening up of India to foreign capital.

The great hope today is that foreign investment will pour into India as soon as the walls of protectionism are demolished with the crowbars of liberalisation. That hope may however turn out to be unreal. Even the physical demolition of the Berlin Wall and indeed the integration of the eastern part of Germany into one national market has not opened the cornucopia of capital. Mr Gorbachov's glasnost fetched him more homilies and humiliation than hard cash. Even Non-Resident Indians (NRIs) have moderated their patriotic fervour with prudence by largely lending their mother country only hot money through short-term deposits rather than putting their money where their mouth is and taking on portfolio investments offered to them.

Neither does the regime, ostensibly carrying out structural reforms, give evidence of attempting to pull the country's economy up by its own bootstraps. After money is borrowed from Peter to pay Paul, there is need not only to repay Peter in a few years but also to avoid repeating the mistake of using borrowed money for the high living, plain thinking style perfected over the last decade. If without additional surplus mobilisation, there is only the offer of public properties to private purchasers, either there will be no buyers for the public sector or private sector investment will fall. The ideology of privatisation is no substitute for actual investment.

At the same time, while much has been said of the need to discipline labour and even a wage freeze has been mooted, there is no corresponding national appeal to capital to endure a dividend freeze. Instead of de-mystifying gold and using it as a means of raising investible capital, surreptitious and shame-faced pledging of gold and knee-jerk gold import policies have only intensified its mystique. There has been no call, as in 1962, for citizens to contribute gold to the nation; no attempt to check brain drain by imposing emigration charges; no move to modernise the infrastructure and stem deindustrialisation by imaginative mobilisation of manpower, food and natural resources.

A crisis of political-economy cannot be solved by mere smartness of bookkeeping. If anything, it damages national identity.

It is the reluctance to call a spade a spade that has characterised Indian politicians and bureaucrats and it is political chicanery of the rulers that spells the greatest danger to the country's political economy and hence to its economic nationalism.

Let us look at only some aspects of the effects of the great modernisation attempt of the last decade, if only to open the political cupboards in which the skeletons of economic mismanagement have been stashed away. Much has been said about the profligate recourse to short-term borrowing under Rajiv Gandhi and also about the flowering of extravagant consumerism of the yuppie generation. It did not require much more than reading the *Economic and Political Weekly* to know what was happening. Week after week, that journal kept the alarm bells ringing but its prognostications were dismissed as the carpings of Cassandras.

Now facts stare us in the face. We shall take just one example of the import-dependence created by the external liberalisation promoted during the mid-1980s. Analysis of figures taken from the *Reserve Bank of India Bulletin* and the *Public Enterprises Survey* leads to dire conclusions.

The data on 600 firms in the pre-liberalisation (1982-85) and post-liberalisation (1986-89) periods show that the net foreign exchange inflow rate (NFIR) for components and capital goods increased by about 23 per cent in the post-liberalisation phase, implying an enormous intensification of import-dependence in this sector. Within the private sector, the NFIR of more than two-thirds of the industry groups registered an increase and it was highest in the transport equipment industry whose NFIR rose by 243 per cent. Not for nothing is the decade of the eighties known as the Maruti age! The data do not include some obvious import-intensive industries like electronics and telecommunications. Had they been included, the picture would have been even darker as even otherwise the share of imports in net value added in these industries increased by as much as 29 per cent in the post-liberalisation phase. The point is that the set in Indian society that has benefited from import-intensification, the Maruti-VCR-cellular telephones set, still rules the roast even as the nation is asked to tighten its belt. That this import-intensification is largely for the indulgence of India's burgeoning consumer class, aimed at the domestic market and not export-oriented, is obvious from the percentage shares of the principal items that constitute India's exports. According to the *Report on Currency and Finance*, 32 per cent of exports are of articles of apparel and clothing accessories, 16 per cent are of gems and jewellery and 19 per cent are of food and live animals. The first two are more often than not the products of sweated labour and the third is outside the import-intensive industrial sector.

If IMF proddings, ideological blinkers and political mythology were not the conditions within which Indian economic policies are being shaped, it would have been obvious that an open door does not necessarily lead to prosperity walking in. Between 1985 and 1989, no less than 4,364 foreign collaborations were finalised and nearly Rs.1,000 crores worth of foreign investments approved. During the same period India's current account of balance of payments deficit went from Rs.2,852 crores in 1984-85 to a staggering Rs.10,975 crores in 1989-90. Neither did exports grow proportionately nor was the economy modernised. What was intensified was economic dualism, with the country split between that limited set which was spoilt with goodies got on loan and the ever-increasing poor.

Indeed, such is the dualism that it can well be described as a veritable "secession of the successful". The NRIs voted with their feet against India; the secession of the others who prospered was no less dangerous. It is only the fact of privilege that prevents this economic secessionism from being recognised as a menace as dangerous as the one we are facing in Punjab, Kashmir and elsewhere. It is referred to more deferentially, with the proper use of polite euphemisms.

But is the attempt to carry out economics by euphemism likely to succeed? The answer must be no. It is extremely difficult to circumvent Indian democratic institutions. The attempt to tame the rich peasants has come a cropper. The vociferous manner in which the rural interests articulated themselves over the fertiliser issue had the finance minister performing the by now familiar Manmohan minuet : one step forward, two steps back.

More is still to come. The fact that in India free trade unions continue to exist, along with a free press, functioning electoral systems and sovereign parliamentary bodies, as institutions of democracy will prevent playing around with organised labour. The organisations of Indian capitalists, FICCI for instance, have already started muttering against the licence given to foreign capital. The federal structure of India will ensure political as well as economic plurality. And, finally, the world has no great interest in seeing that India gets out of its economic morass and becomes an economic superpower.

If India prospers it will only be when it demolishes myths, faces realities and pulls itself up by its bootstraps. These require long-term dedication.

In the euphoria of the recently obtained loans from the IMF, World Bank, etc., it is clear that while these borrowings have helped the country tide over the immediate balance of payments crisis, they have only taken the ship of the Indian economy further into the deep sea of indebtedness. In the context of the palpable relief that India managed not to default on pressing short-term loans, there is little talk about how medium-term and long-term loans are proposed to be repaid. The pie of prosperity is still far far out in the sky.

Even in the short-run, the solutions to economic problems are sought to be found in paradoxes. For instance, the creditors are demanding, and even native commonsense dictates, that the fiscal deficit must be brought down. This implies both curtailing expenditure and raising revenues. These are indeed being attempted.

However, the problem arises in the *modus operandi*. In freezing and even reducing expenditure, the first casualties are non-plan activities of maintenance of existing assets. In the last several months, woefully little attention has been paid to this as the state of roads, dams, embankments, etc. loudly testifies. At the same time, in spite of proclaimed intentions of the de-bureaucratisers and advocates of "small government", there is little evidence of an attempt to curtail wasteful expenditure. It is not surprising in such circumstances that while the assets of the State are declining, the bureaucracy has been treated to fairly large "productivity bonus" all around and the extravagance of ministers is unchecked.

The revenue side presents a similar paradox of cutting off one's nose to spite one's face. It was noticed that collections from customs duties were short of the budgetary targets. This was attributed to the import squeeze. Now, the attempt is to liberalise imports in order to raise more customs duties. The fact is that increased imports have to be eventually paid for through exports. However, the value of exports has stagnated and even declined. It is said, this is in part due to restrictions on imports of components, representing one arc of the vicious circle. In any event, regardless of the various factors that inhibit exports, it does appear that relying on enhanced customs collections through increased imports is another illustration of the attempt to solve a short-term problem by transferring liability to the future.

It was assumed that devaluation would be one method of promoting exports by providing a cost advantage to Indian goods. While the results of that drastic measure are still to unfold, at least a part of the benefit of devaluation has been offset by the fact that prices continue to rise — despite the illusion created by the point to point comparative figures on the relatively moderate *rate* of inflation. This means that domestic cost escalation may yet negate the price advantage of Indian exports.

In order to get out of this vortex of inflation, one of the most important measures that the government has adopted is to put a squeeze on credit by raising bank lending rates. This however has pushed up the costs of working capital and many industrialists are screaming about the results of stagflation. Indeed, the National Council of Applied Economic Research has estimated that the new credit curbs will add 0.5 per cent to the rate of inflation. This could turn out to be the backbreaking straw loaded on the camel of India's industrial renewal.

Meanwhile, those who thought that announcement of a series of policies by the government would automatically open up the flood-gates of foreign investment were obviously being unrealistically over-optimistic. The inflow from loans is far more than from investment and, in a tight global situation of investible capital, it is only logical that foreign investors will take their time to size up India's central as well as state governments and the overall economic climate before putting their money where their mouth is. As such, while advice has been profligate, investment is still miserly.

The answer of the advocates of the policy of liberalisation-globalisation to all these, of the hard-headed economists in government and outside, is curiously non-economic. They invoke "the state of mind" — of investment, efficiency and productivity — which these policies are expected to create. While none can deny that social psychology is an important condition for economic change, orthodox economists would still be appalled at the premium being put on factors other than the bottom-line. It may well be that haste may not induce the speedy laying of golden eggs but it is also an old adage that counting chickens before they are hatched is not altogether wise.

In the context of present-day economics in India, it is clear that short-term pragmatism, overwhelming concern with matters of the moment, can be equally counter-productive. Nothing illustrates this better than the current modes of macro-economic management which is premised on economics without history and politics without sociology.

There are two characteristic aspects of the policy of the moment: one is concerned with gaining economic time even at the expense of political-diplomatic space and the other is with anyhow, somehow preventing uncontrollable distress by "managing" poverty rather than eliminating it. This is the real content of the "social adjustment" discourse which is taking over the language of "structural adjustment".

The IMF wants the government to cut its deficits by a given date. That has to be done, for the consequence would not only be that the IMF does not release another tranche of live-saving loans but also that the whole loan agreement would have to be renegotiated and even more stringent conditionalities might result. Last summer the concern was to avoid default on short-term loans and the deadlines were on a day-to-day basis. Even when the summer of short-term lenders discontent was turned into a glorious tropical winter by multilateral munificence, the preoccupation was with meeting day-to-day demands to adjust structurally.

The most urgent concern of the macro-economic managers is, therefore, to prune the government's deficit. For this, if gold has to be sold, so be it. If revenue has to be raised through enhanced collection of customs duties, import restrictions will be eased. If the government has to raise money by selling its public sector assets, real estate or offshore oil blocks, that will be done. If it means amending laws to convert corporations like Air India or commissions like ONGC into companies so that their equity can be offloaded, that too will be done.

More significant in the context of the long run being overlooked for the short-term is the management of deficit by curtailing expenditure. Not all such cuts affect only unproductive, wasteful and bureaucratic institutions. The foreign exchange crunch has led to import restriction and the effect of that on production and even exports has been widely commented upon. Much more serious is the restriction of development on account of the government's budgetary constraints.

Several years after it was due to have begun, the Eighth Plan is still being debated. Indeed, the new economic establishment, which has its eyes firmly fixed on the immediate present, has in effect ended planning, which is by definition geared to the future. The planning commission has thus become an irrelevance.

Among the items omitted in the effort to bridge the budgetary gap are irrigation schemes, plant and equipment renewal by public sector concerns like coal-mines, expansion and modernisation of the rail and road networks and even adequate supply of fertilisers through the expedience of simply shutting off money for imports and subsidies.

The long-term consequences of such fiscal–structural adjustment are grave. The already poor infrastructure will be further run down. As the State withdraws from even such economic activity, overall development will become all the more difficult as productive agricultural, mining and heavy engineering sectors suffer. As and when private and foreign investment picks up, it will be in "greenfields" and "sunrise" areas. The economic sun will set on India's major labour-absorbing, employment-generating, resource-utilising and wealth-creating sectors, unnoticed by those whose eyes are riveted on the rapidly moving hands of the policy clock and ears

are filled by the staccato ticking of IMF-ordered structural adjustment schedule.

Even in the short term, the profound political and social fall-out
of "adjust in a hurry, repent at leisure" becomes obvious if the
thinking is in weeks or months rather than in a rational time frame.
Only those who divorce politics from economics are oblivious of
this. As it is, the bulk of political class, including even Congress MPs,
is hardly convinced of the logic of the dramatic change in economic
policy. The predicted pruning of public expenditure, "rationalisation"
if not outright retrenchment of labour, slowing down of growth and
double- digit inflation are part of the general political discourse.
Even the finance minister describes the emerging scene as one of
"stagflation" although he still refutes suggestions that what is
afflicting India is actually a recession.

As BJP leaders ride their *raths* and CPM cadres deliberate at their
party convention, as National Front stalwarts set to consolidate their
crumbling organisations through mobilising mass movements and
even Congress MPs anxiously nurse their constituencies during the
parliamentary recess, the whole political class is realising that the
catchwords of politics are "prices" and "unemployment". The
language of politics is turning out to be significantly different from
the discourse of liberalisation.

In such a context, the concern shifts to tomorrow, to the future.
And, then two sets of activities get encouraged. One is geared on
agitation; the other on containment. Both are posited on distress
rather than on development.

The agitations against distress are of two types. The political
right uses the mood against inflation and unemployment to its
advantage. The Germans experienced this outcome of hyper-infla-
tion and widespread closures during the Weimar Republic which
was overthrown by hyped up nationalism and anti-"the other"
racism to establish Hitler's Third Reich. The rumble of the rolling
hindutva juggernaut and the BJPs threat to launch other agitations
soon after that marathon are ominous.

But the Left and populist centre too can revolt against stagflation.
The socialists' resolve to promote "*swadeshi, swablamban, swabhiman*"
(indigenous production, self-reliance and self-respect) and the
unfurling of the Communists' banner against the government are

indications of this. And as the season of agitations on the price rise
and unemployment issues hots up, it will become clear that the last
word has not been pronounced on populist-centrist realignment
either.

In the meantime, the attempt will also be to "manage distress".
Here too there are two variants. One is the desperate "management
of poverty" as by the Bihar chief minister Laloo Prasad Yadav. An
almost complete absence of resources forces him to devote disproportionate interest in the maintenance of hospitals which he calls
"the high courts of the poor where they are sentenced to life or
death". While no industries are set up, no irrigation schemes are
launched, no power projects come up, and even roads are not
repaired, such desperate management of distress has only populist
value. The other mode of managing discontent is through promises
of the "safety net", "social adjustment" and "fund for national
renewal" to take care tomorrow of the problems created today.

However, if the tides did not halt at the orders of King Canute,
time too will hardly heed the hopes of those who barter today for
tomorrow, promising, as Lewis Carrol said, "Jam yesterday and jam
tomorrow, but never jam today."

In any event, if non-economic factors are the ones that have to
be taken into account, then it is also worthwhile to remember that
the most important of such factors is that India has a democratic
polity, one which is qualitatively different from that of South Korea,
Indonesia, Taiwan or even the much-touted Thailand. The populist
urges which reduced the substance of the move to cut fertilizer
subsidies are evidence of only one aspect of such democracy. The
speed with which the finance minister discounted any idea of taxing
agricultural income and the manner in which the agriculture minister denounced the very notion as "perverse" are another illustration of economic populism motivated by power base politics.

Meanwhile, the whole exercise of economic globalisation came
under a cloud of criminality, that of a major fraud committed on the
people and State of India. It got to be known by the rather innocuous
name of "scam" but its import was such that it transgressed the
boundaries not only between India and other nations but also
between legality and crime, between public funds and private
appropriation, and between the interests of the Indian people as a

whole and the unscrupulous greed of those who constitute its ruling set.

It goes without saying that the business of any business is making money. A bank is no exception. However, the Indian banking regulations leave little room to fulfil that aim. For most Indian banks, nationalised in 1969, making a profit is, or was, not an urgent concern. But for the Indian branches of foreign banks, under pressure from their head offices to perform, this was always top priority. This pressure increased in the '70s and '80s when the international banking sector faced a recession. And it is this need to show results that perpetrated the scam.

Once a number of foreign banks had found the loopholes in the country's financial system and started making huge profits, Indian banks too jumped on to the bandwagon. The increase in the profit of the State Bank of India in 1991-92, for example, was a staggering Rs 867 crore.

Every bank operating in India is required to keep over 60 per cent of its deposit base locked in non-profitable or low-profit assets, of which 25 per cent is in cash — called cash reserve ratio (CRR) — and 38 per cent is compulsorily invested in low-interest government securities — termed as statutory liquidity ratio (SLR). Securities are papers issued by the government to borrow money from the banks to pay for the government's own overspending.

The CRR and the SLR are meant to save the banks from going bankrupt. Even if all the depositors come to claim their money on the same day, the cash can be distributed on the spot while the securities can be immediately converted into cash by selling them to other banks. Besides, since the CRR and SLR are stipulations that have to be maintained, every fortnight banks are required to 'square' up their accounts to ensure that they conform to RBI regulations.

These restrictions apart, banks in India are forced to lend 40 per cent of the remaining deposits to the priority sector (agriculture, small scale industry, etc.) at low interest rates ranging between 6 to 10 per cent. This leaves them with only 26 per cent of their total deposits to make profits through lending at high interest rates — the rate for the corporate sector is over 20 per cent.

Some foreign banks realised that they could generate extra profits by controlling the market in government securities. Market makers, who usually work in a cartel of sorts, determine the market rates by buying certain securities and consequently raising its demand and price or vice versa.

For example, the favourite share in the stock market as far the principal "scamster" Harshad Mehta was ACC and he would influence its market price. By buying or selling, Mehta could force other brokers to similarly buy or sell. So what Mehta is alleged to have been for the stock market, say, Citibank is alleged to have been for to the securities market. However, the two markets are quite separate from each other, with RBI regulations prohibiting the diversion of funds from one to the other.

A golden opportunity for manipulation of the market for securities came when the government and RBI decided to increase the interest rate on securities, known as coupon rate, and steadily bring it on a par with the rates on debentures and bonds issued by public sector units and the corporate sector (the interest on the latter was 11 per cent and above).

This meant that the new securities, bearing a higher interest rate, would be quoted at a premium in the market because of the high demand for and low supply of these securities, and the old ones, offering a lower return, would sell at a discount. Thus, if a bank knew in advance of the launch of the new, attractive securities, it could sell the old ones at a higher price (before it sold at a discount) and buy the new ones (before they were quoted at a premium) and make money. This is precisely what some foreign banks did.

This was investigated by the JPC and, according to the first draft chapters, it could not find any direct evidence of the decision to hike the coupon rates being leaked out to some banks. However, the JPC cites one example which provides circumstantial evidence. The draft chapters state that Citibank sold huge quantities of old securities and bought similar quantities of the new ones in November 1991 before the government launched new papers in March 1992. The source of advance information, if any, to Citibank is yet to be identified but it does appear that the decision regarding changes in the coupon rates was not "leak proof".

It did not take some Indian banks long to jump into the fray. B. Ratnakar, ex-chairman of Canara Bank, was the first to enter, followed by other heavyweights like the State Bank of India and

Punjab National Bank. By the late '80s, every bank was frantically buying and selling government securities and, not surprisingly, the volume of transactions assumed unprecedented proportions. The JPC draft report points out that foreign banks alone handled securities transactions worth Rs 6,82,427 crore or 56 per cent of all such transactions between April 1, 1991 and May 23, 1992.

As the total number and value of government securities is huge, there is no physical delivery of paper certificates in buying or selling. All the securities floated by the government are stored in the RBI. The public debt office (PDO) in RBI maintains a register recording all the transactions. For example in the PDO register, SBI might be holding one lakh securities of 2001 which it sells to Canara Bank. The PDO will debit this from SBI and credit it to Canara Bank. However, this laborious manual process takes about two months or even more.

When the volume of transactions increased during the scam period, this time gap between the actual transaction of government securities between banks and it being recorded in the PDO increased considerably — sometimes taking up to nine months. It was this loophole that the banks and brokers exploited to the hilt at the height of the scam.

In many cases, especially of foreign banks, sales transactions cleared through the ledger at the PDO, were found to bounce since they did not have sufficient balances in their accounts. In several other cases they were found to be accepting securities transfers from banks which were known for fraudulent sales. In all such cases, the transactions were effected to generate a short-term cash surplus, which could be siphoned off into the stock market.

Though all such transactions and deals passed through the vetting stone of the RBI, the central supervisory authority failed to take notice right through it all till it was too late and the bubble burst. The "systems failure" — which was the term used by the finance minister, Manmohan Singh, to describe the fraud — was no malfunctioning computer which garbled data but in the very omission or delay in recording the information.

Banks routinely use an instrument called bank receipt (BR) as a record of the concluded transactions, although it has been stated in Parliament that the Banking Regulations Acts running into several hundred pages make no mention of this instrument. If bank A has sold X securities valued at Rs Y to bank B, the former bank issues a BR saying that it owes bank B delivery of X securities. Bank B, in turn, issues a BR saying it owes Rs Y to bank A. Once the PDO records the transaction, the two BRs are discharged by sending them to RBI and the transaction is complete.

The BR is a typed IOU note which is signed by authorised signatories in banks. The Indian Bank Association (IBA) has a standard format for a BR which a number of banks were not following. It is quite easy to forge the BRs and some banks were using ordinary papers as BRs which were not even signed by authorised signatories. This aspect of the scam was no "systems failure" but simple criminal forgery.

The final report of the Janakiraman Committee set up to investigate the scam concludes that the bank–broker nexus was at the root of the scam. But how did this nexus develop?

Although according to RBI guidelines, government securities transactions are supposed to be only between banks, brokers came into the picture because they could easily locate buyer and seller banks. They, with their contacts, could effect quick bank-to-bank transactions for the price of a tiny 0.2 or 0.3 per cent commission. A select group of brokers of proven record were therefore allowed to be go-betweens. Buying and selling in the securities market was, by and large, restricted to maintaining the SLR, whereby 38 per cent of their deposits are invested in government securities.

However, when the coupon-rate "leak" presumably took place and the volume of transactions rose dramatically, RBI's inability to keep pace with recording these bank-to-bank transactions created a time lag — and time enough for the brokers to siphon off funds from the securities market into the stock market. This was, of course, done in collusion with the banks.

While the antiquated system at RBI took its time to record the movement of government securities, banks used their banker's receipts (BRs) to maintain their accounts. With brokers acting as middlemen, these BRs were passed on to the brokers instead of the corresponding buyer or seller bank. The BRs was then being used to establish a line of credit and facilitating brokers' investments in the stock market. Even payments for securities' purchases were made into brokers' accounts instead of the seller bank.

For example, a number of pay orders issued by various banks favouring the Hongkong and Shanghai Banking Corporation Limited were credited to one Naresh Kumar Aggarwala's personal account at Hongkong Bank though there was no letter or memo directing the bank to this effect. And the same account was used to issue pay orders to other banks as well.

Such routing also enabled the broker to gain by the difference in the selling and buying rates of the two banks he would have brought together. For example, Rs 27.30 crore received from ANZ Grindlays Bank on January 13, 1991, was credited to Aggarwala's account. Later, a pay order for Rs 26.90 crore was issued favouring Canara Bank. The broker thus netted a cool Rs 0.40 crore.

In due course, almost all banks joined the bandwagon and the nexus became so strong that some brokers became the favourites for certain banks. And thus began the success story of many a broker. Be it Hiten Dalal, the favourite of Standard Chartered Bank, who handled securities business worth Rs 92,464 crore in a single year. Or Harshad Mehta, whose main dealings were with the State Bank of India (SBI), accounted for 5.5 per cent of the total value of securities transactions worth Rs 12 lakh crore in 1991-92 or N.K. Aggarwala, who dealt for Citibank.

By and large the brokers made their money by investing the security market money in the stock market but there were some like Hiten Dalal, who are alleged to have compounded their folly by introducing forged BRs in the scene. Brokers also used a minor bank such as Bank of Karad, whose board of directors included Bhupen Dalal who also owns a brokerage firm, Bhupen Champaklal Devidas, as a holding bank to legitimise securities actually held by himself. In fact according to the Janakiraman report, Hiten Dalal was the biggest broker in the securities game, followed by Harshad Mehta and Bhupen Dalal. While Hiten Dalal has since been indicted and sentenced to 10 years' imprisonment, Harshad Mehta was kept in custody for 111 days but is now out on bail. Another big "scamster", Bhupen Dalal, originally managed to stay in custody for only one day, but nemesis finally caught up with him too.

Yet another aspect of the scam related to the misuse of public sector resources. In the mid-'80s, the government decided to allow public sector undertakings (PSUs) to float bonds to raise resources for modernisation and expansion. In the beginning, it was decided that these bonds would be sold directly to the public. After the first few issues were floated, there was a general feeling that the marketing expenses for selling such bonds were huge (nearly 10 per cent of the issue amount). So, in 1987, the government passed an order allowing PSUs to sell their bonds to banks who, in turn, would sell them to their depositors. This is called private placement of bonds.

While some of the banks were happy to purchase these bonds and earn an interest of, say, nine per cent tax-free or 13 per cent taxable, others were not. Some of the foreign banks and a few aggressive Indian banks came up with the idea of a portfolio management scheme (PMS).

To illustrate this process, if MTNL raises Rs 100 crore through bonds, or Maruti Udyog collects a similar amount as "booking advance" from customers, the corporations would not require all the money at one go; they can therefore invest the huge sum over a longer period. The banks asked the PSUs raising money to deposit the money which was not required either as short term deposits or under PMS and offered an assured rate of return which was higher than that for fixed deposits. This money would be managed by the banks and invested in stock markets and other profitable instruments to give an attractive return to the PSUs. The PSUs accepted the offer.

The crux of this strategy was that these banks became the market-makers in PSU bonds, setting the market rates for their sale and purchase. Although the objective of the private placement of the bonds was to cut costs for the PSUs, it enabled some banks to take undue advantage and ask for quid pro quo from the companies they dealt with.

The banks benefited because they were in possession of huge funds for periods ranging from nine days to one year, which they in turn invested in the stock market or call money market. The PSUs had the assurance of being able to sell the bonds and were offered remunerative interest rates on the deposits in PMS — anything between nine per cent and 25 per cent.

Curiously, the banks offered an assured return in their PMS. Under SEBI guidelines, no portfolio management agency can give guaranteed returns if it is a risky business.

Apparently, the RBI guideline allowing PSUs to park surplus funds in PMS with "nationalised" banks was later altered to "scheduled banks." Foreign banks cashed in on this, entered the fray and snatched business from their Indian counterparts.

There were many other angles to the scam. Some comprised blatant illegalities; others straddled the thin dividing line between what is legal and what is unlawful. One such element was insider trading. Insider trading, according to technical definition, is trading in the stock market armed with inside information about a company which is not known to the public. Such information could be available to the management, the executives of a company, brokers, lawyers, journalists, bureaucrats, financial institutions. Insider trading is not illegal in India though now there is a demand for making it so.

Harshad Mehta, and some other prominent brokers, are said to have been close to managements in a number of companies. In fact, prior to buying into a company, Mehta would approach the management, disclose his strategy and then buy after getting full information from the company. In the process, the delicate line between right and wrong might have been crossed. Numerous articles on Harshad Mehta, before he was implicated in the scam, reported his close relations with directors of Apollo Tyres, ACC, Reliance. Armed with inside information about these and other companies, Mehta is alleged to have bought a large number of shares, thereby pushing up their prices inordinately high. Other brokers and the middle classes — whose savings had hitherto been kept locked in low interest savings schemes — also invested recklessly in these shares. The inherent strength of a company, managerial competence, past records or future prospects were overlooked.

Thus, for example, shares of ACC, Apollo and Reliance in which Mehta traded heavily went up to Rs 8,500, Rs 400 and Rs 435 respectively. Mazda Industries, which he took over, shot up from Rs 10 to Rs 1,450. Other ailing companies in which he showed interest boomed. Scindia Steam, sick and up for sale, rose in one evening from Rs 15 to Rs 172. Nirlon, a company that left many debenture holders penniless, reached a high of Rs 112. Harshad Mehta was not alone in using his financial muscle in this way but he was certainly the leader. And insiders knew what was going on.

By December 1991 the stock-market was booming. It was obvious, says P.K.Gupta, former Member (Investigation) of the Central Board of Direct Taxes (CBDT), that a lot of money was being made and that certain brokers, who were suspected to be evading taxes on their profits needed to be investigated.

In Harshad Mehta's case his opulent lifestyle, his cars, his properties and his own utterances gave rise to suspicion. There were raids on three groups of brokers in January 1992 and on February 28, 1992, the Big Bull himself was targeted.

The raid on Mehta's house and office premises turned out to be the biggest case in the annals of income-tax (IT) department. At least 80 floppy-computer discs, containing several thousand files, were seized by the IT sleuths. Besides, assets worth Rs 70 crore and share certificates running into hundreds of crores of rupees were confiscated.

The raids revealed that Mehta had defaulted on several counts. He had not filed his returns for the previous two years. His plea that balance sheets of his companies were not ready was disproved when computers, on the codes being cracked, rattled out the concealed balance-sheets.

The IT department does not consider Mehta's subsequent disclosure of Rs 100 crore concealed income tenable. According to the estimates of the department, his taxable income and assets are about Rs 4,000 crore and his IT liability, including interest and penalty on it, based on summary assessment of his known and unknown assets, have been put at Rs 8,000 crores. The latter amount is incidentally nearly twice the amount of total revenue collection — Rs 4,700 crore — by Bombay IT as direct taxes for 1991-1992.

The Enforcement Directorate, the watchdog agency which oversees foreign exchange violations, and the CBI are also investigating possible siphoning off of scam money abroad by Harshad Mehta and his associates who include Niranjan Shah who was first allowed to escape to the UAE and then extradited from there and brought to India for interrogation. When the government launched the NRI immunity scheme — under which NRIs could remit any amount of foreign exchange to the State Bank of India and no questions as to the source of income would be asked — Harshad Mehta's relatives are alleged to have remitted a sum of $ one million from two separate foreign accounts under this scheme. When this was discovered, the finance ministry, bound by the guarantee not to investigate into these remittances, apparently found itself helpless to take action.

Meant ostensibly to attract NRI money and to boost the country's dwindling foreign exchange reserves, the scheme is also said to have become a convenient means of bringing back into the country black money stashed away in foreign banks by bigwigs including Harshad Mehta.

Niranjan Shah, a Bombay-based exporter and a known *hawala* dealer, is alleged to have been the key to all the foreign bank accounts operated by Mehta. CBI sources have said that, in the course of an income tax raid on Niranjan Shah's house in Bombay, the officials stumbled upon documents that revealed a number of transactions between him and Harshad Mehta. One such transaction was the transfer of Rs two crore by Harshad Mehta through *hawala* operations of Niranjan Shah.

Shah's diary is also said to contain names of over 40 persons on whose behalf he used to conduct the *hawala* transactions, that is illegal routing of money abroad. But except for Mehta and his family members, the names of others have not been revealed so far. Shah fled to Dubai soon after the scam surfaced.

Though it has been established that money made in the scam was siphoned off abroad and a part of it was brought back under NRI immunity scheme, the total amount of money thus diverted and the beneficiaries of this process are not known.

Niranjan Shah's involvement in the scam also brings in the drug angle since he has earlier been accused of being involved in the international narcotics trade. Thus, various agencies are investigating whether drug money was involved in the scam or not.

Meanwhile, only the very naive believe that the scam was carried out without political involvement. Serious allegations have, in fact, been made against important politicians and several agencies are investigating the matter. However, even at this stage it can be stated that the scam has exposed and highlighted the corruption that the State has been subjected to in a period when the distinction between what is public and what is private has been sought to be obliterated.

The role that the scam has played in this regard has, of course, been accidental. In actual fact, strenuous efforts were made not only to keep the politician-scamster nexus concealed but even to pooh-pooh the seriousness of the scam itself. The very use of the word "scam" to describe this gigantic criminal fraud was a intended to underplay its significance.

Language often plays interesting tricks on morality. The perception of an act of gross criminality, for instance, can be severely distorted by the words used to describe it. Deliberate linguistic parallax can so shift the enormity of an action as to make it appear innocuous.

Take the massive criminal fraud spanning securities and shares, brokers and bankers, bureaucrats and politicians, foreign banks and native public sector institutions, tax evasion and even narcotics trade. Take all the illegalities, all the immoralities, all the cynical manipulation of public resources, all the betrayal of trust. Take bribery. Take crookedness. Take unprofessional conduct. Take all these and try to take their sting away by finding a nice little innocuous and playful word — scam — to encapsulate them all.

The problem may lie in the fact that in the beginning there was no suitable word. "Scam" does not figure in the 1980s editions of the *Concise Oxford Dictionary* or the *Collins Essential English Dictionary* or even the *Random House Dictionary of the English Language*. No problem. Look further afield. Look at America, where many such frauds have occurred. After all, if the economy is being globalised, so must its language. If such a word is not found even in proper American English, search through slang. The quest will be rewarding, for the word will take the sting out of the scandal.

Finally, it is found. The *Chambers English Dictionary*, 1992, lists it: "**scam**: *skam (slang)* n. a confidence trick, swindle (origin unknown)". Late editions of even the *Concise Oxford Dictionary* recognise it : "**scam** : /*skaem*/*n*. *US slang*/ 1. a trick or swindle; 2. a story or rumour (20th century; origin unknown)".

So there you are. A massive criminality has been reduced to a playful trick. Evidence that stares one in the face is rendered into a diverting fairy tale, an unfounded rumour! In the end, there is the word, and the word itself takes care of the deed. Moral outrage has been controlled and truth has been rendered toothless.

But that is not all. If words can lie, statistics are even better at covering up the truth. Figures, which supposedly responsible chartered accountants and auditors ignored in the performance of their statutory duties, can now be stood on their heads and made to sing a suitable tune. And, if there is a little perversion of fact or logic, so be it.

Take the figures of the money that the foreign banks were forced to bring in so as to cover the losses incurred by them because of shady dealings in securities, etc. Present them as foreign exchange support to India's precarious reserves and, hey presto, a compulsion is made to look like altruism.

Take the galloping figures of a booming stock market unrelated to the fundamentals of the economy or even of the concerned companies. Present them as endorsement of the government's economic policies. And even Harshad Mehta can be beamed on Doordarshan after the budget proclaiming, "India is a turnaround scrip on the global exchange and I am bullish on it". If it recalls the saying that patriotism is the last refuge of the scoundrel, do not worry for patriots can as easily be depicted as scoundrels.

Take even the massive figures of the public money involved in the scam — Rs 5,346 crore according to the CBI and Rs 4,024 crore by the Janakiraman committee. A little disingenuous juggling — discounting claims not registered with the custodian, dismissing tax claims on Harshad Mehta as "wildly exaggerated", assuming his ability and willingness to meet his liabilities, putting a premium on the book profits of banks and public sector concerns without drawing attention once again to fundamentals, ignoring the underselling of public sector shares even during the boom but focusing on the failure to raise money through bonds when the market plummeted — a little twisting of logic and reason can make the scam even look like a public good, an act of benevolence committed by the bright, if a-moral, players, even as the finance ministry, the RBI and other regulators were caught in a spell of absent-mindedness. Indeed, even the licence allowed to foreign banks to subvert the banking laws of the land can be justified as a measure to build up international confidence. It is not for nothing that the Bureau of Frauds promised by the finance minister a long time ago has not yet been required to be set up.

In the end, however, there are still a few problems in converting the crime into a mere playful peccadillo. The first one is that the players fall out with each other. As accusations of bribery and fraud, drug-dealing and money-laundering, of subverting the law and doling out of undue favours fly about fast and loose, the chickens of chicanery begin to come home to roost.

More serious is the ultimate test of reality. The hard reality is the cornering of money by speculators rather than industrialists. It results in intensified stock market manipulation and predatory takeover bids by buccaneer businessmen. A policy geared essentially to bankers and brokers is perilous. When trading in stocks becomes the central focus of businessmen, organisations of high-powered salesmen are set up for selling securities and shares. They sell bad stock when there are no good ones available, for they make just as large a commission on the sale of dubious shares as on sound ones.

The superstition on which the scam was based is the faith that the stock market regulates itself. It calls for and secures the reduction of the statutory liquidity ratios of banking institutions because it considers these as penalty put on good and "smart" bankers for the benefit of poor ones. It holds that high stock market prices represent high demand and hence the government needs to continue giving support to such an economy of profiteering. This superstition encompasses Puritan economic fundamentalism : that life must be made as uncomfortable for the poor as possible to induce them to work and work ever harder; to give relief to those who work would destroy their self-respect.

The prevalence of such superstition shows that the dinosaurs of economic thinking are not yet extinct. Some of them occupy the treasury benches and sit on the right in Parliament. Others chant the incantations outside. The scam is the manifestation of precisely such economic superstition. And, after all is said and done, even scam remains a four-letter word.

Topsy turvy economics may cope with such facts. Politics based on an integrated India may find such sectoral disparity altogether more difficult to come to terms with. Wishful thinking is a bad substitute for political economy. And an essential element of political economy is economic nationalism, one of the defining characteristics of nationhood itself. It is this that is today in the process of being re-defined.

IV

The recent revival of interest in the legend of Chanakya can be ascribed to the fact that it is as much an allegorical statement of present day reality as a depiction of the political situation in the fourth century before Christ. The story centres around the character of Vishnugupta Chanakya who came to be known as Kautilya, the devious one, on account of his advocacy of the complex rules of statecraft. However, before the precepts of Kautilya on statecraft could be put into practice, a State had to be created. In other words, the notion of Indian-ness had to be forged into the reality of a nation through the invention of a State structure. Those who seek to claim legitimacy for their idea of an India premised on *hindutva* could do well to acquaint themselves with the context and content of the *Arthashastra*, that most ancient secular text of India whose intellectual pedigree and lineage have been traced with historical rigour by Damodar Dharmanand Kosambi.

There was no India at the time when Alexander's troops crossed the Hindukush after having ravaged the Persepolis. There were a number of mutually warring monarchical and republican *janapads*, the most important of them being the low-caste, non-Vedic kingdom of Magadh which was immensely rich not only on account of the fertile Gangetic plains that it commanded but also because of its access to the iron-rich Jharkhand. And yet, in spite of the existence of relatively or absolutely autonomous regions and peoples, there was the incipient *idea* of an India, an entity that included the tribes of the Punjab but excluded the Bactrians, Persians and the Greeks. It was this idea of India, outlined by his predecessors like Katyayana, Kaninka Bharadvaja, Dirgha Charayana and Pisuna that Kautilya sought to concretise. He discovered that the only way to do so was by institutionalising the rule of law.

The rule of law was not based on according a superordinate position to one communitarian or religious grouping among the many that existed but by making all subordinate to one set of political-economic rules. Indeed, nearly two thousand five hundred years before religious majoritarianism became the fashionable mode of defining nationhood, the *Arthashastra* polity recognised that pluralism, heterogeneity and even heterodoxy were not incompatible with uniform codes of political action. In fact, the first practitioners of pan-Indianism, Chandragupta Maurya, and his successors, notably Asoka, recognised that the existence of multiplicities is a *sine qua non* of Indian unity.

The *Arthashastra* also recognised the role of the· market in forging the identity of India. Common coinage, common excise rules, common taxation, State-promoted infrastructure and private enterprise were all seen as essential. However, even two and a half millennia ago, while the philosophers of Indian-ness rejected religious or ethnic singularity as determinants of nationhood, they were also not so reductionist as to posit only the economic factor as the defining characteristic of an Indian identity. This is in sharp contrast to the political simplification that is propounded today by overt and covert proponents of *hindutva* and those who worship at the altar of the market.

But if rule of law defined India in the time of the low- born, non-Hindu Chandragupta Maurya who administered it from Patna, what is it that characterises the identity of India today when Laloo Prasad Yadav metaphorically occupies the same seat? The posing of the question itself may appear absurd to those who think in the cliches of the linear movement of history. And yet the apparent absurdity itself raises basic questions about the definitions of Indian-ness.

Centuries of Brahmanical hegemony, institutionalised first through the *coup d'etat* of Pushyamitra Sunga, have not made this issue irrelevant. They have not sufficiently fossilised the polity to prevent so-called low-born people, like Shivaji Maharaj and today's "Backwards", from seizing and legitimising power. They have not fractured Indian-ness enough to answer simplistically why the Monghol Chinghiz Khan is regarded as a non-Indian when his descendant Akbar is as Indian as they get. They have not been able to petrify the economy to such an extent as to prevent the political-economic kaleidoscope from turning to create ever new patterns of development. And, neither the brahman nor the bania nor even the brahmanical bania — represented by the hegemonistic traders from across the seas — has been able to reduce India to the mere representation of an imperfect market.

The Indian identity is still defined by the rule of law. In our context, the rule of law is the Constitution "ensuring liberty of thought, expression, belief, faith and worship; equality of status and of opportunity; ... promoting the dignity of the individual and unity of the nation". That majoritarian *hindutva* is *ipso facto* antithetical to this concept of Indian-ness is evident from the fact that the very person who drafted the Constitution, Babasaheb Ambedkar, was constrained deliberately to renounce Hinduism and embrace the Buddhist heterodoxy just as Chandragupta Maurya had become a Jain. In fact, aggressive assertion of *hindutva* has only limited itself by driving a wedge between Hindus and Sikhs with the latter asserting a counter-point exclusivism. Majoritarianism by its very self-definition is divisive because no majority can be perpetuated without creating minorities.

The essence of Indian-ness however is shifting perceptions of minority and majority. And the political articulation of this with the concept of the nation is democracy with the ideal of equity. It is the cement of electoral democracy, even such as it is, which holds up the structure of the rule of law within which the concept of the Indian nation is secure. It is this which distinguishes India, with all its political flabbiness, from the brittleness of the Soviet Union. Those who like to think of themselves as nationalists but have no objection to the abbreviation of democracy would do well to reflect on the role of democracy in keeping the nation united.

But democracy itself can survive only on the basis of the ideal of equity. And equity can have many meanings. It can be the content of interpersonal relationships, inter-group transactions and inter-regional cohesion. Even the market, iniquitous as it is in many respects, is a stable feature of India because, in a political economy characterised by many elements of feudal hierarchy, it represents a relative democracy: it is through the operation of the economic as well as political market that the "Backwards" have inched ahead of the "Forwards" in the power race.

However, along with the advocacy of *hindutva*, majoritarianism and simplistic notions of a value-free market, there is also an insidious attempt to formalise, if not curtail, democracy. The move is to separate the ideal of equity from the forms of democracy; in other words, to divorce democracy from republicanism. The ideologues of the BJP proudly assert that their appeal is premised not on concrete issues affecting the people but is *bhavatmak* (emotional). Their practice too demonstrates that mythology is the most important ingredient of their politics. On the other side, among non-*hindutva* politicians too there is the attempt to bypass the issues of equity through serious political manipulation.

This is a sure-fire recipe for disaster for the very entity of India. To take just one example of the counter-productive effect of dispensing with inter-regional equity, it should be clear to all that it does not take much for a State like the Soviet Union to fragment. In the context of developments in Kashmir, Punjab and Assam, the perils of dispensing with inter-regional equity cannot be over-stressed. Similarly, democracy cannot be divorced from the issues of social and political equity if it is to continue to provide the very definition of Indian-ness.

India was invented once on the basis of the rule of law. It is time to re-invent it on the basis of equity as well.

CHAPTER 1

CONCEPTS AND CATEGORIES

Along with the constantly diminishing number of the magnates of capital, who usurp and monopolise all advantages of this process of transformation, grows a mass of misery, oppression, slavery, degradation, exploitation: but with this too grows the revolt of the working-class, a class always increasing in numbers, and disciplined, united, organised by the very mechanism of the process of capitalist production itself. The monopoly of capital becomes a fetter upon the mode of production, which has sprung up and flourished along with, and under it. Centralisation of the means of production and socialisation of labour at last reach a point where they become incompatible with their capitalist integument. This integument is burst asunder. The knell of capitalist private property sounds. The expropriators are expropriated.

— Karl Marx (1974)

In today's world, Marx has become unfashionable and in India at least there is a revival of Manu. As the baby of historical method is being thrown out with the bathwater of repressive statism, even concepts like class are being given up for the more amorphous, but intellectually comfortable, categories like 'caste', 'tribe' and 'ethnicity'. If this process continues unabated, the people themselves and history too may be given up for more tangible concerns of geography and *realpolitik*. In India at least the trend is already discernible with academics lending respectability to the planners' and policy-makers' switch from concern with 'target populations' to 'area development'. From rejection of one type of totalitarianism, we are being pushed into once again accepting the time-worn cliches of another type of totalitarian *sarvodaya*, the undifferentiated community, the development of all. This suits not only the prevailing politics but even the intellectual laziness of those who are tired of trying to unravel the complexities of concepts and find comfort in the security of categories. For such people, description is an easy substitute for analysis and descriptive labels replace the effort of conceptualising processes.

Even otherwise, in recent years there has been a tendency of using descriptive labels in this context. The use of the term "subaltern" has now become quite generalised and has received legitimacy through professional currency if not through tracing its origins in Gramsci's writings. Even earlier, sociologists who shied away from "class" were quite prone to use "status groups", "hierarchies", "segments", etc. The use of the term "under-class" must be seen in that context.

The advantage of "under-class" is that it is multidimensional and relativist. Quite obviously, the under-class is relative to the superordinate or "over-class", but, by continuing with the class concept, places the very discussion within the context of the mode of production. Even if today "proletarian" is a term surrounded by confusion and obscured by the changing nature of capitalism itself, the facts that society continues to be differentiated and the mode of production remains iniquitous continue to provide validity to the concept of "under-class". It is therefore that, risking the danger of sounding anachronistic, we persist in beginning with a quotation from Marx.

In social sciences, there is a strong tendency to disaggregate social formations in order to study them discretely. Thus, even studies of capitalism are carried out by taking capital by itself, separate from labour, and analysis is attempted of its characteristics, nature and future.

However, in the realm of political economy, and even more in the area of political praxis, it is apparent that such a disaggregation is patently absurd. Capital is not only unable to stand without labour, but even its conceptualisation without its 'integral antithesis', the working class, is impossible. Indeed, methodologically it makes ample sense to try to analyse capitalism in terms of its mirror image, the working class. This is especially fruitful in the context of underdeveloped capitalism as in India where structural specificities have so blurred the essential general characteristics of capitalism that often academic analysis flounders on the rocks of abstruse mode of production debates and is unable to even identify capitalism itself. However, even in such a situation, the most abstract analysis cannot deny the existence of a vast multitude of poor, hungry and labouring people — the set that constitutes the working class. And, given their composition as a working class, it is possible to deduce the nature of the capitalism that is responsible for the state of their existence.

In the Indian context, there has been much confusion about the nature, composition and state of the working class. The confusion has been confounded by the continued existence of caste, tribe and other social groupings which are articulated with class in various ways at different times. Indeed, this has led to some academics to even conclude that in India the concept of class cannot be used meaningfully and that as such the working class is something of a myth; to them the 'wholesale' concept of 'ethnicity' appears more meaningful.

II

SOME THEORETICAL CONSIDERATIONS ON CLASS

> Class political consciousness can be brought to the work-
> ers... only from outside of the economic struggle, from
> outside of the sphere of relations between workers and
> employers. The sphere from which alone it is possible to
> obtain this knowledge is the sphere of relationship of all
> classes and strata to the state and the government, the
> sphere of the interrelations between all classes.
>
> V.I. Lenin (1976).

In the realm of practical politics the world over, and particularly in India, the working class has been so fragmented that, in most cases, it is possible to identify only workers in this or that union, industry or sector and hardly ever the proletariat as a whole. Ironically, much of this fragmentation has been carried out in the name of organising the workers. Indeed some of them have been organised, but most organisational attempts have been restricted to the formation of sectional, economistic and self-isolating trade unions formed in the mirror image of the various divisions of capital itself.

The most serious of these divides segmenting the working class has been the urban-rural chasm; and the political, ideological and even conceptual basis of this divide has been an appalling lack of theoretical clarity regarding the use of such concepts as 'mode of production' and even 'class'. An analytical concept of Marxist theory has tended to be used (during the long and tortuous mode of production debate) as a descriptive term, to the extent that people have talked of "the mode of production in agriculture", a logical extension of which could become nonsensical rubrics like "the mode of production in West Bengal agriculture", or worse still, "the mode of production under the Akalis of Punjab". The very posing of the question : "What is the mode of production in Indian agriculture?" is a theoretically impermissible use of the category. In the context of conceptualisation and politics of the working class, not only has the imprecise use of 'mode of production', separately and discretely for agriculture, industry, etc. confused issues but also the confusion has been further confounded by simplistic notions of 'class' itself.

In many discussions of the working class, by making the workers into *objects* of their own ideological exercises carried out by scholars and politicians, rather than *subjects* of human history, the working class has been reduced into a *thing*. 'It', the working class, is assumed to have a real existence which can be defined almost mathematically — so many men (and hardly ever women) who stand in a certain relation to the means of production. Once this is assumed, it becomes possible to deduce the class-consciousness which 'it' *ought* to have (but seldom does have) if 'it' was properly aware of 'its' own position and real interests (Thompson 1968). Thus the working class is segmented and reduced from being a historical process and phenomenon into a category, well-defined and easily recognisable.

Many scholars concerned with working class action perpetuate this conceptual fragmentation. Some of them do not recognise even the possibility of existence of a working class in India: when they throw out their finely meshed sociological nets, they draw out not class but the familiar fishes of 'caste', 'tribe', 'sex', and sometimes even 'peasants' and 'artisans'. At best these discrete phenomena are bundled together into the descriptive term of working classes. Such scholars too are looking for the working class as an easily recognisable category rather than an active process and, since they come up with only a multitude of people with different occupations, incomes, status-hierarchies, etc. instead of a packaged and labelled bundle, they conclude that indeed the working class has not yet fully emerged and its consciousness has been invented by displaced, disgruntled, subversive intellectuals merely to disturb the harmonious co-existence of groups performing different social roles.

These Parsonian pedants "who have stopped the time machine and with a good deal of conceptual huffing and puffing, have gone down to the engine-room to look, tell us that nowhere at all have they been able to locate and classify a class....Of course, they cannot find it, since class is not this or that part of the machine *but the way the machine works...* not this and that interest, but the *friction* of interests—the movement itself, the heat, the thundering noise" (Thompson 1968).

Other scholars, who have a less static view of class, do look for the movement. But for many of them movements in history are not caused by flesh and bones human beings but by the disembodied economic forces which are capable of being reduced to algebraic formulae. For them therefore there is no need to concern themselves with actual workers, and statistical derivations and deductions suffice.

For many others, indeed for many who actually bother to look at the activities of real, live, workers, the workers become a class only when they institutionalise themselves into organisations: they require definite, card-of-membership of a class before they award their recognition. And since class relations and class consciousness often consist of the experiences of different groups — factory workers, artisans, agricultural labourers, people belonging to different castes, tribes and sexes — and are cultural *phenomena* not nearly as definite and matter-of-fact as the scholars would like them to be, only partial recognition is granted: the working class is the section assembled into organisations the scholars are familiar with, e.g., trade unions; the rest — agricultural labourers, domestic workers, the unemployed, etc. — lie in the great beyond.

It is this partial truth that scholarship on the working class in India continues to labour with, not admitting that "class is a social and cultural formation (often [but not necessarily always] finding institutional expression) which cannot be defined abstractly, or in isolation, but only in terms of relations with other classes; and, ultimately, the definition can only be made in the medium of *time*— that is, action and reaction, change and conflict...A class...[is]...a very loosely defined body of people who share the same congeries of interests, social experiences, traditions and value-system, who have a *disposition* to behave as a class, to define themselves in their actions and in their consciousness in relation to other groups of people in class ways...class itself is not a thing; it is a happening" (Thompson 1968).

That this happening is a process of *self-discovery* and *self-definition* is seldom recognised, with the result that while scholars try to fit the working class into tight little compartments which can be easily classified and labelled, politicians try to push the working class into exogenously fabricated political schema. But the process cannot be forced: in spite of the fact that scholars are concerned with either sociological categories or economic forces or merely with organised structures, the working class continues to happen and make history in its own ways, and in spite of the fact that politicians scream themselves hoarse about their pet theories of "worker-peasant alliance", "vanguard role of the working class", etc., the industrial workers, by and large studiedly avert their eyes from agricultural labourers being bonded and enslaved, Dalits being burnt, tortured and raped. That till today there has not been a single significant nation-wide solidarity action on these issues by the 'organised' working class is not merely accidental; nor can the working class be glibly dismissed as having become a "labour aristocracy." Explanations have to be found in the very nature of the industrial section of the working class itself and its organic relationship to others in the specific historical and political-economic context of India today. These explanations are not readily available.

The reason for this rather long introductory note to a discussion of the making of the Indian under-class, particularly in the context of the development of capitalism, is that in considering the process of class formation, we *ab initio* reject the conceptual and political fragmentation of the under-class or, to use a more 'scientific' and yet more unfashionable term, the working class — with which we are concerned—into rural and 'urban' discrete segments. We consider the concept of rural proletariat to be just as inadmissible as that of the 'mode of production in agriculture'. The many and varied links within the working class—located in urban or rural contexts—have been amply demonstrated, and we will have occasion to discuss some of them later. Suffice it, at this stage, merely to enter the caveat that in our consideration of the long and winding historical processes of class formation and rural (and urban) transformation, when we refer to the under-class or working class, we do so to an organic whole, whose very conception has to be holistic, unfragmented and processual. It is necessary, indeed, to understand the processual rather than categoric nature of 'class' itself.

III

CLASS AND CLASSIFICATION

The owners merely of labour-power, owners of capital and landowners, whose respective sources of income are wages, profit and ground rent, in other words, wage-labourers, capitalists and landowners, constitute the three big classes of modern society based upon the capitalist mode of production...

The first question to be answered is this: what constitutes a class?...

Karl Marx (1974)

Unfortunately, Marx himself could not complete this discussion of class and the manuscript of *Capital Vol.III* breaks off just as he poses the question. Nevertheless the considerable discussion of the question of the concept of class which has gone on both before and after Marx and indeed in other works of Marx himself can be considered useful if only to arrive at particular and specific class situations rather than posit the general laws, valid in and of themselves, for which positivistic social science has been constantly searching (Dos Santos 1970).

In the first place, the concept of social class was not a creation of "displaced intellectuals (like Marx) who want to disturb the harmonious co-existence of groups performing different 'social roles'...". As Dos Santos points out, the concept was present in the works of Aristotle, the New Testament, Thomas Aquinas, Babeuf, Adam Smith, Saint-Simon, Proudhon and Rousseau, to mention only a few in the mainstream of Occidental social philosophy. In the East, the edicts of Confucius and Manu are based on the acceptance of the existence in society of classes. The notion of class was identified with the very functioning of society. What Marx did was to give the notion of class a scientific dimension and, moreover, make it the basis for explaining society and its history. Even where he made mistakes, as in describing pre-colonial India as composed of undifferentiated village communities living in self-satisfied idiocy (Marx 1976), his analysis was predicated on the axiom that "all hitherto existing history is the history of class struggle" (Marx and Engels 1976b).

Nevertheless, despite the basic importance of the conception of social classes in Marx's work, he did not give it the same rigorous and systematic treatment that he gave other concepts; his major work, *Capital*, breaking off just at the chapter in which he starts to deal with social classes. In addition, the fact that in several earlier works, Marx used the notion, sometimes rather loosely, gives rise to a series of ambiguities used by both his epigones and opponents to attribute a crude notion of class to him and then to use and abuse that notion for their own purposes.

Let us trace what Marx himself has to say on the subject. In the Second Volume of *Capital*, he says that in a developed capitalist society there is only a capitalist and a proletarian class (1957:348). The former who are called the bourgeoisie are described in the *Communist Manifesto* (1976b) as "owners of the means of social production and employers of wage-labour" and the proletariat are said to be "the class of modern wage-labourers who, having no means of production of their own, are reduced to selling their labour power in order to live".

In his unfinished final discussion we have seen that he asserts that three classes—capitalists, proletarians and landowners— constitute, in their mutual opposition, modern society.

The confusion is worse confounded by his specific historical treatment of particular 'classes' e.g., the landowners, "owners of large tracts of land and ...almost always feudal in origin" (Ollman 1968). In the 'Introduction' to the *Critique of Political Economy* (1951a), the landowners are included as one of the "three great social classes", whereas in *The Eighteenth Brumaire of Louis Bonaparte* (1951b) Marx treats them as a section of the bourgeoisie, claiming that "large landed property, despite its feudal coquetry and pride of race, has been rendered thoroughly bourgeois by the developments of modern society". His treatment of the petty-bourgeoisie, the peasantry and "that dangerous class — the lumpen proletariat" at different places in different ways further emphasises the need to draw integrated methodological conclusions on the concept of class following the methods used by Marx himself in relation to other concepts.

But before coming to Marx and the Marxists, let us take the error committed daily on the other side of the ideological divide. The body of thought which calls itself "non-Marxist" assumes that any notion of class is a pejorative theoretical construct imposed upon the evidence. It is sometimes denied that class has happened at all and sometimes, by a curious inversion, the dynamic view of class is passed over to a static view by which it is asserted that 'it' —in particular the working class— exists and can be defined with accuracy as a component of the social structure as long as such definition is bereft of any action element like class-consciousness. Then the scientistic concept is used to merely bottle, label and put on display specimens of different sections of humanity.

But class is not a mere category: in everyday life it is a relationship, not a thing (even though it has fallen into the seemingly neo-Hegelianism of the distinction between "thing in itself" versus "thing for itself"). Class, as history has borne out, is a historical phenomenon: a social and cultural formation arising from processes which work themselves out over a considerable historical period. "If we stop history at a given point, then there are no classes but simply a multitude of individuals with a multitude of experiences. But if we watch these men over an adequate period of social change, we observe patterns in their relationships, their ideas, and their institutions. Class is defined by men as they live their own history, and in the end this is its only definition" (Thompson 1968).

But why would these "non-Marxist" social scientists let men live their own history and define themselves? Just as the Marxist method is predicated on history, the non-Marxist social science (and politics) has its bread and butter coming from trying to halt the time machine in both the present and the past in the interest of the much-vaunted status quo and scientific objectivity and, to mix a much mixed metaphor, take a slice of time, place it under powerful microscopes of positivism and trace the a-historical cross-sectional patterns which are static, perhaps sociological, often econometric, psychometric or otherwise mathematical. These scientists forget that while mathematics (and history) are the methods of all sciences, in the study of social situations, the social sciences have to put temporal, dynamic, historical analysis before static mathematical processes. It must be noted that not only sociologists and such like make this mistake but even those historians who take history to be a subject and a craft in itself and not a method of all sciences. In carving out their medieval craft guilds, they not only reduce history to antiquarianism but also transform themselves from scientists and practitioners of humanity to nostalgists and obscurantists. And having obscured their visions thereby, they cannot experience and perceive class but expect it to be placed before them in silver platters with watercress around it! And even then it is doubtful if they will recognise it as anything (sic) but a dead object.

But class is live. It cannot be preserved in formaldehyde. And if it is to be perceived, it can only be done historically and on several interdependent levels of analysis which have to go through the process of progressive concretisation (Dos Santos 1970). It is also only possible to arrive at an explanatory level of analysis when the empirical descriptive level is inserted into an abstract theoretical picture. This however is not an easy process as there is the danger of putting abstraction above concretisation or vice versa with the twin dangers of seeing classes either as "personifications of abstract relationships" or as conglomerates of completely volitional individuals. Classes as active historical phenomena indeed either go up in the hot air of high "mode of production" theory or are left to flounder on the rocks of unconscious practice.

In Marxian understanding classes have to be of course located within modes of production, but these modes of production themselves are not cut-and-dried rungs on a historical step-ladder on which humanity jumps convulsively. Modes of production too are historically dynamic and the dynamic is motored by antagonistic human components. Social classes are a fundamental expression of these antagonistic relations. Consequently, the concept of social classes is formed, even theoretically, within struggle. And, while class struggle is predicated on class consciousness, it is not possible to reverse the process by first discovering the nature of consciousness, then determining the level and nature of class struggle and finally to identify the contending social classes. The concept of class consciousness in Marxism does not correspond to the vulgar empirical idea of the consciousness that individuals have of their class status.

> We cannot judge of such a period of transformation by its own consciousness; on the contrary, this consciousness must be explained from the contradictions of material life, from the existing conflict between the social forces of production and the relations of production (Marx 1951a).

Thus, consciousness here has to be dealt at a theoretical rather than empirical and psychological level. At the same time, classes and class consciousness cannot be studied without reference to the concrete historical forms of production. What are involved in the study of classes through this method (as opposed to the method of vulgar sociology) are not operational categories established by more or less arbitrary or free premises (ideal types) but "essential" categories that are constituted by reality itself and derived from it; hence, in that sense, not categories at all but specifically historical phenomena. It is important not to confuse class structure with social stratification, as many sociologists have done, nor the psychology of classes with their class consciousness. By class consciousness is meant the systematic expression of interests of social classes; by class psychology, the mode of thought and feeling of determinate human groupings in a given situation or at a given instance. We will return to this issue of class consciousness later; suffice it to say for the present that it is "the historical reduction of relations among men to class relations that explains the historical possibility of unmystified class consciousness, i.e., consciousness that is aware of itself as class consciousness" (Dos Santos 1970).

Marx himself can be faulted on many of these counts. His own use of the term "class" is at times "group", "faction" or "layer". However, the implications of this disorder for Marx's class analysis of society should not be carried too far since, through his empirical studies and theoretical writings, he does use one set of albeit interwoven criteria for understanding what constitutes a class and his own work makes it clear that by conceptualising this unity of apparently distinct social relations, "class" is inextricably bound up with the specific reality of the unity so posited. This conceptualisation of class which takes into account "identity of revenues", "sources of revenues", consciousness of uniqueness, cultural affinity, the very opposition to another class, etc., also establishes that Marx viewed class as a complex rather than a simple relation. The thread that runs through all these criteria is the hostility a class displays for its opponent classes. For the capitalists this can be seen in their hostile relations to the workers and the landowners in the field of production, politics and culture. Of the bourgeoisie, Marx says, "The separate individuals form a class insofar as they have to carry on a common battle against another class: otherwise they are on hostile terms with each other as competitors" (Marx 1942). The common battle is fought on as many fronts as there are criteria for constituting a class, but it is the fact of the battle that earns the label of class, in the full sense of the term if the battle is carried out on all fronts. Marx says of the proletariat, for instance, "Thus this mass is already a class in opposition to capital but not yet a class for itself" (Marx 1941). The missing factor in this case is class consciousness, the proletariat's comprehension of its life situation and its acceptance of the interests and enemies which accrue to it.

Elsewhere Marx is even more demanding and requires the existence of a class-wide political organisation for the 'recognition' of a class. For example, Marx speaks of the programme of the First International as helping "the organisation of the workers into a class" (Marx 1941). He is even more explicit in this regard when he talks of the French small-holding peasants: "Insofar as millions of families live under economic conditions of existence that separate their mode of life, their interests and their culture from those of other classes, and put them in a hostile opposition to the latter, they form a class. Insofar as there is merely a local interconnection between these small-holding peasants, and the identity of their interests begets no community, no national bond and no political organisation among them, they do not form a class" (Marx 1951b). It does appear that while in the economic and cultural sense these peasants are a class, as regards class consciousness and politics, they are not. Of course, the latter two are closely interrelated. Increased class consciousness advances the cause of political organisation by creating greater interest in it, while organisational activity should heighten class consciousness. The fact that these two at times do not exist is related to the development of the mode of production: "The organisation of revolutionary elements as a class supposes the existence of all the productive forces which could be engendered in the bosom of the old society" (Marx 1951 a); and, since the engendering of all productive forces is itself a historical phenomenon included in the development of capitalism, Marx asserts that class is a "product of the bourgeoisie". This is an assertion which seems to contradict the other famous premise that "all hitherto existing history is the history of class struggle" (Marx and Engels 1976b).

The answer to this apparently Catch-22 situation is again in remembering that for Marx "class" is a complex relation based on many criteria which are historically specific in time and space. Thus, the relevant criteria in each case hinge on the answer to the twin questions of "Who is the enemy?" and "Why are they the enemy?" Marx's concept of class is historical, based on his analysis of capitalist class society, and with that perspective of human development in general, and it is with this specific historical content that the concept of class has to be used today.

What are the implications of all these for the working class involved in the process of social transformation in India?

IV

CLASS COMPOSITION AND CLASS ACTION

The real fruit of their battle (between the workers and the
bourgeoisie) lies, not in immediate results, but in the ever-
expanding union of the workers...

Karl Marx and Fredrick Engels Å(1976b).

In approaching the problem of class composition and class action, it
is worthwhile to go into a brief discussion of the distinction made by
Marx between class-in-itself and class-for-itself. A comprehensive
discussion of these concepts exists elsewhere (Byres 1981); so we
will merely abstract some portions from it and go onto trying to
apply those concepts to the specificities of the Indian situation.

The notion of class-in-itself, which has been said to embody
the 'hard core of class' (Westergaard and Resler 1976)
concentrates one's attentions upon the structural characteristics which develop in any process of class formation.
These involve men and women with a common relationship
to the means of production, a common relationship to the
appropriation of the surplus product, and a common relationship, therefore, to one another; these relationships
giving rise to an objectively given, common set of economic
interests vis-a-vis other classes (other interests). Class-for-
itself, on the other hand, entails a perception of these
interests, and a willingness and capacity to pursue them
through organised collective activity (class action), and it
directs the analysis towards ideas, institutional forms,
behaviour and the possibility of struggle. The crucial medi-
ating element between class-in-itself and class-for-itself is
class consciousness, which transforms the former into the
latter, though never in a mechanical way... class consciousness cannot be a mere by-product or reflex of structural
characteristics. How class interests are perceived and pursued depends upon the synthesis of a whole complex of

factors: the structural   characteristics of the classes in question, the inherited historical situation, the nature of class action taken by opposing classes, and, perhaps, organisational initiatives which may be partly independent (Byres 1981).

If in this manner class-in-itself is perceived as an amalgam of interrelated structural characteristics, a proper analysis of the process of working class formation in India should take us away from a sectional analysis of segments of the population to an analysis of relationships existing between those segments. In trying to understand just one aspect of one of the structural characteristics of the Indian working class-in-itself, with particular reference to the rural existence and transformation, we will take an element of the relationship between three segments of the working class: the urban workers in the old industrial sector, the rural agricultural workers and poor peasants and the interlinking migrant "casual poor". In all these segments, of course, are women and children and the relationships between sexes and between adults and children are important, though often ignored, components of the structural characteristics of the Indian working class-in-itself.

While studies of industrial workers in India have repeatedly noted the rural background of industrial workers, they have, by and large, failed to recognise and explain the persistent and structurally perpetuated nature of agrarian links maintained by different segments of the working class. There has been a registration of the evidence for an interpenetration of industrial and agrarian labour in the literature on internal migration, urbanisation, industrial sociology, etc., without coming to explanations for the phenomenon, arising out of the tendency of treating workers as a collection of single individuals and their links with the agrarian sector as so many personal choices. This simply ignores evidence which not only demonstrates the importance of kinship networks in gaining jobs (Holmstrom 1984) but indeed the evidence which demonstrates the two- way flow of remittances which makes the very existence of the two segments possible.

V

VILLAGERS IN THE CITY: WORKERS IN THE VILLAGE

The foundation of every division of labour which has attained a certain degree of development, and has been brought about by the exchange of commodities, is the separation of the town from the country. One might well say that the whole economic history of society is summed up in the movement of this antithesis.

Karl Marx (1976).

In the context of the emergence of the working class, Marx saw this antithesis between the town and the country as inexorably leading to de-peasantisation on the one side and proletarianisation on the other, leaving the worker with nothing else but his own labour power which too he is forced to sell. Marx's own historical writings pointed in this direction as only a general process which had specific aspect in specific time and place. But orthodox 'Marxists' studying the division of labour and the exchange of commodities, the progress of capitalism, predicated this into a law and sat down with their revolutionary horoscopes to work out the exact dates for the disappearance of the peasantry and the emergence, like the rising sun at an appointed time, of the proletariat. Only this did not happen. The peasantry continued in spite of its being wished away and the working class was present at its own making. Further they did not observe the command that "the twain shall never meet". This confounded the scholars and politicians whose simple schemes capital and labour refused to follow.

For many years, scholarship on the peasant question and the relationship between peasants and workers got embedded on the shoals of mystification and de-mystification of concepts and categories. The increasing sophistication of academics did not take into account that, in the final resort, learning is not "a question of dialectical reconcilation of concepts" but "of understanding of the real relations" (Marx 1973), whose conceptual format would give help in the commitment to define dimensions of oppression of men by men and of the ways to struggle against them. Thus, in the quagmire of 'scientificism' (which, for instance, considered Marx's *Capital* more 'scientific' than his *Eighteenth Brumaire*), the peasantry, as a living organic entity, was forgotten in the interest of studying capitalist transformation.

In any case, capitalism was taken to mean 'de-peasantisation'; industry would, according to this approach, outstrip, subordinate, and finally destroy peasant agriculture; so what was the need to waste time over the genus "potato" in the "sack of potatoes"?

Other scholars, who did not go so far, concerned themselves with studying ways in which capital penetrates agriculture and finally conquers it through a conflict of disembodied inhuman 'forces'. Yet others, nearer to the ground, were absorbed in the economic phenomena: the study of production relations, 'market relations' and the gradual disappearance of the peasantry through the process of 'differentiation'. The logic of commodity relations and exploitative capacity of the richer peasants indicated a necessary polarisation of the peasants into rich and poor, and eventually into 'rural' capitalists and rural proletarians. And, as for production, it would inexorably move through the stages of serfdom–peasant farming–agriculture to finally agri- business.

The Marxists indulging in the 'mode of production' debate followed the process of differentiation as a law of nature and received nods of approval from neoclassical economists. In spite of them however, once in a while, political activists like Lenin and Mao suddenly conjured up the differentiating, disappearing peasantry into a major political force: in their hands peasants seemed to be transformed from derivations and deductions to armies and actors. But every time the dust settled down, the scholars got back once again to their horoscopes to work out the dates for the disintegration of the peasantry in the face of the onward march of industry, capital and the nation-state.

Only, disintegration was not necessarily inevitable. Without doubt capitalism transformed agriculture and differentiation played an important part in the capitalist transformation, which often represented very significant structural changes. The theoretical and factual claims in support of this are valid. It is the interpretation of this as the axiomatically necessary and *exclusive* pattern, which is not. The model should lead to an increasing capital accumulation at the top. Such a process would de-peasantise, create a reserve army of labour, procure jobs for many of the newly pauperised turning them into proletarians and extending capitalism in the classical sense. This did not happen. The agrarian surplus accumulated neither in the village nor in the towns nor even in the country, but in a metropolis thousands of miles away. What followed was a polarisation indeed but a twisted one in which the downward trend was not matched by an upward one, i.e., what occurred was not differentiation and proletarianisation of the majority, but a process of pauperisation expressed in the phenomena of "surplus population", "rural under- employment" and "culture of poverty". It was not a "reserve army of labour" which was produced, for there is nobody to call on those reserves. The peasants did not dissolve and differentiate into capitalist entrepreneurs and wage labourers, nor were they simply pauperised. They persisted, while gradually transforming and linking into the encapsulating capitalist economy which pierces through their lives.

The scholars have been proved wrong in their optimistic, classical unilinear view of capitalism. They had seen it as aggressive, constructive, overwhelming and supra-energetic in its capacity to spread. Like the finger of Midas which turned everything it touched into gold, so also capitalism was expected to turn everything it touched into capitalism. This did not happen. The capacity of capitalism to milk everything and everybody around it is doubtless; it is capitalism's capacity or need (in terms of optimisation of profits and accumulation of surplus) to transform everything around it into replicas of itself, which is not. The peasants are a case in point. The alchemy of capitalism did turn them from baser metals into higher ones but often they became 14-carat and not necessarily 24-carat gold.

Peasants continued to exist, though in the economy as a whole, many of them were marginalised being both within agriculture and outside it. They serve capitalist development (or lumpen-bourgeois development of underdevelopment), though in an indirect manner, by a type of permanent "primitive accumulation", offering cheap labour, cheap food, cheaply captured markets for profit-making goods. They produce also healthy and stupid soldiers, policemen, servants, cooks and prostitutes; the system can always do with more of each of these. And of course, they, i.e. peasants, produce tasks and troubles for those scholars and officials who puzzle over "the problem of their non-disappearance"(Shanin 1978).

In addition to all these, the peasants also produce two other important commodities for the urban sector: food and labour. The exchange of these commodities transcends the separation between town and country. About the transfer of the first, food and raw materials, considerable amount of critical research now exists which has started breaking down notions of economic dualism (Breman 1976,1977). However, regarding the second, i.e. labour, several types of mystifications still exist. One concerns labour in the rural sector itself. Considering the fact that a very large segment of the working population consists of landless agricultural labourers, there seems to be a strange reluctance to expand the numbers of what is thought to be the 'category' of the working class. Even granting that the production process within which agricultural labourers are engaged gives them a limited world view, there is still no justification for the almost caste-like exclusiveness which the leaders of the industrial working class enjoin on the organisations of their followers, considering that both agricultural and industrial workers form a "loosely defined body of people who share the same congeries of interests, social experiences, traditions and value systems" and may indeed have a *disposition to behave* as a class. This latter point is more evident if the seasonal nature of the agricultural labourers' production process and the considerable migration patterns are taken into account. Regardless of this however, agricultural workers and industrial workers are not only segregated by politicians into separate organisations (when they are organised at all) but also the organisations are mediated by the political parties and leaders. Even academics generally tend to accept this segregation and rarely include the agricultural workers among the working class.

Another aspect of the mystification of the rural-urban labour nexus is with regard to the industrial workers. It seems that the only thing which is not disputed about them is that they exist (as individuals; whether they are a class is of course debated). The classical studies of the industrial workers (Mukherjee 1948; Morris 1965) traced their origins to the countryside. This was verified by 'social anthropological' researchers (Sheth 1968; Kapadia and Pillai

1972; Lambert 1963; Niehoff 1959; Ramaswamy 1977; Saberwal 1976;) although some sample surveys gave them the "quantitative treatment" and cut them off from the peasantry (e.g., Sharma 1970 and 1973).

However, detailed research on the subject has left no doubt about the rural origins of much of the industrial workforce. The interrelationship between workers in urban and rural settings is expressed clearly through the medium of migration and remittances (Byres 1979). The statistics of increasing urbanisation accompanied by sex disproportions in Indian cities point to migration being a significant factor, and although accurate statistics on remittances by rural-urban and rural-rural migrants are not available, the volume is by no means inconsiderable.

Figures of sex disproportions point to features of the capitalist political economy which have serious bearing on both industrial accumulation and rural stagnation/transformation. That this is an important issue is clear when we notice that old industrial centres like Bombay and Calcutta have sex ratios of roughly 600 women to 1000 men. In many other industrial areas like Dhanbad too there are only about 700 women per 1000 men. These figures do not even touch on intercensal temporary migrations of men and, on account of various factors, can be taken to be gross underestimates.

Nevertheless, on the basis of available statistics, if the sex disproportions in the major industrial centres of India are taken to be significant, a number of interesting conclusions can be drawn. The sex disproportions point to a situation where at least a large number of industrial workers lead 'bachelor' lives in the city. This means that the reproduction of labour is taking place away from the city. In other words, the agricultural sector, in particular the workers' families engaged in subsistence and other cultivation 'back home', subsidise exploitation of labour by capital in industry, with the consequence that workers can be paid less than subsistence wages. In spite of this however, living in animal and even worse conditions (Desai et al. 1972), the worker manages to remit small amounts of money to the family in the village. The family remaining behind, deprived as it is literally of its 'manpower', is neither able to intensively cultivate the little bit of land it might have, nor is it totally de-peasantised because the petty remittance acts as its buffer between pauperisation and prosperity. In some cases, as in Kerala and Punjab and some districts of Bihar where the amount of remittances is relatively high, they have even stimulated the land market and formerly landless people have started buying land in an ironical process which can only be described as 're-peasantisation'. In general however, the poor family in the village remains poor; subsistence cultivation continues; process of differentiation grinds excruciatingly slowly and the generalisation of wage labour seems to have been replaced by a generalisation of non-wage labour both through this process in the village and the 'housewifisation' of women (Mies 1979) and their decreasing participation in the wage labour force in the cities (India 1975).

The continued reluctance of Indian capitalism to bear the full costs of maintaining and reproducing the existing and future labour power of the working class—namely the costs of maintaining working class families and in many cases, the worker himself in times of childhood, old age and illness, and in some cases even during the working period—is even present in the agricultural sector. The extremely low level of wages and unwaged labour mean that the workers are pushed to a situation of finding or suplementing subsistence through non-marketable and non-priced 'waste' or by-products like fruit kernels, gleanings from harvested fields, minor forest produce and other items of a food-gathering system. Indeed in north India, there is a large caste group at the margins of the agrarian economy known as *Musahars* — those who eke out existence through eating field mice.

And yet in spite of the evidence, attempt has still been made to arrive at a concept of the "working class" without taking into account the female and rural half of that class.

It is obviously wrong to see the 'proletariat' as merely urban, industrial and predominantly male. The figures of agrarian proletarianisation in general and those relating to women in particular give the lie to such a concept.

Capitalism is obviously transforming the class position both in the urban and rural sectors, and of both men and women and 'proletarianising' large sections everywhere; only it is doing so in different cases in different ways. And yet, understanding of the effect of this process for the organic unity of the working class in India is not apparent even in 'radical' scholarship on the subject. This may be because theorists of the family, sexual division of labour and even the 'modes of production' have taken 'radicalism' to be synonymous with reductionism, "collapsing what is rational for capital (division of the working people into apparently different 'classes') into what is real", as Humphries (1977) has acidly put it.

CHAPTER 2

CATEGORIES INTO CONCEPTS

Against the vagueness of class has emerged the relative clarity of ethnicity. Class after all is an intangible concept whereas ethnicity is in essence a tangible grouping of people. Further, the concept of ethnicity has gained intellectual respectability on account of its linkage with the struggle for decentralisation and democracy while class has lost because of its unfortunate association with simplistic, even vulgar, proponents of what was seen as the command economy and political totalitarianism.

The issue of ethnicity has also gained currency because, in one sense, it does not need definition. Standing as it does between the individual and the State, it is an easy replacement for the other vaguely defined level of social organisation, civil society. Indeed, as society turns less and less civil, the primordialist appeal of ethnicity rather than the institutional structure of the State gains in appeal. And, precisely because of the very nature of primordialism which makes it "close to nature", ethnicity becomes an instantly graspable concept. At its very basic level, it expresses the herd instinct of the animal variety and therefore feeds on the instinctive rather than the conceptual.

But ethnicity is neither a species characteristic nor is it one which refers to intra-group ordering. It has its uses only as an indication of a loosely defined 'set identification' where it is necessarily located in the 'us' – them conundrum which vitiates any concept of humanism.

Nevertheless, the fact is that in the last several years, 'ethnicity' has not only gained intellectual respectability but it has also acquired tremendous power as a political phenomenon. In the struggle for decentralisation and democracy, the issues of identity, and hence ethnicity, have gained importance. It is significant that neither socialism as it has been practised nor capitalism can be premised on the self-identity of the individual or the broad species identity that takes the philosophical form of humanism. Both therefore have to seek intermediate identities and, under capitalism, ethnicity is one such convenient group identity.

The term 'ethnicity' is employed to describe groups of people whose consciousness about their identity is sometimes more powerful than even the concepts of nations, States or nation-States. This is a new meaning of ethnicity and it is still developing beyond the boundaries of the earlier concept which identified it with 'race' to encapsulate language, religion and culture.

But language, religion and culture have been combined earlier too, either with or without race, to form a compound which has been labelled 'nation'. In fact, till recently, almost all attributes of ethnicity were also ascribed to nation and nationalism and it is a moot question as to when and why the distinction between the two concepts arose. One explanation is that, unlike ethnicity, nationalism has an essential economic content and it is that, along with other factors, which posited it against colonialism and in some cases even against capitalism itself. As the ideological hegemony of capitalism asserted itself on account of a variety of factors, it was found convenient to promote the culturalistic concept of ethnicity to counter both the holistic concept of class and the socio-economic concept of nation.

Be that as it may, even without going at this stage deeply into the discussion on nation, it is apparent that till recently in much of social discourse, the term 'nation' has been used in much the same sense as 'ethnicity' is used now. This is particularly so when nation is posited against the State and examined in the light of capitalism itself.

The discussion of State and capital has often been vitiated by mystification on the one side and oversimplification on the other. Those who consider themselves to be the acolytes of Adam Smith chant the mantra of the market with full and touching faith in the mysterious powers of "the invisible hand" to make everything perfect in this most perfect of all possible worlds. Spanning the ideological divide, the heirs of Hegel marvel at the State as "the march of God on earth". And, on the other side, simple-minded materialists limit the examination of society to the means and relations of production. All three underrate social and cultural factors.

An interesting contribution in respect of the body of historical materialist thought is the addition of the category 'conditions of production' to those of the 'forces and relations of production'. These include the different geographical, historical, even anthropological — in short, cultural — contexts in which production takes place.

The geographical context is obviously very important because most production is still dependent on the variables of land, water, mineral resources and so on. It is also on this account that cultural contexts, identities, self-definitions, ethnicities are localised in the geographical or territorial sense. Nicos Poulantzas (1978) refers to "history of a territory and territorialisation of history — in short a territorial national tradition concretised in the nation-State", but, given the process of de-Statification of much of human activity, the same territorialisation phenomenon finds articulation with non-State or even anti-State ethnicity.

At the same time, both the processes and conditions of production are getting increasingly "globalised" and local control over these is getting abbreviated. In such a situation, the by now almost classical paradigm of alienation finds increasing expression. Consequently, while people lose control over themselves in the realm of production, they also seek to assert their group identities in the localised cultural context.

"Ethnicity possesses features which may well be illustrated in a parallel vein. There emerged a conflict between the attempt to establish a modern, integrated, frequently bourgeois State, and the parochial parameters of the smaller self-identifying communities which the State attempted to subsume. In conditions when the capitalist mode of production had not totally assimilated the whole of the nation, where class formation itself was still correspondingly incomplete, where remnants of older modes of production, social formations and cultural differences persisted, the necessary material conditions were at hand for regimes of crisis, for ethnic conflict and possibly for the collapse of the whole project of bourgeois nation-building. The material premises of ethnic conflict, and the flawed project of modern nation-building on a capitalist and frequently authoritarian basis are, therefore, not difficult to see" (David and Kadirgamar, 1989).

Indeed, the same observations have been made earlier about nationalism in a period when nationalism, rather than ethnicity, was the currently fashionable term.

Writing in the context of the emergence of European nationalism, Munck (1986) asserts: "Nations existed before capitalism," and goes on to elaborate as follows:

Yet it may be necessary for Marxism to recognise that a nation possesses a unique collective subjectivity, structured by language and a common economic history, which is specific to a particular people. To say that a social group has a common history and that it constitutes a particular type of community is by no means to deny the conflict between social classes which compose it. It is only to recognise that the concept of nation existed before the bourgeoisie created the nation-state.

Apart from the somewhat nebulous idea of the 'structuring by language', these remarks may be forcefully applied to the proposition that separated ethnicities existed before colonialism.

A commission of French Marxists (1970) makes much the same point when it says: "Behind the nation-state there exists another relatively independent concept, that of nationality. Nationality designates the community of culture of peoples, determined by an identical history and material conditions of existence."

The problem with such a concept however is that it has no historical concreteness. In the Indian context, for instance, it can be easily asked whether "the community of culture of peoples" refers to the colonial, pre-colonial, pre-Islamic or pre-Aryan period. It is also a concept which is static and does not take into account the changing natures of such "communities of culture". Again, in India, an observation has been made that the whole process of development of culture can be described as the merging of a tribal stream into a general one. We shall see the historical details of such a process later but even at this stage it is necessary to refer to the famous "composite culture" of India which creates its celebrated "unity in diversity". Without a historical understanding based on the dialectics of cultural evolution, a concept of ethnicity is frozen in time, mostly in one slice of the present, and in fact negates the past in a vicious way. The future of such a social form is beset with grave peril.

It cannot be denied that in the process of the very emergence and articulation of specific ethnicities, the self- definition of other ethnicities is crucial. Similarly, in historical terms, the significance of the State in the evolution of ethnicity is profound. "Where a linguistic-geographic unit, for example, persisted for a millenia (sic) as a State and a separate entity of social production, the persistence of ethnicity, or its revival in the sphere of social consciousness a few years or decades after this State form is subsumed by another, is not an anomaly, but something to be expected. Where the material basis is destroyed for longer periods, the old ethnic consciousness is displaced by a new one — the Goths and Vandals became German. Ethnicities disappear and new ones emerge" (David and Kadirgamar 1989).

It is interesting and instructive to note the example of Germany in this context of the definition of ethnicities. Till the Middle Ages, the Germans of today consisted of a large number of tribally and locally defined groups. It was only the sustained State activity under Fredrick the Great in the eighteenth century that transformed these various ethnicities into articulating themselves as a German nation, a process that was philosophised by Hegel and actualised through ruthless realpolitik by Bismarck. In the 120 years period subsequent to the "unification of Germany", there have been many ups and downs in the self-definition of Germans. The conflict over Alsace-Lorraine, the ceding and re-capture of Saarland and parts of the mineral-rich Ruhr, the rise and fall of the "pure" German state under Hitler with its need for lebensraum, the fact that for 45 years one part of Germany was constituted as a separate State and social system, and most recently the trend of subsumption of German identity in a broader European identity — all point to the chequered career of ethnicity there.

What emerges from this case however is that the very definition of ethnicity is dynamic and while it is conditioned to a large extent by the State, its basis is in fact in the material realm of production and material culture.

What determines which ethnicities are 'selected' as poles of activation? Not culture, nor ideology, nor some nebulous structuring by language or religion, but an actual material history. Surprisingly, it is the study of ethnicity, thought to be a non-historical material concept, which has persuaded us of the inadequacies of an idealist, that is anti-historical materialist, cognizance of history. Superficially, ethno- politics appears to be determined by identity and culture, but they themselves are selected, transformed and set in motion by palpable material linkages. The dialectics of conflict, in turn, further transforms ideology and constrains the material premises in new ways (David and Kadirgamar 1989).

Now, given the fact that both ethnicity and class have bases in material culture, what is their interrelationship? While a few decades earlier a view was that class overrides ethnicity and even nationalism, it appears today that ethnic loyalties persist over class solidarity. It is not clear today as to how this conflict will resolve itself in the ultimate analysis; hence for the present it is essential to investigate the reasons for the tensions between the two.

There are many aspects of both ethnicity and class and therefore many modes of their mutual articulation. The dissonance between the two arises from many sources. In their seminal book *Ethnicity*, David and Kadirgamar (1989) outline them in the following manner.

The absence of capitalist/class homogenisation is one aspect of the tension between class and ethnicity. The other is that the principal classes which form the poles of capitalist production relations, the bourgeoisie and the proletariat, are numerically swamped by other population groups. These include intermediate groups such as the middle class, and the petty- bourgeoisie properly speaking, which does actually occupy some intermediate position within the capitalist mode. There are also large segments which belong to survivors of pre-capitalist production relations or to bastard or peripheral or client production conditions which have sprouted around the principal capitalist mode.

It is to be expected from their location in the production process, and this is confirmed by experience in political activity, that religious and ethnic ideology, culture and custom, play a far more important role with these classes than it does with the principal classes at the theoretical poles — the bourgeoisie and the proletariat. The ideological parameters of these classes, therefore, need to be considered further.

Although the working class may be fractured along ethnic lines, and although the bourgeoisie is prone to racial and religious prejudices, the vital and active repository of ethnic consciousness in the Third World is this larger collection, for convenience usually referred to simply as the petty bourgeoisie, both rural and urban. The middle and upper strata of this class — traders and money-lenders, teachers, monks and mullahs, small businessmen and the ubiquitous agents and politicos — constitute the true repository of racial, linguistic or religious consciousness. Because of their education and money, they also succeed in giving leadership to the larger petty bourgeois mass of peasants, city lumpen and also to landless rural labour. When, due to the great numerical preponderance of these classes, the tide grows, a section of the organised working class too begins to succumb.

There is a reason why this particular segment of the petty bourgeoisie functions as the source of modern ethnic consciousness. It is only indirectly to do with the fact that indigenous teachers, monks and mullahs have been close to local culture and may perhaps have championed religious or linguistic causes against colonialism and the westernised elite in previous decades. It is more directly to do with social mobility in the post-colonial phase.

The rising expectations of the better-off stratum of the petty bourgeoisie, especially its aspirations for its children, converge on such issues as white collar employment and the professions, education and social acceptance. It is inevitable that a 'limited' programme such as this (limited as opposed to social transformation), given the parameters of ethno-consciousness out of which this class has issued, leads to competition and intolerance. Intolerance engenders conflict when the crisis of the economy shrinks the cake in relation to numbers and aspirations.

The class power of the bourgeoisie, which exists in the economic and social plane, functions in the political sphere through State power. In the context of the relative balances of power described in the previous paragraphs, it is not possible for an effete Third World bourgeoisie to hold State power except through alliances and adaptations with other classes. This is true even of military dictatorships in the Third World. The State power possesses a relative autonomy from class power, but that is not our point here; this autonomy does, however, explain how these class alliances are mediated.

Even in developed capitalism, the hegemonic bourgeois ideology has to accommodate and diffuse working class power through, for example, reformism and parliamentary democracy, if it is to hold State power. All the more so in the far less advantageous position that the Third World bourgeoisie occupies; an unholy alliance with some or other petty bourgeois sector is the only way to hold State power (David and Kadirgamar 1989).

It is seen that the material and historical specificity of many countries was such, however, that these, in turn, made ethnic oppression or discrimination necessary. This is the history of the articulation of ethnicity with class in at least the first phase of ethnopolitics.

The important point is that both ethnicity and class are essentially political phenomena. While the first draws on culture, religion and language and the second on relations of production and, to an extent, region, both find themselves only when they make their appearance on the political plane. And, this is not the only commonality among the two. They also meet and dialectically interact through politics. For instance, it is clear that new expressions of ethnicity are not mere revivals of old divisions. Ethnicity itself is transformed dialectically by the crises and contradictions of class society, the weaknesses and strengths of contending classes and by the exercise of class power through the State. Similarly, class too is often expressed through the medium of constructed ethnic identities.

Using an earlier terminology, Ernest Gellner (1983) wrote of a similar phenomenon: "Nationalism is not the awakening of an old, latent, dormant force, though that is how it presents itself. It is in reality the consequence of a new form of social organisation, based on education-dependent high cultures, each protected by its own State."

David and Kadirgamar (1989) have made an excellent summary of the various historical specificities which contextualise the manifestation of ethnicities. They present what they call the "dynamics of manifestation" schematically within the general framework of imperialism and global capitalism and the international balance of power:

1. The extension of the bourgeois mode of production into the residual regions of the economy entails marginalisation or pauperisation of communities, genocide of tribal people and the manipulation of sectional interests.

2. The weakness — structural [arising from the incomplete penetration of the nation by the dominant mode of production, the enormous political weight of the rural petty-bourgeoisie and peasant masses, and the threat to bourgeois political hegemony from sometimes powerful working class movements — economic and ideological) of the bourgeois class or the bourgeois-landlord alliance, which inherited State power from colonialism, forces its ruling groups into variegated political alliances with sections of the petty bourgeoisie for the purposes of holding on to State power. Reactionary ideologies are the cement of these contracts; 'necessary' material-political alliances reflect themselves in the political-ideological plane, the sphere of consciousness, as hegemonic ideologies.

3. The attempt to correct the unequal treatment meted out to different communities during the colonial period especially during the formation and expansion of the administration, bureaucracy and the army bedevils ethnic relations. Because of the reactionary alliances and ideologies, the organs of State which are being built or expanded are frequently ethnically flawed, internally. This has important repercussions in many countries since the State is the big spender, the major employer and the provider of education, health and other services.

4. Not merely mass poverty and the apparently endless failure of economic growth, but even more sharply a crisis of expectations deeply affects the Third World. While there is indeed much absolute poverty, there is also relative poverty — relative to what every educated youth knows to prevail in advanced countries. There is an impatience for a decent life, education and a place in the sun. When leftist ideology apparently fails to provide a quick answer to these expectations, false consciousness usually breeds crass racism or

religious intolerance.

5. Even when economic growth does take place, the dynamics of the development itself exacerbates social tensions at another level and in more complex ways. The condition in Punjab, India's most prosperous state, is the story of a ferocious ethnicity whose roots lie in more complex socio-economics than poverty and discrimination. The roots lie in the deformations of retarded capitalism.

These ideas are put together in Munck's remark (1986), "In other words, uneven development can cause nationalism, whether at the poor or rich pole of the process." However, he goes on to add, "We could argue that uneven development explains the economic basis of national divisions, but as with much of Marxism it leans towards economic reductionism".

6. The authoritarian State arises from the weakness of the bourgeoisie, the corruption and nepotism of the ruling classes and the ferocity of the cycle of violence and counter-violence in relation to national minorities. The authoritarian State is the harbinger of terror, violence and torture, but the ease with which ethnic militancy assimilates violence, often degrading and meaningless, leads to its own degeneration.

7. The only partial homogenisation of global power has sometimes resulted in an "anarchy in interstate relations in the periphery" (Arrighi 1982). To this can be added the fragmentation of the nation-State itself in many cases.

8. The ease of communication and transaction on a global scale in modern times, has stripped State power of its monopoly of physical force. This is a crucial technical change that has breathed life and stamina into armed ethnic movements.

9. Foreign involvement in ethnic militancy has proved to be a double-edged sword and the specific variations are numerous.

This variety of factors, features and phenomena related to the unfolding on ethnicity (and, for that matter, class struggle) demonstrates that in any case the formulae of nationalism were deeply flawed. Laclau (1977) had made this point earlier:

"Let us take an example: nationalism. Is it a feudal, bourgeois or proletarian ideology? Considered in itself it has no class connotation. The latter only derives from its specific articulation with other ideological elements. A feudal class can, for example, link nationalism to the maintenance of a hierarchical- authoritarian system of a traditional type—we need only think of Bismarck's Germany. A bourgeois class may link nationalism to the development of a centralised nation state in fighting against feudal particularism, and at the same time appeal to national unity as a means of neutralising class conflicts — think of the case of France. Finally, a communist movement can denounce the betrayal by capitalist classes of a nationalist cause and articulate nationalism and socialism in a single ideological discourse — think Mao for example."

It is possible to make similar observations about ethnicity. For instance, Randhir Singh (1990) concludes about the Sikh extremist movement that much of it is a product, even a reactive outcome, of the politics of the ruling classes as has been practised in Punjab in recent years. "Nevertheless, it is correct, and not unfair, to assess the overall character of this movement to be socially reactionary, communal and divisive, anti-communist, even fascistic" (Singh 1990).

David and Kadirgamar (1989) point out that "In discussing the crisis of ethnicity it is essential to appreciate that there is an important difference between supporting the rights of an oppressed minority and harbouring illusions about the political programmes of many ethnic 'liberation' organisations. The political and economic programmes put forward by these organisations are often untenable and are, sometimes, downright reactionary. In other cases they may indeed possess a healthy and progressive thrust. Frequently, we have a third variant, a somewhat garbled programme, but in the realities of struggle, such movements subordinate the progressive content to terror, fundamentalism and plain ignorance."

The crisis of ethnicity manifests itself in two ways — as a crisis of the programme, which is seen more and more clearly to be untenable, or as a crisis of the dynamics of struggle, that is a dead-end or a no-win situation.

These painful manifestations include on some occasions an alienation of the 'national liberation' organisation(s) from the very peoples they intend to represent, and sometimes even their reduction to small, sectarian groups or armed bands, and in some cases intense factionalism and even internecine slaughter of great ferocity.

Given this mixed record of ethnic assertion, a consequence of its mixed nature itself, the question that arises relates to the modes in

which social groupings can arise or can be deliberately fashioned so
that while alienation of the individual is prevented, the oppression
of the State too is combated. And, in that context, repeatedly we
come across the two paradigms of primordialism and institutionalism. The mediation between the two can be through class.

In the following pages we will look at aspects of Indian history
and the contemporary situation in order to discover the dialectical
relationship between these two. And in doing so we will try to get
a view of India, "from the worm's eye" as it were. We shall also see
the evolving nature of some of the many pluralisms which constitute
India. Drawing on the work of various scholars, we shall try to get
a fix on at least one moment of the changing kaleidoscope that
represents India and humanity itself.

CHAPTER 3

'TRIBE' IN INDIA: FROM
ETHNICITY TO CLASS

If we stop history at a given point, then there are no classes
but simply a multitude of individuals with a multitude of
experiences. But if we watch these men over an adequate
period of social change, we observe patterns in their relationships, their ideas and their institutions. Class is defined
by men as they live their own history, and, in the end, this
is its only definition.

E P Thompson (1968)

Although it is obvious that definitional exercises are not always
fruitful in considering social complexities, it is necessary in the
present context to attempt to define the subject if only with the
intention of clearing some conceptual cobwebs which obscure the
relationship between what are called 'tribes' and are the staple of
ethnicity and class. Pathy (1982 etc.) has done this admirably and
the following discussion draws heavily on his work.

It is particularly important in the Indian context to assert that
'tribe' cannot and should not be related to 'race' as that fallacy has
often been repeated by ethnographers and anthropologists who have
presumed in their use of the term 'tribe' for certain communities
common ancestry and specific genetic characteristics. It is not
coincidental that such a presumption has been accompanied by
political domination of these communities. It is also not merely
accidental that before colonialism, outsiders who came into contact
with such communities referred to them as 'peoples', 'kingdoms',
dwellers of particular regions, etc., and only exceptionally as 'tribes'.
It was only in the heydays of colonialism i.e. by the end of the

nineteenth century, that colonial administrators and anthropologists labelled sections of the subject people as 'tribes'.

In the Indian historical tradition, both in terms of ancient literature as well as contemporary folk terminology, there is no equivalent of the value-loaded term 'tribe'. The nearest concept is that of the Sanskrit *janah* which denotes an agglomeration of individuals with a definite territorial kinship and cultural pattern (Choudhary 1977:6-12). Prior to the colonial annexation of parts of India inhabited by such groups, most of the presently called 'tribes' were either unconscious of their ethno-tribal identities or called themselves "people" vis-a-vis outsiders (Pathy 1982:6). Instead, the issue of *juxtaposed identity* was very important in the demarcation of self-identity as the latter was neither conceptually autonomous nor, in practical existence, particularly distinguishable. Alongside, such terms (e.g. Atavikas, Girijans, Vanvasis, etc.) as were used for these people by the 'outsiders' also referred to their location (as dwellers in hills and forests, etc.) rather than to distinct racial features.

This is not surprising in the Indian context where the intermixing of 'races' such as the Australoid, Mongolian and Caucasian had gone on for so long and had penetrated so deep that even the emergent vocabulary was particularly non-racial, using for instance the term Aryan (*Arya*) to denote behavioural rather than significantly racial characteristics. Neither did the evidence of adherence to particular religions indicate racial categories, as the very evolution of Hinduism was the product of the interaction of various popular-cultural streams (Kosambi 1975). Even the spread of Islam and Christianity in India was not among racially specific groups but through conversion of large number of various peoples. Thus, it was only with the coming of colonialism, whose perpetrators conceived themselves as racially distinct, alien and superior, that there was a systematic search for racial categories and gradations in India.

In particular, during the nineteenth century, when colonial capitalist expansionism faced formidable opposition from 'forest-dwellers', primitive groups, etc. (as contrasted with the relatively simpler subjugation of the mainstream population), many of these 'peoples' were termed 'tribes' and attributed a-historical racial characteristics which were borrowed from the experience of colonial expansion in America, Australia and Africa. They were simplistically distinguished from Hindus and Muslims on the assumption that they were animists while the others were not. On the economic scale, they were placed as being 'backward' food-gatherers or shifting cultivators. On cultural criteria, obviously artificial and alien, they were described as being 'primitive'. On juridical grounds, since they were difficult to tame and subject, many of them were classified as being 'criminal'. And on the chronological scale, they were put as the earliest inhabitors of India—the aboriginals, autochthons—whose repeated subjugation by waves of 'outsiders' provided the 'logical justification' for colonialism too. In the interest of the requirements of different phases of the colonial administration, they were either brutally suppressed or subjected to special regulations which at best amounted to paternal despotism.

These communities were given different appellations and thus most such 'peoples' have come to be known today by names they did not recognise themselves, while several widely dispersed masses of people were brought under a blanket nomenclature. A number of cognate groups of people were arbitrarily divided into several communities among the Indian 'non-tribal' people too. In the Census of India in 1931, serious attempt was made by the colonial administration to list the "primitive tribes"' and it was discovered that while the "forest tribes"' of 1891 had numbered 16 millions, in 1931 the "primitive tribes"' numbered 22 millions. Shortly thereafter in the Government of India Act of 1935, they were redesignated and were called "backward tribes"'. After Independence, special provisions were made for the administration of these peoples and they were listed in separate schedules of the Constitution, thus becoming known as "scheduled tribes"'. Even after Independence the numbers of such 'tribes' kept going up: from 212 in 1950 at the time of the adoption of the Constitution of India it became 427 in 1971. Together they constitute about 7.5 per cent of the total Indian population today.

In short, 'tribe' in India is essentially a politico-administrative category and has hardly any specific racial or even socio-cultural and economic characteristics. Critical sociology has been asking, "Should the juridical category of scheduled 'tribes', which may grind a political axe, be our guide to impose the invidious distinction of tribals and others on the Indian society?" (Mukherjee 1974:180).

Still, in spite of such questions and the knowledge that the classification of people was ad hoc, unscientific, based on stereotypes and images and geared to administrative ends, for all practical — and even most academic — purposes, "a tribe is a tribe which is included in the list of scheduled tribes" (Pathy 1982:10). A political categorisation of society has been reified into becoming social reality. And further, the reality has acquired stability as the official list has been so axiomatised (on account of protective discrimination which it implies) that critical scrutiny is prone to be dubbed a reactionary political move and definition of tribe *ipso facto* an irrelevant academic exercise.

It has been demonstrated, as is discussed in detail later in this chapter, that the common definitional attributes of 'tribes' are (1) oldest inhabitants of the land but with shallow histories; (2) common name, territory and language; (3) strong kinship bonds with endogamy and distinct taboos; (4) single social rank and political organisation; (5) distinct customs, moral codes, religious beliefs and rituals; (6) high illiteracy; (7) common ownership of means of production or simple economic profession at subsistence level; and (8) low level of technological development. If all these indicators are taken to be necessary for a community of people to be called tribe, then apart from very few communities of almost exceptional nature, most of those listed in the statutory schedules are excluded. On the other hand, in India almost any community would be able to claim to be a tribe on the basis of a few of these attributes. In other words, unless all these attributes are grouped in some way, sequentially or transferably, there can be $[(2^8 -1)=255]$ variants of tribe which would nullify, or at least drastically reduce, the analytical relevance of the concept.

Hence what is required is the identification of the most significant and necessary denominator which not only characterises the community but also determines its transformation, i.e., if that factor changes, the system itself tends to change (Pathy et al. 1976:403).

It is therefore also necessary to examine two other important aspects in this context: (i) the distinction, if possible and necessary, of tribe from other social aggregates like peasantry, caste and class, and (ii) the contemporary self-perception of the concerned people.

Historically, even this analytical exercise is difficult to carry out as not only have multi-ethnic formations existed in many situations but indeed, "the entire course of Indian history shows tribal elements being fused in general society" (Kosambi 1975:27). In fact, even the isolation and consequent backwardness of so-called 'tribes' is not necessarily an ancient phenomenon. The very colonial policy of calculated unevenness of production, forced isolation of 'tribes' and, ironically, the development of modern transport which changed and even destroyed traditional trade routes and systems, encouraged and in some cases even created conditions of relative isolation rather than accelerate the processes of fusion and integration. In other cases, as for instance that of Palamau in Bihar, the opening of the cotton route through it, resulted in creation of periodic labour shortages on account of facilitated migration, and led to the attempt by the landowners to secure workers for the peak seasons through the system of bonded labour (Mundle 1978).

Some anthropologists (e.g. Roy Burman 1975:33) have concluded that it was with colonialism that the "isolated" and the "primitive" was born. Such a view is obviously sweeping and extreme, not taking into account all aspects of social development—exceptional or otherwise, but what can certainly be said is that colonialism changed the context and level of tribal–non-tribal social interaction to suit colonial interests.

In the context of tribals' exchange, interaction and integration with others, it is also interesting to note that at least one-fourth of the number of declared — 'scheduled' — tribes today are spread in three or more states in India. Gonds are found in eight states; Bhils in seven; Khonds and Savaras in six; Mundas, Oraons and four others in five; and no less than 16 other 'tribes' in four states each. The spread of an individual tribe is not necessarily contiguous, implying a great degree of mobility. Another very important aspect in this context is that many of the 'tribes' are settled cultivators, internally stratified and practically indistinguishable from other peasant groups. Thus not only is geographical isolation not a significant feature of tribal India but in fact a large segment of the tribal population forms an integral part of peasant society and is thus a general participant in the processes of rural change.

An analysis carried out nearly twenty years ago of the occupation of 384 'tribes' revealed that as many as 234 of them are agriculturists while only 71 small 'tribes' depend on hunting, fishing, other forms of food-gathering and animal husbandry, 56 'tribes' depend primarily on trade, commerce and handicrafts and 40 others live by selling their labour (Danda 1973). Among tribal cultivators, who constitute about 85% of the tribal working population, there are marked disparities in land-ownership: while 10.62% of households own more than 15 acres, 54.71% own less than five acres (Pathy et al. 1976: 403-04). In spite of such evidence, however, many Indian anthropologists, following classical colonial ethnography, continue to depict 'tribes' as small, self-contained, self-sufficient, isolated, homogenous and autonomous communities, not amenable to class-analysis and class action and essentially static and a-historical.

One group of anthropologists has however admitted that the 'ideal' social aggregate of tribe is merely conceptual and, if it existed at all it did so only in the (undefined) past; and that what exist today are 'tribes' in transition (Beteille 1977; Desai 1977; Dube 1977). Even this realisation is nevertheless restricted, not critically re-examining the notion of lack of internal dynamics in tribal society. The transition in fact is largely seen as sociological rather than politico-economic, a shift from 'tribe' to 'caste' (Mandelbaum 1970 : 573-619; Sinha 1958). It is stressed that "the direction of tribal change is clear and predictable, virtually all 'tribes' are now shifting toward *jati* characteristics, a movement which has greatly accelerated as communications have impinged more closely" (Mandelbaum 1970:593). In fact, some sociologists have even gone so far as to call 'tribes' "backward Hindus" (Ghurye 1943).

These analyses, while correctly rejecting the earlier paradigms of physical and cultural anthropology, which took an unhistorical and static view of 'tribes', do not come to grips with economic and political processes and internal dynamics among the 'tribes'. Most such social anthropologists have preferred to consider them in light of caste, as points of a social continuum (Bailey 1961; Haimendorf 1948; Sinha 1965). It is only relatively recently that a few attempts have been made to understand some Indian 'tribes' as differentiated peasant societies (Bose 1981; Mandal 1975; Misra 1979; Pathy 1982; Roy Burman 1975; Sengupta 1982; Shah 1976,1979; Upadhyay 1980; etc.).

This realisation of 'tribes in transition' and their characterisation as 'peasants' is a significant advance in Indian ethnology as it does away with the perspective of timeless, unchanging, undifferentiated conglomerates eking out subsistence existence in confrontation not with other men but with the elemental forces of nature. It is not that earlier anthropology totally ignored the existence of hierarchy in tribal societies but its concern was with 'sacred', 'ritual' or 'pollution hierarchy'. In contrast, social anthropology recognises today a different kind of hierarchy, 'secular', 'politico-economic' based on the devolution of economic and social power (Bose 1981), and change among the 'tribes' is now sought to be understood on the basis of the secular principle of class (Das 1984).

Even this advance however is impeded by various factors, the most important of which transforms history to being one separate specialised social science rather than a method of all social scientific inquiry. Thus, even while correctly identifying 'tribes' as components of peasant society, or for that matters in certain cases of industrial organisation, the attempt shifts to cross-sectional analysis, at given points of time, of various existential and behavioural features rather than to understand social dynamics, where attention is paid on forces of change through internal organisations of tribal societies and their connections with the various dimensions of the obtaining political economy (Pathy 1976;Upadhyay 1980). Even in the latter case, the issue of how the external forces articulate themselves within the tribal organisation is little attended. The external forces are simply juxtaposed with the internal organisation, and, in that sense, at the theoretical level there is not much difference between the two perspectives of change (Pathy 1982:39- 55).

A widely accepted theory on the articulation of the external and internal factors in the dynamics of tribal societies is in fact based on the curious paradox of disarticulation through physical displacement of tribal groups from their original habitat by non-tribals. The confusion inherent in such a proposition is confounded by parallel theories of integration and absorption of tribals in the 'mainstream society': "There is considerable evidence to suggest that several groups were pushed out of the areas where they were first settled and had to seek shelter elsewhere. And there are several groups, now absorbed in Hindu society, which can make an equally tenable claim to being original, or at any rate, very old inhabitants" (Dube 1977:2).

In light of such illuminating complexity before coming to the contemporary situation of tribals in India, it is worthwhile taking a brief, albeit sketchy, overview of the historical processes that seem to have led to the present.

The dislocation theorists begin with the assumption of 'tribes' being pushed back into inhospitable terrains by the waves of Aryan invasions of India (Bhowmik 1982:297), an assertion made by racist colonial administrators and repeated *ad infinitum* (and some may say, *ad nauseum*!). Not only does such ethnographic scholarship ignore that in many respects the Aryans themselves seem to have been constituted of what would appear to be 'tribal' formations, but given historical evidence of their stage of production vis-a-vis that of the Indus Valley civilisation as well as the very sparse population of the vast and fertile lands of India in that period, there was neither the necessity nor, for that matter, the possibility of large-scale displacement of aboriginal populations.

Some historians at least have looked at this theory of displacement far more critically than conventional anthropologists. Thus, "the historians therefore cannot but doubt the theory that a large number of Aryans conquered northern India, enslaving the existing population and thereby establishing their language and culture, both entirely alien to the indigenous tradition. It has to be conceded that, if there was a conquest, it was limited to parts of the extreme north. It was more likely that groups of Aryan-speaking people migrated into northern India, and settled and mixed with the indigenous population. The culture that resulted evolved from this interaction" (Thapar 1975:26-27).

The displacement theorists and some tribal populists too, then pose the question of how in that case it is that 'tribes', by and large, inhabit the less fertile parts of India today if they were not pushed back from the more fertile river banks. The answer to this is found in the specific activities of production that respective groups were engaged in. The agriculturists and traders who dominated the Indus Valley civilisation inhabited the river banks of Western India and some coastal and other outposts; the pastoral Aryans spread out in due course also along the lush river banks eastwards, clearing forests as they went along by burning them, and the hunters and gatherers continued in the uplands which were more suited to their appropriation of subsistence: "Primitive man would live best in thinner marginal jungle, not in territory now bearing deeper, cultivated soil; that is, the best localities for the food gatherers were approximately where they are found today" (Kosambi 1975a:41).

These separate modes of social existence of course did not mean that they were not articulated with each other. There were not only trade, political and cultural contacts (Chattopadhyaya 1968:178-79) but each one took over aspects of the very production activities from the other. It is interesting to note that a number of agricultural implements mentioned in Vedic literature like *Langala/hala* (plough) and *Kuddala* (spade) are of Mundari (tribal) etymological origin (Singh 1985). Rituals were profitably exchanged between groups to make alliance (Sharma 1975:9-11) and composite material cultures developed over time. With increase in economic surplus, social formations appropriate to the process of its expropriation by some from others [like caste (Klass 1980)] and need for the emergent state and ruling class to subjugate specific groups of people to gain access to vital natural resources [like the conquest of present-day Chhotanagpur and Orissa by Ashok in the 4th century B.C. to establish control over sources of iron ore (Kosambi 1975,1975a)] led to further stratification and segmentation on the one side and emergence of commonality in culture, society, economy and polity on the other.

There were periods of centralised rule when the marginal groups were either sought to be subjugated through force of arms (Chattopadhyaya 1968) or pacified otherwise (Thapar 1974) or integrated into the obtaining state structure through marital alliances or incorporation into ritual hierarchies by religious sanctification (Kosambi 1975a:171). There were other periods of political fragmentation, when feudalisation was ascendant, during which the tribals, like others, formed small kingdoms. As early as the first century B.C. the Bhils of Malwa had their own little kingdom which soon disintegrated (Kosambi 1975:43), a process which was replicated many times by different tribal peoples like Mundas (Roy 1982:65-80), Gonds (OMalley 1976:84), Bhuiyas and Binjhals (Singh 1982), Chutiyas and Kacharis (Guha 1967), Khasis (Mishra 1979) and many others.

A feature of these states was that their subjects neither completely belonged to a particular tribe nor all the members of a tribe belonged to a single State (Pathy 1982:67). As the stability of these States depended on economic prosperity, their rulers took measures to increase production by encouraging the settlement of exogamous agricultural and artisan groups. In order to further stabilise their kingdoms, several of the rulers married outside their own 'tribes' to try to obtain the legitimacy of Kshatriya status (Kosambi 1975a:192).

In terms of control over land and territory, the favourable land-man ratios prevented alienation of lands of particular groups from becoming a major issue. In fact, in the early part of Mughal rule there was still a shortage of labour for cultivation throughout the country and thus a mixture of cajolery, economic inducements as well as terror was used to keep the tillers of the land at work (Habib 1963:115-18).

Along with the small 'tribal' kingdoms, there were numerous petty tribal chiefdoms which relied heavily on shifting cultivation and long-distance trade. These social formations were relatively, but only relatively, more isolated and kept to their indigenous customs and traditions more rigidly; in the case of small units of hunters and food gatherers articulation with external structurers was limited.

The Hindu and Mughal kings, by and large, accepted the limited authority of tribal chiefs and kings. This was rational from their point of view. Under the political economy of feudalism, it was neither possible to completely integrate the people into a single socio-cultural whole (Sharma 1965) nor was it necessary, as acceptance of tribal leadership rationalised the divisions in society which insulated the central power from organised resistance. Some of the Mughals in fact had a calculated policy of protecting the interests of the tributary chiefs even at the cost of the royal revenue (Jain 1979). The tribals were of course encouraged to reclaim waste and forest lands and incentives for this were offered to both tribals and non-tribals. Thus, under Akbar for instance, a policy of peaceful peasantisation of tribals in the long-term interest of the state was pursued and when this policy was reversed either by the Mughals or by the Marathas, not only did the 'tribes' rise in violent revolt (O'Malley 1976:79) but peasant insurrection generally assumed tribal overtones and resulted in downfall of empires (Habib 1963).

In sum, tribal India was unevenly composed. By and large, the 'tribes' enjoyed relative autonomy with the hegemony of the paramount power seldom strictly imposed on them. The food-gathering communities reproduced themselves with little interference and the peasants among the 'tribes' were subjected, at worst, to similar extortions as levied from the peasants in general. Some 'tribes' were in fact better-off than the general peasantry; the Santhals for instance were considered tribal groups but were internally structured with varying degrees of stratification, with the divisions being most marked between tribute/rent-receivers and actual producers. There was a complex system with distinct and yet interconnected levels of tribal existence in pre-colonial India.

To start with, the British followed a policy of benign neglect or non- interference towards most of the 'tribes', and in particular towards those who were located away from the area of their immediate concern. To the extent that the British were forced to come into contact with the relatively remote tribal areas, they recognised the feudatory States subject to their paying tribute. A similar policy was adopted towards the hill chieftains also; they were accorded recognition under the colonial administration as petty kings and in some cases, as those of the Lushais and Khasis, they were made the *de facto* owners of communal lands (Chaube 1982). This indirect rule suited the early colonialists: "The very recognition and upholding of their (chief's) right tended to render the British negligent of the need to worry much about the support of the people" (Dena 1979:72).

However this happy state of affairs did not continue for too long. In their quest for secure revenues, the British imposed on different parts of the country several land revenue settlements which clearly unsettled some traditional systems. Through the zamindari land tenure system known as the Permanent Settlement which was introduced in the eastern part of India, ownership of land was conferred on zamindars and actual producers were reduced to the position of tenants. In due course, several levels of under-tenures developed and every level made ever-increasing demands on the producers. Sub-infeudation, insecurity of tenure, rising land rent, increased pressure on land on account of pauperisation of artisans and population growth created immense burdens on the less fertile tracts. While peasants generally suffered, the Adivasis were even more oppressed.

In the western part of India, a different land revenue system known as the Ryotwari Settlement was introduced. Here too rigid enforcement of high revenue assessments led to growing indebtedness and alienation of peasant holdings.

Simultaneously, in order to increase revenue in the interest of capitalist accumulation, the colonial power encouraged cultivation of waste lands in both regions, thereby increasing pressure on tracts inhabited and cultivated by the tribals. Large areas of forests were reserved and used for commercial exploitation. The natural habitat of the tribals was further disturbed by increasing immigration on account of encouraged mining and exploitation of various natural resources. Large-scale mining and location of manufacturing industries in the mineral-rich areas led to the conversion of large segments of the tribal population into wage labourers.

Even earlier, the cash economy had penetrated the tribal areas. Colonialism created the demand for money to pay land revenue and various other taxes and levies. Heavy excise duties, forest imposts, etc. added to the burden of the tribals and indebtedness increased by leaps and bounds. In the primitive agrarian set-up, such usury and indebtedness naturally led to the strengthening of agrestic servitude and new forms of bondage emerged. By 1918, in just one tribal district of Bihar, Palamau, no less than 60,000 kamias (debt slaves:bonded labourers in modern parlance) were reported to be in existence (Singh 1969).

The coming in of the railways and other modern modes of transport on the one side destroyed traditional trade routes and on the other propelled into the area aggressive commerce carried out in unequal circumstances, leading to further immiserisation, indebtedness and servitude among the tribals. Primitive accumulation was the rule of the day and to that end even slavery was used. Systems of indenture of labour were devised to take away large numbers of tribals to work on tea gardens in Assam (which were located on lands vacated from the local 'tribes'), to be chain-ganged into coal mines and to slave on plantations even outside India (Singh 1982; Mintz 1977; Omvedt 1980; Tinker 1974; etc.) As Das Gupta (1976,1983, etc.), Mukherjee (1948), Chakraborty (1978) and many other scholars have pointed out, the origins of much of the industrial section of the working class in India were also in systems of unfreedom.

At home too, the tribals were faced with shrinkage of their means of livelihood and breaking down of their traditional ecological equilibrium (Mitra 1977). Rapacious exploitation of agriculture and forests led to repeated droughts and floods which further worsened the situation. And, as forests became physically limited and access to them restricted by laws and regulations, the mobility of the tribals practically disappeared. The cumulative consequence of all these was that land became more scarce than labour (Pathy 1982). Both became marketable commodities; but the market operated less according to capitalist principles than according to the diktat of the usurer and his colonial master (Upadhyay 1980; Das Gupta 1976). As such, the traditional land relations became obsolete and the differential interests of the internal structural units became more conspicuous. Land alienation, de-peasantisation and impoverishment were the order of the period, a period which continues in many respects for the tribals in post-colonial India too.

The exploited and oppressed tribal segment of the emergent working class struggled against colonial rule and against the native exploiters whom that power protected. The British had faced formidable challenge in the very conquest of many tribal areas when they tried to impose their direct rule and at every step of their expansion or introduction of significant new measures, resistance flared up. During the nineteenth century, most of the numerically strong and settled tribal communities fought against colonialism as it was perceived in their immediate context. The Santhals rose in revolt in 1855-57, 1869-71, 1882 and 1885 against both the British and their subservient landlords and money lenders; so did the Mundas in 1789,1808,1811,1818,1820,1832,1857,1887-90 and 1895-1902. The Oraons took up arms in 1895-97. The Kols revolted in 1824,1839 and 1844-46. So did the Bhils of Gujarat in 1809-28,1846 and 1857-59. The Koyas rose against their feudal oppressors in 1803,1852, and 1879-80. The Kolis staged their insurrection in 1831-32 and the Saoras between 1839-60. These were but a few of the numerous anti-colonial and anti-local exploiter movements of 19th century tribal India (Gough 1974: 1391-1412).

Most of these movements centred around land and forest issues and the major thrust was against forced dispossession of land, oppressive taxation, forced and indentured labour and reservation of forests. The additional issues were the excise policy, use of force to cultivate cash crops, attacks on cultural and religious practices, etc. Many of the movements were short- lived, reformative, messianic or emulative and were primarily directed against landlords, contractors, usurers, traders and other 'native' exploiters and apparently only secondarily against the edifice of the colonial State. Nevertheless, they posed a serious enough threat to the State, its law and order, its allies and subordinates for the British power to try to combat them through different means, ranging from brutal repression, promulgation of measures like the Criminal Tribes Act, settlement of 'loyal' subjects in 'troubled' areas in an effort aimed at re-peasantisation, incorporation of some tribals like Bhils in specially raised police corps and, finally, some ameliorative legislation banning alienation of the land of the tribals to non-tribals, thus trying to halt de-peasantisation. Repression worked, but only for a while, and the ameliorative measures remained largely ineffective owing to lack of sustained, organised and united struggle on the part of the tribals as such and lack of political will to enforce such measures on the part of the State.

In the twentieth century, with the strengthening of the nationalist movement, tribal struggles, like working class struggles in general, also became a part of the anti-colonial crusade though, by and large, they retained their autonomy and repeatedly raised local issues in addition to the broad national issue of freedom. The Oraons participated in the non-cooperation movement in 1920-21 and the Mundas, Saoras, Varlis, Gonds, Kolams, Koyas, and others too took part in varying degrees in different phases of the anti-colonial campaign.

Increasingly however, the peasant and/or working class content of these subaltern movements asserted itself and the movements themselves, albeit local, limited and sporadic, got radicalised. Some of the more important agrarian movements had significant tribal participation. Thus struggles like the Hajang unrest (1944), Tebhaga movement (1946-48), Telengana uprising (1946-51), Naxalbari movement in 1967 and the subsequent 'Naxalite' upsurges in Bengal, Srikakulam, Koraput and Ganjam, Chhotanagpur, etc. were either predominantly or significantly tribal. Other 'lesser', more localised, movements among the tribals took place and continue to take place even today (Breman 1974; Das 1983; Desai 1977; Danagare 1974; Mies 1979; Sundarayya 1977; Upadhyay 1980; etc.).

In the meanwhile, along with being part of the anti-colonial struggle and simultaneous and subsequent struggles against Indian exploiters of various sorts, another type of movement which developed among some of the more numerous 'tribes' and in the areas predominantly populated by tribal peoples related to regional autonomy (RSU 1982). In certain cases, the 'tribes' were not easily reconciled to integration into the post- colonial Indian state structure and struggled, sometimes even with arms to maintain their independence. The Nagas (Misra 1979) and the Mizos of northeastern India are cases in point. In due course, for a variety of reasons, they now seem to be giving up what was known as their 'secessionist' politics and most of them have settled for autonomy within the Indian union but it has been a long and often bloody process.

Indeed in north-eastern India, the process has resulted in fragmentation of the amalgamated Assam state and the formation of different states composed of separate preponderant tribal groups. But even now the story is far from complete. In Tripura, the tribals are agitating against the massive inflow of 'outsiders', mainly Bengalis, and in Assam itself a long-drawn struggle is going on (among both Assamese plains and other tribals and non-tribals) against similar immigrants (Misra 1982). While the Marxist government in Tripura tried to establish some kind of an equilibrium by undertaking special measures for the tribals to bring down conflict levels in the state (though violent incidents continue to take place), in Assam and Mizoram through 'top-level' accords attempts were made to break the political stalemate. The accords recorded only limited successes.

Another significant movement of tribals for regional autonomy is in what is known as the Jharkhand area comprising several districts in Bengal, Bihar, Orissa and Madhya Pradesh (RSU 1982; Sengupta 1982). An aspect of this movement is that it is pan-tribal, carrying within its fold different communities who are united in opposition to exploitation by dikus (outsiders). The multi-community movement has had a long history here with organisation like the Chhotanagpur Unnati Samaj (1915) and Adivasi Mahasabha (1938) having come into existence several decades ago on the realisation that struggles of single tribal communities, howsoever valiant, would in the end not achieve the purpose of ending exploitation.

The Jharkhand movement itself has had two strands, one dealing only with the interests of the tribals, and in fact ignoring the internal differentiation among them, and the other struggling against exploitation in general, if possible with the association of the exploited among the non-tribals also (Roy 1982). Indeed, the demand for autonomy is only a part of the Jharkhand movement, covering as it does issues of industrialisation, wages, living conditions, work situations, ecology, sharing of the benefits of modernisation and development, land alienation, indebtedness and bondage, traditional modes of livelihood, and cultural assertion through the development of regional languages (Sengupta 1982).

The movement has had several phases, militant and moderate, radical and conservative, mass-oriented and constitutionalist/electoral, and the State too has responded at different times through coercion and repression, accelerated economic development 'from above' and ameliorative legislation, populist slogans and attempts at co-optation, etc. (Singh 1977). At different periods and in different parts of the Jharkhand region, the movement has had as its vanguard coal-miners, railway workers and other exploited people and a grand unity has been forged calling for the transformation of Jharkhand (land of forests) into Lalkhand (land of the people). At other times the movement has restricted itself to the following of certain charismatic leaders belonging to particular 'tribes' (Dhar 1980). However, in spite of its various modes and phases, the Jharkhand movement has remained essentially popular, militant and against different kinds of exploitation and oppression. And, as long as the issues behind the movement — and there are many — are not solved, its embers will glow and occasionally burst into flames.

In other parts of India too there are fires underground. By and large, the processes of uneven development have resulted in the tribals being left behind in the race for deriving benefits from progress and modernisation. At the same time, many of them have lost their traditional occupations; their ecology has been badly tempered with; they have been converted into 'primitive' agrarian communities or wage slaves living at the margins of subsistence; the natural, mineral and other resources in their areas have been taken away and their culture has been under siege. All these result in sporadic radical agrarian and industrial movements and other struggles against exploitation and oppression and occasionally issues of regional autonomy too have been raised in various areas which have large tribal concentration. Thus, movements have erupted in Uttarkhand (Uttar Pradesh), Gondwana (Madhya Pradesh), Bhilwara (Rajasthan), the areas in and around Bastar in Madhya Pradesh, Andhra Pradesh, Maharashtra and Orissa, and struggles against moneylenders, landlords and outsider exploiters, including State and private capital, have taken place among the Varlis in Maharashtra, the Girijans in Andhra Pradesh and among Adivasis in various other parts of the country (Singh 1982). The present spurt in 'tribal class' movements led by the Peoples War Group has added an important ideological dimension to ethnic assertions.

For today, the 'ethnic' minorities who are broadly known as 'tribals' *Vanvasis* (forest-dwellers), *Girijans* (hill people) or *Adivasis* (aboriginals) are waking up after centuries of exploitation and are becoming components of a 'class in the making'. The articulation of this 'class-in-the-making' may not follow classical 'proletarian' patterns but, given the specificities of Indian capitalism itself, that is not surprising. What is noteworthy is the emergence of class solidarity.

CHAPTER 4

RELIGION, NATIONALISM AND CONSTITUTIONAL ORDER

It is not given to journalists, in the ordinary pursuit of their profession, to witness a momentous event in two takes, at first as a rehearsal and then as the actual happening. The voodoo politics of the Hindu extremist Bharatiya Janata Party (BJP)–Rashtriya Swamsewak Sangh (RSS)–Vishwa Hindu Parishad (VHP)– Bajrang Dal combine made that magical experience possible in Ayodhya in December 1992.

The assembled journalists were first treated to a simulated demonstration of how the Babri masjid could be demolished with crow-bars and pickaxes and the debris cleared with ropes. The exercise was staged by the Amritsar wing of the Bajrang Dal and was photographed. The pictures were even published in newspapers which little realised that this was a mere dress rehearsal of the actual *shramdan* (gift of labour) that the BJP president L.K. Advani had spoken of during his second (w)*rath yatra* through which he re-enacted the journey to Ayodhya which he had attempted earlier in 1990. It is not without significance that Advani resumed his interrupted ride atop the voodoo juggernaut from Varanasi in BJP-ruled Uttar Pradesh and not from Samastipur in Bihar where in 1990 he had been forced to dismount and arrested on the charge of inciting communal tension. Discretion is, after all, the better part of such valour which thrives on exhorting others to shed blood in the cause of propagation of mythology!

In any event, journalists got to witness the actual performance of predetermined vandalism on Sunday, 6 December, 1992. The only problem was that when the real event happened, the journalists were prevented from photographing it, recording it or reporting about it. They were beaten, their equipment was destroyed and they were kept in virtual imprisonment under siege for six hours.

Six real-time hours on that fateful Sunday have greater significance than the fictional celluloid *Nine Hours To Rama* that created a furore some years ago. The coincidence of six hours in many sets of happenings could not possibly escape anyone but the most naive. It took six hours for the three domes and the walls of the Babri masjid to be demolished. It took six hours for the UP chief minister Kalyan Singh to draft a one-line letter of resignation. It took six hours for the Central cabinet to be summoned and to dismiss Kalyan Singh after he had resigned.

And, during those fateful six hours, time itself was made to stop: it was ensured that troops could not move, journalists could not report, the conscience of the nation could not be stirred and the muscles of its awesome State could not be exercised.

Only the naive could ignore the coincidence of the six hours. Real-time evidence exposes that picks and spades, ropes and chains, burning tyres and effective barricades were readily available. Evidence also exists of the voodoo leaders who had ensconsed themselves in their so-called "control room" gleefully receiving news of the desecration and the vandalism. Even the "moderates" exhorted the frenzied crowds to blockade the entry points so that the Central security forces could not enter. The entrances were dutifully blocked.

Only the naive will believe that the act was as spontaneous as the coincidental ready availability of the "bricks and shovels" that had been mentioned by Advani earlier during his journey. Enough evidence exists now to prove that finally when the Rapid Action Force (RAF) moved in to clear the site nearly 40 hours after the demolition, the leaders on the spot once again called on the crowds to assemble in large numbers and block the entry points. The drill had obviously been laid down earlier.

In the actual event, the site was cleared by the RAF in only 40 minutes, albeit 40 hours too late, for in the meantime a makeshift temple was erected on the spot, the idols which had been removed during the demolition were hastily reinstalled, an efficiently executed pogrom against Muslims was carried out in Ayodhya and neighbouring Faizabad and a communal conflagration was unleashed in different parts of the country. However, in Ayodhya itself, when the State decided to act, the only display of force in clearing the ground was the beating of the ground with sticks as *kar sevaks* ran away from the scene. Only the naive will believe that the ground could not have been metaphorically struck earlier.

But naiveté is in fashion today. He who has been fooled most, he who was the most gullible, he who believed the dissimulators even as he disregarded the warnings of others and even of his own machinery, viz. the Prime Minister of the country, is the most responsible person. In his hands must the destiny of the nation lie!

The naive may also be taken in by the charade of constitutionalism which apparently prevented pre-emptive action which could have saved a historical building, saved the lives of nearly a thousand innocent people and saved the face of Republican India in the comity of civilised nations. If the Constitution prevented action against the UP state government under Article 355 which enjoins on the Centre the responsibility of maintaining internal security, its Article 356 also does not provide for the sacking of a chief minister who has already resigned!

Even after the event, naivete does not seem to have subsided : it is as rampant as when the promises and assurances of the voodoo politicians cast a spell on the functionaries of the Indian State. This is in spite of the fact that after flouting the National Integration Council, disregarding the Supreme Court and befooling the executive and battering the Press, Parliament itself was immobilised by slogan-shouters who proclaimed that what had been enacted at Ayodhya was only the trailer (*jhanki*) and that Mathura, Kashi *baki hain* (Mathura and Kashi still remain to be similarly treated).

The spell of voodoo politics of the BJP–VHP–RSS–Bajrang Dal combine is still allowing only mesmerised knee-jerk action even as in its subconscious the Indian State realises that it has been pushed into a position in which it has no option but to hit back in a fight to the finish.

In response to widespread revulsion among ordinary citizens at the vandalism in Ayodhya and keeping in mind the other national and international ramifications of the fascist vandalism at Ayodhya, the State has already made four announcements of policy measures of utmost significance. It has committed itself to: (1) rebuilding the Babri masjid; (2) banning communal parties; (3) taking the strongest possible action against those guilty for perpetrating, aiding and abetting the vandalism; and (4) fixing responsibility for administrative lapses and taking disciplinary action, including prosecution, against persons in various positions of authority who were found negligent or otherwise wanting.

It is, however, obvious that meeting these commitments will not be easy for a State whose political acumen as well as administrative competence has come under a cloud. To take just the issue of banning of communal organisations, the fact that various administrative and legal considerations prevented the notification to this effect being issued for several days after the announcement is not without significance. And, when the notification was issued, several other problems appeared.

First, the question of dual, triple or even quadruple membership of organisations has to be sorted out and it will have to be decided if action has to be taken even against members of organisations which have not been banned if they also happen to be active in banned bodies.

Second, the issue of what happens to such persons' membership of Parliament will have to be addressed.

Third, the question of implementation of the ban orders will arise. Quite obviously, the BJP state governments of Rajasthan, Madhya Pradesh and Himachal Pradesh were not likely to implement the ban and other related legal provisions with the commitment that the law demands. In such a situation, they were dismissed by the Centre using Article 356 of the Constitution. Now, the Madhya Pradesh High Court has held the dismissal as illegal and violative of the federal character of the Indian polity. Whatever the Supreme Court decides on the appeal made to it on this matter, it appears that elections are the only way out of the impasse. But there lies the rub: such is the spell cast by the voodoo politics, that there is apprehension that the voters will be swayed by religious considerations and thereby democracy itself will be perverted and sabotaged.

Fourth, if voodoo politics prevails over electoral democracy, the very character of India will change. The implications of this are ominous.

Fifth, the cleanest option of obtaining another mandate from the people in the qualitatively changed circumstances obtaining now is also not without problems as a large section of the political class is clearly unwilling to face the electorate. The announcement on the rebuilding of the Babri masjid has also become much more problematic on account of the reinstallation of the idols which had been removed earlier. The attempt by the Congress to play the "soft Hindu" game to wean away voters from the "hard Hindu" BJP led to worship being allowed in the temple. Now the situation has been extremely complicated; how the government copes with internal and external demands on this matter will be a test of its will, commitment to secularism and adherence to the legal principle of restoration of status quo ante.

The administrative action taken against some officers of the UP administration has, in the meantime, a clear aspect of the search for scapegoats. The fact that Mr Kalyan Singh has openly asserted that administrative decisions were taken by him should have indicated that the officials were mere spineless pawns but, instead of proceeding effectively against the real culprits, attention has once again been focused on surrogates. This is of a piece with the practice of evading reponsibility and passing onus on to lesser mortals. When limpets rule, small fry are sacrificed.

Finally, the vandalism in Ayodhya and the ad hoc response to it have made India much more vulnerable to international pressures than ever before. The damage to Indian nationhood has been so severe that it can only be remedied by sustained and systematic display of political will in upholding the Indian Constitution. Meanwhile, as the State dithers, even the shame of the charge on the practitioners and ideologues of the voodoo politics that they have firmly placed themselves outside and squarely against the constitutional scheme of things is being diluted. While it is a fact that those who cannot even control their own cadres can no longer pretend to be a party of governance, the ad hoc responses of the State are once again enabling them to seek political respectability.

This is inevitable when naivete becomes the characterising feature of political leadership. At the end of this chapter of the sorry tale whose denouement is still in the future, it needs recalling that, faced with fascism, only the naive believe that they are safe and the attacks will be confined only to those on their neighbours. As was realised in Germany, first they came for the workers and the naive stood by. Then the communists were attacked and again the naive watched. Then they came for the Jews and the naive were helpless. And finally when they came for the naive, there were none left to protest.

Once earlier too, Neville Chamberlain had allowed himself to be taken in by a false promise of "peace in our times". Only the naive will fall for that trick again and, if they do, a terrible price will have to be paid once again. Meanwhile, voodoo politics will thrive on myth and superstition, communalism and revanchism, and will engender counter-point religious fundamentalisms. These pose a threat not only to the Indian polity but also to its very civilisation. And they have serious implications for the rest of the world.

One of the major problems which arises in this respect springs not from the political characterisation of religions without due regard to what they actually mean to the people who practise them as faiths. In particular, Hinduism has been subjected to a vicious politicisation and it is that which has informed much of the expression of Hindu ethnicity, identity and inherent majoritarianism.

It is important therefore to begin with asking the question, what, after all, is Hinduism?

India does not lack simple-minded souls. There are many today who spout a simplistic religiosity — a caricature of the immensely complex traditions of Indian philosophical thinking — in the faith that their put-on religion encapsulates the commonness of common sense. Indeed, there are many born-again pundits who peddle religion now with the same zeal with which they earlier propagated hard-headed, this-worldly, a-religious realpolitik. It is no surprise, therefore, that in the hands of such fair-weather preachers of theocracy, the very Ram of the *Ramcharitmanas* is distorted and Goswami Tulasi Das himself is turned into a two-dimensional cardboard character.

That there is not only literary richness but also an eclectic and even syncretic splendour in Tulasi Das is cynically brushed aside as the short-sighted plans of bringing India under a theocracy are prepared. Tulasi Das himself would have had little patience for such atavistic narrow-mindedness which characterises today's burgeoning bazaar clergy.

In his *Kavitavali*, Tulasi Das himself exposes the ugly underbelly of Hinduism as it actually exists in society. Even an article in

Organiser, the otherwise unabashed medium of *hindutva* myth-making notes, "From his verses in *Kavitavali*, we get a lot of information about the then prevailing caste barriers, evil practices in Hindu society, the degeneration of high caste Brahmins, especially of Kashi (now Varanasi) and the sufferings undergone by him for rendering the *Ramayana* in folk language and for his unorthodox ideas".

Among the "unorthodox" ideas of Goswami Tulasi Das was cultural syncretism and disregard of the sectarian bigotry of those who appoint themselves the arbiters of "correct" socio-religious practice. In one poem, Tulasi Das not only rejects being tied down to a fixed place in the caste and even religious matrix but also describes his own peaceful abode in a mosque, a structure just like the one which has been demolished by those who today take his name in vain. *"Dhoot kaho, avadhoot kaho, rajput kaho, julaha kaho kovoo/ Kahoo ki beti se beta na beyahab; kahoo ki jaat bigaar na sovoo/ Tulasi sarnam ghulam hai Ram ko; jako ruchai so kahe kachhu vohoo/ Maang ke khaibo, masjid mein soibo; laibe ko ek na daibe ko dovoo."* (Let anyone call me either a cheat or a mendicant, a rajput or a (Muslim) weaver/I have no son to marry to anyone's daughter and (thereby) defile his caste/Tulasi is well-known as the slave of Ram; everyone is free to call him by any name he chooses/He lives by begging for alms; he sleeps in a mosque and is free from any kind of obligation, either to give or to take).

Today, however, not only has the *bhakti* of Tulasi Das been defiled by an artificial and aggressive *hindutva* but the very flexibility of Ram himself has been finished by fossilising him into a stylised icon. It is well-known to those who are familiar with the cultural traditions of India without subscribing to the narrow-minded big-otry of political pseudo-religion that, in deference to the wishes of others, Ram himself took on different forms (*roop*). The *Balkand* of *Ramcharitmanas* describes how when he incarnated himself in the form of the four-armed Vishnu with all his weapons, Kaushalya entreated him to become a child: *"Keejey shishoo leela, ati priyasheela"* and Ram obliged. Similarly, when Tulasi Das refused to bow to his Krishna form (*Ka varnaun chhavi aap ki, bhale bane ho nath/Tulasi mastak tab navey, dhanush baan lehu haath*), the icon changed: *Kit murali kit chandrika kit gopiyan ke saath/ Apane jan ke kaarane Sri*

Krishna bhaye Raghunath. (For his devotee, Krishna gave up his flute and even his gopis and became Ram).

This flexibility is a far cry from the attempt of today's votaries of political *hindutva* to freeze Ram into mundane icons of Ramlalla which are surreptitiously installed, removed and reinstalled through acts of vandalism. Indeed, there is disjunction even between the icon of the infant Ramlalla on the one side and of the warrior Ram which is projected through the *hindutva* public relations campaign. It is the simplification, even vulgarisation, and the attendant politicisation of religion that put political pseudo-religion squarely against spiritualism and philosophical discourse.

It is not that Hinduism does not have contradictions but the contradictions within it, which reflect its evolution over time through interaction with various philosophical and ethical systems, give it the intricacy of a richly woven tapestry. Take, for instance, the very concepts of the meaning of action (*karma*) as outlined in the Gita itself. At one place (2.55), it notes, "*Prajhati yada kaman sarvan Partha manogatan/Aatmanyevatmanaa tushtah sthitprajnastdochyate* (He who has forsaken all desires, he alone is truly wise). At another place (2.37), however, Arjun is exhorted to indulge in action (war) not with the attitude of one who has forsaken all desires but with the prospect of very real reward: "*Hato va prapsyasi swargam jitva wa bhokshyase mahim/Tasmadu-ttishthha Kaunteya yuddhaya krittanischayah*" (O son of Kunti, if you die you will gain heaven; if you win, you will gain a kingdom. You have gain on both sides; hence get up and fight).

The simple-minded version of *hindutva* being currently popularised and politicised ignores such dialectics and complexities and adopts only that aspect which suits its current, this-worldly purpose. Indeed, as it abuses religion by turning it into a self-righteous crusade, it even ignores the call of Krishna himself recorded in the Gita (18.66), "*Sarvadharman paritajya mamekam sharanam vraja/Aham tvam sarvapapebhyah mokshayishyami ma shuchah*" (Give up all religion and come to me; I will free you from all your sins). Those who create armies of vandals to fight in the name of a created, constructed and politically contrived dharma obviously have nothing to do with the call to abjure all religion and seek spiritual solace. The self-appointed soldiers of political *hindutva*, led by the mendicants who constitute the bazaar clergy, have little realisation and no appreciation of the syncretism of Indian cultural tradition and even of its religious discourse. They fail to catch the echo of "*Buddham sharanam gachchami*" in the Gita's "*Mamekam sharanam vraja*" (Come into my shelter). They do not notice the integration of the pre-Vedic Mother Goddess cults into the post-Vedic Hinduism in, for instance, the Durga Saptashati. Even in contemporary and popular Ram worship, they ignore the use of Akbar-esque characteristics of *Jharokha* darshan, for instance, bestowed by Tulasi Das himself on Ram : "*Ram jharokhe baith kar sabka muzara leit*".

The reduction of philosophy to religion and of religion from the abstract *nirgun* (formless) to the concrete *sagun* (with characteristics) and of even *sagun* to a uniform *moort* (iconistic) does not derive from the cultural traditions of India. Indeed, it would not be wrong to say that the vandalism perpetrated at Ayodhya has nothing to do with either culture or civilisation. It models itself only on the political maxim of the Mahabharat "*Anyo dharmah samarthanam nirbalanantu chaparah* (There are separate dharmas for the powerful and the weak) and ignores the teaching of Vyas, the compiler of the Mahabharat : "*Ashtadash puraneshu Vyasasya vachandwayam/ Paropkarah punyay, papay parapidanam*" (There are only two truths in the 18 Puranas : helping others brings merit and hurting others is sinful."

Those who have made it a deliberate political policy to grab power by hurting others, indeed by creating "the other" among Indians, have not only gone against the Constitution and rule of law but also against religion. They have glorified an unfair version of a weak, deceitful and cowardly Ram about whom Bali ruefully said "*Dharam hetu avatareu gosain/Marehu mohi vyadh kinain*" (you, who had come for the cause of righteousness, ended up killing me like a cruel, cunning and unfair hunter who hurled weapons while hidden from view)".

When militant Hinduism seeks to define itself today, it can only do so with reference to "the other", rather than autonomously and based on its own internal characteristics. This is evident in the attempt of the Rashtriya Swayam Sewak Sangh (RSS), Bharatiya Janata Party (BJP), Vishwa Hindu Parishad (VHP) and the Bajrang

Dal to find foci for Hinduism in one or three or 3,000 mosques. The shadow of revanchism hangs heavily on the definition of Hinduism today.

It is readily acknowledged that the term "Hinduism" is not self-explanatory. It refers to a highly complex religious and social configuration which has developed over many centuries. It is full of variation in terms of theological, ritual, regional, local and social differences and offers as many perspectives.

Heinrich von Stietencron (1990), has identified three major approaches towards Hinduism which, he feels, would be relevant for "a discussion of trends and processes partly inherited from the past but operating, directly or indirectly, in our own time".

The first approach relates to the abstract level of concepts comprising theology and philosophy into a system which might be called "religious conceptualisation". This system provides man not only with a goal or a reason of being and with rules for communication with superhuman powers but also with a complete world view (Weltanschauung). It therefore includes cosmogony and cosmology, i.e. origin, structure, function and purpose of this world and all conceivable other worlds; and it includes *achara*, i.e. correct or appropriate behaviour of the individual within these worlds. Although such religious conceptualisation gives meaning to lived religion, the two are by no means identical. Lived religion usually lags far behind the conceptual construction.

A second approach to Hinduism therefore would be to perceive and describe it as it is in actual practice : in all its multiform expressions, influences by theological goals, by ritual practice, by traditions of tribe, clan and family, or by traditions of *jati* and varna, of caste and class. Such Hinduism is profoundly influenced also by the social setting in a pluralistic society which has more than one religion, more than one tradition, more than one god, more than one holy scripture, more than one language, one caste, and, last but not least, more than one level of income and education. The result is that lived religion in a pluralistic society tends to exhibit almost endless varieties and syncretisms.

A third way of looking at Hindu tradition is by seeing it in terms which are more contemporary: as a huge market where all kinds of goods and tools are offered for sale. Such a market offers intellectual and emotional goods; it offers values and meaning, and justification, and legitimation in large variety. Like every good market it also offers the necessary tools for producing these goods : ritual, yoga, *vrata, tapas, prayaschita,* meditation, *teerthayatra, dana, guruseva* and every other variety of *sadhana.*

This commercial analogy to explain Hinduism is of course somewhat imperfect as the transaction is coloured by *sanskara* and is not one of free choice : whatever your father and mother chose from among the goods and tools and used at home as well as what you yourself picked up from the market becomes your own, your actually valid and used religious tradition.

Sanskara thus imparts an element of inspired selectivity to the otherwise laissez-faire of Hinduism. The selection is based on "education" as well as individual choice and, of these two, education provides for continuity while choice adds personal experience and detracts what does not arouse interest any more.

All oral and written tradition is dependent on this element of choice : choice of those who first told or wrote down a story or an idea or a prescription, and choices of those who transmitted, copied and changed it, commented on it, emphasised particular aspects of it, or transformed it beyond recognition.

The Hindu chooses from his own tradition, but he also chooses new elements which did not belong to the tradition. Foreign values, for example, if socially viable and intellectually attractive, can be integrated by the medium of myth, an authoritative story or a legitimising tale of a miracle.

It is also possible that the new elements are identified with already existing values which are being activated in a particular context and thereby the inclusion assumes greater weight. The concept of *nishkama karma,* for instance, had been available in Hindu tradition for centuries, but it was invested with a new meaning and became socially relevant in the nineteenth century when it was identified with social engagement and responsibility in the sense of Christian ethics. The popularisation of *bhakti* after Hinduism's encounter with sufism and the revival of interest in the Gita by Tilak, Gandhi and Vinoba Bhave following their interaction with Christianity are not mere coincidences.

Indeed, Hinduism has always had the tendency which the

Indologist Paul Hacker (1990) called "inclusivism". To avoid or diminish conflict by integration-cum-subordination is typical for all tradition-based societies. In Hinduism, for this purpose incentives can be offered which promise rise of status against acceptance of certain symbols of orthodoxy as in the case of so-called Sanskritisation.

While all these can be individual choices, there are times when choice of values, certain aspects of tradition, a different perspective with regard to the past and to the future become a collective affair. The Ram revival is one such exercise.

In this context, it is interesting to note that the worship of Ram himself has strong political overtones. Jurgen Lutt (1990) has demonstrated that the switch from Krishna Leela to Ramraj was at least partly the fall-out of a scandalous court case, "the Maharaja Libel Case" in 1861 which exposed the "immoral activities" of the spiritual heads of the Vallabhacharya sect. Gandhi himself came from a Vallabhacharya family, was turned away because of rumours about "immoral matters" concerning its priests and went over to more sanitised Ram worship.

The last two centuries in particular have seen at least three major phases of change in Hindu self-perception. The first phase started in the late 20s of the nineteenth century when Rammohan Roy attempted a major reassessment of Hindu tradition and directed his attention to important social reforms.

Subsequently, a wave of reasserted awareness of indigenous ancient values, which were supposed to have been suppressed during centuries of Muslim and Christian domination, swept through the Hindu intellectual elite. Curiously, this reassertion was aided and even abetted by European Orientalism, Indology and Indo-European Comparative Linguistics which have even been characterised as "the prehistory of Hitler and his Aryanism".

In India, the most characteristic feature was a discovery or construction of a national culture which could be proudly posited against the world. In order to create and polish up such a national culture, several vigorous reform movements started to break away from multiform Puranic and Tantrik religion based on idol worship which, following European aversion to pagan rites, were condemned as superstitious by the Arya Samaj for instance. In contrast, the choice of Vedanta and a few selected items from Vedic tradition served as the basis for purifying society and rediscovering its spiritual values.

Wilhelm Halbfass (1990) demonstrates that the move from "pagan" folk religion to more metaphysical Hinduism also prompted Swami Vivekananda, for instance, to discover and propagate "practical Vedanta". The political face of such "practical Vedanta", which influenced Aurobindo and Radhakrishnan, Golwalkar and Rajagopalachari, played a significant role in the public culture of modern India. On the other hand, there continued to be rigorous critics of Advaita Vedanta, like Dayanand Saraswati and Debendranath Tagore, who questioned its ethical, social and political applicability.

Curiously, while Vivekananda toyed with "practical Vedanta", his "master" Ramakrishna was constructed by the Calcutta middle class, as Partha Chatterjee (1990) has shown, as an expression of the fear of the material world and the humiliation of subordination, of a lack of faith in the claims of reason and modernity, and of the loss of the sense of community. It is this theme that emerges from a critical reading of *Kathamrita* which throws light on the crucial questions about nationalist ideology as the construction of gender, the appropriation of the popular, the classicisation of national culture and the divergence between the state-forms of nationalism and its cultural forms.

The next major change in Hinduism came in the political context of the coming of Independence. It revolved round the question of the future of India: industrialisation versus rural self-sufficiency, the secular versus Hindu state. Both Gandhi and Nehru, though led by different visions, objected to the Hindu option and the secular state won. But one of the undercurrents of the Gandhian Ramrajya was also the shifting of emphasis from the strictly purified Vedanta to *bhakti*. Simultaneously, through other Hindu assertions, the epics and Puranas were reinstalled and, the Hindu universalist claim with theistic overtones was strongly felt and dreaded by the Muslims. This contributed in no small measure to Partition of the country.

When Independence finally came, the Vedantic image of Hindu tolerance was drowned in the bloodshed of Partition and the sacrifice of Gandhi, only to reappear unshaken by these events. The secular state was born.

With this state, the political and cultural unity of India became the dominant concern : all-India rulers like Asoka and Akbar were highlighted. Abolition of the caste system, integration (and even Hinduisation) of the tribals, education campaigns based on a pan-Indian curriculum, and even the industrialisation and land reform measures were designed to promote, or rather to create, a cultural unity of India.

Under the surface of this Nehruvian current, there have been opposing trends. Separatism, regionalism, casteism, communalism, etc. are polemic designations of some of these. Behind them are two larger and worldwide movements. One is religious fundamentalism. The other is regionalism. Hinduism today stands at this crossroad.

In this context of changing Hinduism, various strands of its tradition can be examined to identify what indeed is Hinduism. One examination reveals for instance that it is time the essentialist definitions be discarded. Friedham Hardy (1990) has made a radical reassessment of the Vedic heritage by looking at the thirteenth century Tamil text *Acharyahridayam* which reveals that the broad processes of "Hinduisation", "brahmanisation", "Sanskritisation" or "The Great Tradition" may in fact always have been countered by sophisticated centrifugal tendencies of regionalisation. "The Tamil Veda" for instance is accessible to all and the new religious ideal of devotion (*prapatti* or surrender) supersedes the old *varnashramdharma*.

Lest this "de-Sanskritisation" in the cultural context of the Dravidian Tamil Nadu be dismissed as peripheral to "mainstream Hinduism", it has been demonstrated by Dr Gunther D. Sontheimer (1990), following D. D. Kosambi, that mass and popular Hinduism includes many "non-classical" elements which are characterised as "folk religion" which cannot simply be categorised as "Little Tradition". Its phenomena are widespread and form distinctive patterns which can be found all over India. The deity of such "folk religion", like the Pandhârpur Panduranga, does not live in a Puranic heaven but is earthbound like the devotee. The deity is *urga* (powerful), and *jagrit* (wakeful) rather than *saumya* (otiose). Its *moorti* is a corporeal, sentient being, not a *pratika* (symbol) into which the god is invoked by *mantrochharan*.

In view of the widespread nature of such Hinduism, it is

interesting to note the Sanskritising, symbolising attempt of the homogenised Hinduism of today's politicised Ram *bhaktas*.

In the end however, after having traversed the fields of Indology, the only real self-definition of Hinduism is vis-a-vis "the other". More and more, as virulent communalisation of Hinduism shows, "the other" is the Muslim, the Sikh, the *dalit*, the *adivasi*. A series of studies by Gyan Pandey (1990), Veena Das (1990), Javed Alam (1990) and others demonstrate this unequivocally.

Where does this simplification, even vulgarisation, of the immensely rich, complex and dynamic Hindu tradition leave the simple-minded Hindu votaries of Ram who can only define their being vis-a-vis Babar?

Meanwhile, their own artificial edifice of undifferentiated Hindu society has been seriously breached by the secular assertion by not only the *dalits* and *adivasis*, now grouped under the statutory categories of scheduled castes and tribes (SC/ST), but also by the relatively ritually higher Sudra and Vaishya segments who have found a political economic identity under the label of "other backward castes (OBC)". While constitutional provisions for reserving government jobs for scheduled castes and tribes have existed ever since India constituted itself into a modern democratic republic as a generally accepted policy of positive discrimination and affirmative action, the recently announced reservation of a percentage of government jobs for the OBCs, following the recommendations of the Mandal Commission, has upset the ideological-political applecart of those who propagate undifferentiated Hinduism.

The welter of analytical confusion which has grown along with civil disorder in recent times has tempted political theorists to simplify further their already simple concepts of State and civil society in India. Unable to cope with the unfolding complexity, they have sought to pin India down on an invented grid where the vertical lines represent religious divides and the horizontal lines correspond to caste hierarchies. This two-dimensional matrix, devised by the Indologists from whom modern-day sociology proudly claims its ancestry, is used as India's exotic pattern for the development of a true 'civil society'.

It is weakness of imagination which characterises much academic and political analysis that limits their conception of contemporary India to just the two factors of religion and caste. It would appear from reading the currently fashionable literature that if one understands the Hindu-Muslim and caste dichotomies, one can grasp all that is relevant in India's social and political existence today. It is this kind of simplified, even vulgarised, civilisational analysis that ignores not only reality encompassing the Indian millions but even dismisses manifestations of significant processes of change or, at best, seeks to interpret them within the limited religion-caste paradigm.

For instance, the very entity of India, its civilisation, culture, polity and nationhood are sought to be constricted by such analysts within the strait-jacket of Hinduism; it is Hindutva which is thought to be the essential element of Indian nationalism. Whatever be the vague, imprecise definition of Hinduism underlying this theory, in the end it is defined in terms of a religious order whose parameters are set by a group of self-styled custodians of its spirit. Thus, Hinduism increasingly means devotion towards the *Vaishnavite* Ram as the superordinate deity in the Hindu pantheon. The delightful and exciting complexities of polytheism, of pluralistic philosophical and moral discourses, of the many diverse subaltern traditions are sacrificed at the altar of this synthetically homogenised and consumerised religiosity. Even the myriad expressions of Hindu polity are negated by the supremacy accorded to the political pronouncement of the RSS supremo in Nagpur on Vijaya Dashmi day.

Even worse, the Hinduisation of the very concept of Indian nationalism excludes the active participation in it of religious minorities as well as of those 'Hindus' who do not accept the version of Hinduism ordained from Nagpur by the RSS. The Little Traditions which have so enriched Indian culture are crushed under the juggernaut of commercially-blessed BJP *rath yatris* attempting to ride to power via Ayodhya.

Simultaneously the potency of Hindutva is sought to be bolstered by equating it with the essence of the Indian State itself. As the State is projected, through a perverse neo-Hegelianism, as a work of art, humankind's highest achievement, "the march of God on earth", so is Hindutva sought to be made the informing principle of such 'civil society' as exists in India. It escapes such neo-Hegelians that the State is neither the final form of social organisation nor is it inherently 'transcendent' or 'sovereign'.

Indeed, in today's situation, as Ronald Inden (1990) points out, other institutions may be seen to rival or even to dominate supposedly discrete nation-states or politics — the multinational corporations, the international financial bodies, the 'free world' led by the United States of America.

In a context where the pressure is to 'internationalise India', an intellectually consistent political analyst may well ask, "What price Hindutva, the socio-religious system unique to India and shared only with Nepal, as the informing principle of nationhood?"

In the discussion of Hinduism, the misconceptions about caste, which is considered an essential element of Hinduism, also, curiously, owe their origins at least in part to an incomplete, incorrect and mechanistic adoption of the Hegelian ideas of the state in general and of the 'exceptional' nature of state and society in India. Hegel believed that "A State is a realisation of Spirit, such that in it the self-conscious being of Spirit — the freedom of the Will — is realised as law." On that basis, he went on to observe that in India "the proper basis of the State, the principle of freedom is altogether absent: there cannot therefore be any State in the true sense of the term". "This", Hegel held, "is the first point to be observed: if China may be regarded as nothing else but a State, Hindoo political existence presents us with a people, but no State."

Hegel continues his analysis of India's malformation to add that in India "independent members of society ramify from the unity of despotic power. Yet the distinctions which these imply are referred to Nature — they petrify and become rigid, and by their stereotyped character condemn the Indian people to the most degrading spiritual serfdom. The distinctions in question are the castes."

Caste is thus in Hegel's representation not merely a form of social order peculiar to India as exemplifying the most extreme of the unenlightened ancient societies. Through this limited, and wrong, imagination of India, an imagination mechanically borrowed by subsequent sociologists who dress themselves in Hegelian hand-me-downs, caste, and consequently, India itself was seen as static, a rigid, unchanging hierarchy which imprisoned humanity.

The fact is otherwise. Empirical evidence and critical theory have demonstrated that caste is neither unchanging nor is it even peculiarly "Hindoo". For all his imperfections, and they are many, even B.P. Mandal (1981), the author of the controversial Mandal report on reservations for "other backward castes", realised this: his understanding of caste is of a hierarchical order but one which is relative to given dimensions of space and time. The same caste is `forward' in one region and `backward' in another. And caste characteristics of `forwardness' and `backwardness' cut across boundaries of religion. Indeed, even in as pathetic an intellectual exercise as indulged in by Mandal, the picture of caste that emerges is not of a static and lifeless arrangement of social building blocks but of an unruly, ever-growing, verdant social jungle.

In the apparent anarchy of the social jungle however, there is one overriding aspect of order. It was perceived by the Orientalist Charles Eliot: "In the jungle (that is Indian society), every particle of the soil seems to put forth its spirit in vegetable life and plant grows on plants, creepers and parasites on their more stalwart brethren. The jungle is not a park or garden. Whatever can grow in it does grow. The Brahmans are not gardeners but forest officers" (cited in Inden 1990). It is the metaphor of the Brahmans as forest officers that is apt. In the inherently disorderly Indian society, it is the Brahmans and Brahmanism that laid down the kind of law that existed.

Today, the attempt of the promoters of *hindutva* is to turn the luxuriant jungle of India into a park through whose paths their *raths* can roll unhindered. And, the Brahmans and neo-Brahmans have been turned into tamed and paid park attendants whose job is to pluck out socially undesirable weeds.

However, the very fertility of the Indian soil and the infinite ingenuity as well as plurality of its human soul stand in the way of such ordained ordering. It is true that, in the conditions of the modern age, some organisation is inevitable but the organisation can be multi-faceted, complex and multidimensional. It is the limiting of the very imagination of India to confine it to merely the two dimensions of religion and caste that stands in the way of the evolution of a modern civil society responsive to the various needs of diverse cultural, regional, class and group identities. Modern civil society does have to be created, even invented in India. The citizen has to be ensured security, equity, liberty and civilised governance. The day-to-day needs of survival and growth have to be met.

But this is a creative endeavour which goes beyond the narrow confines of caste and religion and raises questions of class, culture, gender, regional and ethnic identities. Such a creative endeavour cannot subsist on a mixed diet of Hegelianism and Hindutva. It has to grapple with the issue of cultural-religious pluralism in a republican polity and contend with the many minorities that constitute the kaleidoscopic Indian reality.

On definitional grounds, the issue of religious minorities, on the face of it, does not appear to be as complicated as those of tribal or caste minorities. The very fact that people divide themselves by declaring their adherence to particular religions would appear to simplify their classification into majority and minority categories.

However, even this classification is not as simple as it seems even on institutional criteria because there are different religious groups which are covered by the same personal laws and civil codes governing various aspects of social existence and there are few, if any, significant differences in the broad secular and material cultures of different religious denominations. Racially of course it is nonsensical to distinguish between people belonging to specific religions. The issue of majority-minority classification according to religion is further complicated by the continuing debate on the dividing line between a sect and a full-fledged religion. Thus, even in this respect, the task of determining religious majority and minorities is not simple, a fact which was realised even in the framing of the Constitution of India where the problem was sought to be neatly side-stepped by unanimously resolving that "for the word 'minorities' wherever it occurs, the words 'certain classes' be substituted"! (Wadhwa 1975: 5).

It is important to note in this context that the very concept of majority and minority in religious terms is an outcome of a modern consciousness of population numeracy, in particular of the Census exercises that were undertaken in the 19th century. Before head counts of people were announced, it was neither possible nor necessary for communities across the land to identify themselves with any degree of preciseness and to seek similarities or differences with others outside their immediate ken. There was thus no general

"Hindu" community and people defined themselves with reference to their specific modes of worship as localised Shaivites (worshippers of Shiva) or Shakts (worshippers of the Mother Goddess) or Vaishnavas (worshippers of the various incarnations—Ram, Krishna, etc. of Vishnu) and so on. Indeed, in the pre-modern preiod, it is doubtful if even the Muslim *ummah* (global community) had any more than a symbolic meaning, if even that. The Censuses, however, not only counted people but also pigeonholed them and made it possible for them to seek self-definition in terms that were set for them by external enumerators. In an ironical sense, therefore, primordialism was the result of modernism.

In modern India, thus, Hinduism is the declared religion of the majority of the population, and Muslims, Christians, Sikhs, Buddhists and Parsis are important religious minorities. Before proceeding with discussion of their respective situations in the overall Indian social and political pluralism it is, however, necessary to enter one more caveat about even the above rather simple statement. By no means can it be said that the Hindus, who in terms of religious declaration, constitute the majority of the population are, even in terms of their beliefs and far less in terms of other secular aspects of culture, homogenous.

It is facile but not altogether untrue to say that the number of gods in the Hindu pantheon is legion and the Hindus are extremely divided among themselves as worshippers of respective gods and goddesses. And this is not all. Among the Hindus, even those who worship the same god(s) may do so according to different modes and thus belong to different sects. Further, they may belong to various orders headed by different teachers (gurus) and accordingly can be even more sub-divided. And so on.

To complicate matters more, even discrete religious and ethical/moral systems like Jainism and Buddhism have been incorporated in the broad framework of Hinduism and a large number of Hindus (and even some Sikhs) believe that Sikhism is not a different religion but only a sect within Hinduism. This creates a religious-cultural complexity which is difficult to disentangle.

Nor is the situation among the Muslims simpler. Apart from the two major Islamic sects - Shias and Sunnis - which are both present in India in significant numbers, there are also sub- groups like

Ahmadiyas, Bohras and Ismailis, and followers of various *pirs* (holy men) and Sufi *fakirs* (religious mendicants who established systems of devotion different from Islamic orthodoxy, marked the cultural confluence of Hinduism and Islam and became popular among both Hindus and Muslims).

The Sikhs too have their share of heterodoxy, the most prominent being the Nirankaris who are rejected (and even physically attacked) as non-Sikh by the orthodox but who have significant following among the masses. Although Sikhism has its origins in rejection of the caste system, it has its share of untouchables, known as Majhabis, Kabirpanthis, Ramdasias, etc. whose social and cultural position is so similar to the Hindu *dalits* that they are even governed by the special legislative provisions meant for Scheduled Castes in spite of not being Hindus. On the other hand, similarly placed and even worse-off members of the Scheduled Castes who have got themselves converted to Buddhism are deprived of 'protective discrimination', leading to Buddhists distancing themselves from Hinduism although the latter claims Buddha to be one of the incarnations of its God.

Among Christians, the broad divisions are of course, between the Catholics and Protestants but they are further subdivided among different orthodoxies like Roman, Syrian and Greek, on the one side and various episcopal orders or other groups like Baptists and Adventists on the other. Only the Parsis are relatively free of schism and heterodoxy. But their small numbers make them not only a minority but a minuscular community which is gradually dying out.

With this variety of complexities obtaining in India, it is nothing but gross simplification to talk of percentages and numbers. And yet, for lack of any other system of broad classification, it may be stated that the distribution of major religious groups is as follows: Hindus 82.72%; Muslims 11.21%; Christians 2.60% and Sikhs 1.89%. Thus, all religious groups, other than Hindus, are numerical minorities and many sects among Hindus too distinguish themselves from the "majoritarian" community.

The largest group among the religious minorities is that of Muslims. In spite of the fact that the proportion of Muslims in India has been significantly reduced on account of partition of the country in 1947, the absolute numbers of Muslims in India is still so large that the Muslim population in India is third highest in the world, after those of Indonesia and Bangladesh. It is ironical that there are more Muslims in India than in Pakistan which was carved out as a 'homeland' for Indian Muslims. This historical, and political, irony is at the root of many of the problems of Muslims in India who are spread over almost the whole of the country and are unevenly distributed. Their largest concentrations are in minuscular Luccadive, Minicoy and Amindivi Islands (94.37%); Jammu and Kashmir (65.85%); Assam (24.03%); West Bengal (20.46%); Kerala (19.50%); Uttar Pradesh (15.48%); and Bihar (13.48%). Thus, in one Union Territory, the Laccadives groups of islands, and one state, Jammu and Kashmir, Muslims are not minorities but constitute the majority religious community.

It is neither possible nor necessary here to trace the Hindu-Muslim divide in India which led to the traumatic partition of the country and left in its wake such a state of bitterness that not only led to several wars between India and Pakistan but also to a serious communal problem in secular India. Suffice it to be noted that there is little historical evidence of sustained communal hatred operating at the popular level prior to colonial rule. There were, of course, instances of rulers of one community or the other imposing discriminatory measures against subjects belonging to faiths other than their own but, as often as not, these could be traced to 'reasons of State' rather than those of religion alone (Shakir 1980: 75). And in any case, at the level of the ordinary people, peasants and artisans, as they were exploited almost to the point of being reduced to mere subsistence survival by practically all regimes, religious rivalries hardly mattered. It is significant that at the popular level, the religious response to prevailing state of affairs, expressed through the Bhakti movement, Sufism, etc., was in terms of amalgamation of faiths rather than fuelling of mutual hatred.

The picture changed with the coming of the British, though in their case too the causal factors in promotion of a policy which resulted in dividing Hindus and Muslims were geared to 'reasons of state'. *Divide et impera* as the foundation of British rule had been suggested for adoption as early as 1821 and the application of this maxim was first tried out in the reorganisation of the Indian army after the great revolt of 1857. Only after it proved to be successful in that formal and structured system was it actively promoted in civil society at large in terms of differential education, personal laws, etc. and finally even through the setting up of separate electorates based on communal representation (Shakir 1980: 75-81).

Of course, the British design was furthered by short-sighted Indian politicians, the Indian social and economic elite and bigots among both communities. As British rule neared its end, the communalisation of Indian policy which it had indulged in, actively encouraged by self-seeking and foolish Hindu and Muslim politicians, led to terrible communal carnages. The people and the country were divided even as British rule came to an end (Akbar 1985).

After Independence, India tried to set up a secular polity, free from religious interference in temporal affairs and promoting 'fraternity' with equality under law. These noble ideas as well as considerations of realpolitik, of having to function in a multi-religious, multi-cultural context, did have some measure of success and overtly at least 'exclusivist' politics tended to retreat. The Congress party, for a long time, retained power by consolidating its support in what was known was the Harijan-Muslim-Adivasi block in the electorate (Kothari 1970). The Communist parties and other leftists too gained significant support among the minorities on account of their secular professions which were, by and large, substantiated by their record of action. The organs of the State were purportedly non-communal and the progress of capitalism seemed to lead towards wiping off distinctions of creed in economic, cultural, educational and social interaction.

However, 'passion-politics' was by no means eliminated. Hindu chauvinism, led by the Rashtriya Swayamsevak Sangh (RSS) and its political organ, the Jan Sangh which in its current incarnation is known as the Bharatiya Janata Party (BJP), made great strides in the Hindi heartland, Gujarat, Maharashtra, Punjab and lately even in Kerala. Occasional foolish utterances and actions of Muslim communalists were grist to the mills of Hindu communalists (Smith 1963: 477).

The situation changed qualitatively for the worse with the aggravation of the Babri Masjid – Ram Janmabhoomi dispute in the mid-1980s. The then Congress government cynically allowed the unlocking of the gate of the disputed monument which had been closed on judicial orders. The consideration of the Congress was to secure support among Hindus. However this did not fetch electoral dividends that were expected. Instead, the genie of communal strife which was let out could not be effectively bottled back for years. The organisations which benefited most were the BJP behind which was the Vishwa Hindu Parishad (set up to counter the conversion of oppressed Harijans to other religions) and Muslim fundamentalist bodies. In a desperate attempt to capture political power through invocation of a religious majoritarian consciousness, the RSS-BJP-VHP-Bajrang Dal combine has pulled mouldering pseudo-historical data out of academic cupboards to reinforce its claim of the Babari masjid at Ayodhya being "a symbol of national shame" as a mosque allegedly built by a Muslim invader in the early sixteenth century after destroying an ancient Hindu temple. Fortunately, manufactured myth cannot stand the glare of genuine scholarship, and hence the attempt to commandeer academics into becoming the handmaiden of bigotry was proved false by a host of academics, among them, Sushil Srivastava (1991).

In the first instance, the RSS-BJP-VHP-Bajrang Dal case and the more surreptitious arguments of closet communalists in the government and its "outside supporters" rest on a perversion of the many poetic traditions of Ram articulated by Valmiki and Kamban, Namdev and Tulsidas, Eknath and Krittivas.

Second, those who suffer from a poverty of imagination and have to assert the historicity of Ram's Ayodhya, were hoist with their own petard. If Ram is dragged into the domain of history, then problems of factual reconstruction arise. Prof H.D. Sankalia of the Deccan College, Pune, and Prof B.B. Lal, former director-general of the Archaeological Survey of India (ASI), proceeded on the assumption of the present-day Ayodhya being Ram's Ayodhya. The eminent scholars soon struck the shoals of evidence denying the antiquity and divine omnipotence of Ram. Prof Lal's archaeological research demonstrated that the earliest human habitation at Ayodhya could not have been before the seventh century B.C. And, as a good scholar, Prof Lal concluded that if indeed Ram ever was in Ayodhya, he could not have predated the period of the Buddha by more than a century or two. As he himself pithily remarks on the basis of his evidence, "For indeed, can anything be earlier than the earliest?" Prof Sankalia went even further and concluded that if Ram was indeed a historical figure, his area of operation was severely limited and the superhuman feats ascribed to him were no more than the exercise of poetic licence by Valmiki.

This delimiting of Ram through rigorous historical enquiry brings us to the third level of intellectual archaeology of myths : if Ram was a mundane historical personage, what is the legitimacy of Ram Janmabhoomi as "sacred space"? Regarding the birthplace itself, reference to literary and religious texts like the Ayodhya Mahatmya lead Srivastava (1991) to arrive at identification of at least two different sites. One is the Ram Janmabhoomi located on a grid whose referral points are Sita Paksthan (*Sita ki rasoi*), Kaikaiy Kop Bhawan (40 yards away), Sitakerp and Sumitra Bhawan (30 yards away). The other is the Ram Janmasthan whose referral points are Vighneshwara Temple (1,000 yards), Lomasa Rishi ashram (500 yards) and Vasistha ashram. There are several other claims regarding the actual birthplace in Ayodhya itself, not to mention one made by Punjabi University scholars that he was born in Ghuram in Punjab, the paternal home of his mother Kaushalya!

Let us go to the fourth level : what happened to Ayodhya after the seventh century B.C.? Excavations carried out by Prof Lal and Prof A.K. Narain of the Banaras Hindu University reveal that the habitation passed on without interruption to the Sunga period. Subsequently, legend, called into service by the VHP, talks of Vikramaditya of the Gupta dynasty having built a Ram temple at Ayodhya. However, archaeological findings of Prof Lal show that no Gupta layers were found in the excavations.

For the moment skipping the period before the site was reoccupied in the eleventh century, we proceed to the fifth level: did Babar destroy a Ram temple and build a mosque at Ayodhya? Srivastava (1991) and others doubt if Babar ever went to Ayodhya. Interestingly, in 1885-86 when the legal suit relating to the Babri masjid-Janmabhoomi dispute originated, Mahanth Raghubar Das, a noted Hindu priest, contended before the judicial magistrate of Oudh that the mosque had not been built by Babar as declared by the district judge, Col. J.E.A. Chambier.

On the basis of a careful reading of the controversial inscription of Babar's general Mir Baqi and other sources, Srivastava (1991) concludes that it is possible that the 'Babri masjid' may have been no more than an earlier ugly Jaunpuri- style mosque which Mir Baqi might have renovated and dedicated to Babar.

We now come to the final level of historical inquiry : although there is no conclusive evidence of the existence of a Hindu temple consecrating the birthplace of Ram, what is the possibility of there having been some other ancient structure at the site? In this context, the accounts of the Chinese travellers Fa-hein and Huen-tsang, the archaeological excavations done by A. Cunningham in 1862, the motifs on the carved stone pillars found in Ayodhya, all suggest that the site was a Buddhist stupa. The possibility of the destruction of this Buddhist site by Brahmanical onslaught, which desecrated even the Mahabodhi temple at Gaya, cannot be discounted.

The conclusion is that reverting to medieval barbarity of counter-point destruction of monuments of India's composite cultural heritage is self-destruction and the defence of elements of this culture is not the responsibility of any particular community, though one community can be singled out through fascistic propaganda to be made "the other" vis-a-vis which ethnic-religious tensions can be exacerbated.

In the communal situation in India, there are of course economic and other tensions too that add to religious-ethnic conflict. In spite of declaration of secularism, neither the machinery of the State nor the economy at large showed proportion of employment of Muslims which with an overall population of 10 to 12%, got a representation of merely 3.6 to 5.3% in the All-India Services, 0.2 to 0.9% in other Central Services, and around five per cent in the country's highest legislature. The ideal of 'equality of status and opportunity' is obviously far from being fulfilled (Wadhwa 1975: 153-54). In other bodies also like Chambers of Commerce, boards of directors of public and private sector companies, etc. the Muslims have been highly under-represented (Shahabuddin 1984).

Generally lagging behind Hindus in terms of possessing economic assets and being able to take advantage of such educational facilities as exist, it is not likely in the near future that the non-elite Muslims will catch up with the elite belonging to other religious communities (or even the small Muslim elite) in India. Proportionately, there are more Muslims among petty cultivators, artisans, agricultural and other labourers and the urban lower middle class. And there they suffer double discrimination, by virtue of being both Muslim and poor.

But the one most important way in which Muslims suffer are through communal riots (Shah 1983: 29-33). Communal riots are essentially urban phenomena and have to date, mercifully, not taken place in any major way in the countryside. "Regardless of which side starts the riot (this is often impossible to determine objectively), the Muslims are generally the relative losers in terms of lives lost and property destroyed" (Smith 1963: 414). And communal riots have become a recurrent phenomenon of Indian life, occurring ever so often in different areas and occasioned by different reasons. Official reports released from time to time indicate that there has not been a single year since Independence when communal incidents, large or small, have not taken place. Indeed, the number of riots has gone up alarmingly: there were 65 riots on an average in a year in the `fifties, the number increased to 257 in a year in the `seventies and there were 427 in 1980 (Shah 1982). A very serious aspect of these riots in recent times is that they have started occurring even in `non-traditional' areas like Gujarat and Assam and in not only large cities and industrial centres but also in small towns and suburban situations as in Bhagalpur in 1989. Finally, of course, in the wake of the destruction of the Babri masjid in Ayodhya on 6 December 1992, the riots which spread to many parts of the country, including Bombay and Calcutta, have helped in creating the ground for high-tech terrorism which thrives on the communal divide.

It is not possible to analyse each communal riot because of lack of accurate and systematic information but, by and large, it can be said that the religious issues ordinarily only provide the cover for the battling out of other social or economic matters. An important aspect is that, in addition to loss of life and property, many Muslims are forced to change their occupations as a result of communal riots (Gupta 1976). "When we were not free, communal disturbances were considered to be the handiwork of an alien government and it was hoped that communal relations would improve once it was gone... Since the birth of the Republic, the Government of India have been taking manifold steps to curb this evil... to control and check the communal menace. No safeguard, constitutional or legislative, is greater and more meaningful for the minorities than the actual protection of the life and property of its people from physical violence. So utility and merit of the safeguard are in the working and implementation and not merely in the writing of it in the fundamental law of the land. To proclaim the goals and ideals is one thing; to realise them in practice is, however, quite different and even difficult" (Wadhwa 1975: 155-56).

At this point, in the present consideration of the communal question in India, it is necessary to make a few points, both general and specific. A specific aspect of communal rioting which has not received adequate notice concerns intra-communal riots like those recurrent ones between Shias and Sunnis in Lucknow (Uttar Pradesh) among Muslims of different persuasions even though their impact is minor compared to the damage done by Hindu-Muslim riots. Much more in-depth investigation and analysis of causes and processes of such rioting are required. It is important in this respect to draw attention to two major aspects of the communal problem.

One relates to the situation of Pakistan. Events there have shown that even four decades after Partition, the so-called "ideology of Pakistan" premised on the first deliberate creation of a Muslim "homeland" has not guaranteed equality of life and opportunity for all Muslims. The fact of the non-integration of *Mohajirs* (immigrants from India) and their existence as a virtual "fifth nationality" (in addition to Punjabis, Sindhis, Pathans and Baluches) there has blown the myth of Pakistan for Indian Muslims. This, added to the gradual, even if painfully slow, expansion of opportunities in India itself has led to Indian Muslims increasingly seeing India itself as their homeland and therefore attempting to fashion their future here itself both as general Indian citizens as well as a distinct religious group present in the pluralistic polity of India.

The second aspect relates to the overall integration of the Indian market. While, as pointed out earlier, Muslims generally constitute the lower end of the Indian economic spectrum, nevertheless the curious growth of the Indian economy as an integrated whole, ranging from Stone Age tribes through feudally organised guilds of artisans to 'modern' high-tech industries, has found a place for everyone, even Muslims. And, no amount of social and cultural distinction therefore can insulate this section of the population from the political-economic forces that operate generally.

A general aspect of the communal situation, particularly concerning Muslims, is the realisation that religion by itself, in the face of other antagonistic contradictions, cannot bind people together. The historical experience of the breaking away of Bangladesh from Pakistan, which was artificially created as an Islamic State without reference to geographical contiguity, regional imbalances, linguistic and cultural factors, etc., shows that when secular issues arise, religion recedes to the background. The experience in India too would tend to indicate that whatever class politics have taken root, communal considerations are relatively weakened. We shall come back to this aspect in discussing other aspects of minorities in India also. However, it must be recorded, that as of now the secular consciousness is still weak and that, combined with various social and economic issues, results in a fair amount of political articulation in communal terms, a dangerous portent not only for secularism but for India's very entity (Akbar 1985).

A major issue confronting Muslims in India is that of their personal laws. As yet no uniform civil code governing matters like marriage, divorce, adoption, guardianship of children, inheritance and succession exists for all citizens of India in spite of the injunction to this effect in the Directive Principles of the Constitution (Article 44), nor has it been possible for legislation to be brought about on this aspect. This is particularly so because Muslim orthodoxy, which has received encouragement by the rise of Islamic fundamentalism in West Asia in recent years, has opposed any such measure (it may be noted here that the legislation of a civil code for Hindus through the enactment of the Hindu Code Bill and various other laws in the 1950s was similarly opposed by orthodox Hindus and could be carried only with difficulty).

Some non-Muslims have also pragmatially accepted the position that separate personal laws for different communities will have to continue given the politically 'sensitive' nature of the problem. In 1951 itself, the then Law Minister, Dr B.R. Ambedkar said, "In our country... the profession of a particular religion carries with it the personal law of the person. You cannot get away from that position" (cited in Luthera 1964: 96). Similarly, the Law Minister in 1970,

Govinda Menon, remarked, "Article 44 of the Constitution, laying down the Directive Principle that the State should endeavour to bring about a uniform civil code for all communities, should be read along with Article 25, a fundamental right which laid down that the existing religious rights of all communities should be allowed to continue" (cited in Wadhwa 1975: 158).

A major controversy which arose in this regard is the Shah Bano case, an instance of a Muslim woman considered eligible for receiving alimony under the general civil laws but subjected to discriminatory provisions under Muslim personal laws which were indeed retrogressively amended for this purpose by a purportedly secular government. Interesting and important legal and moral questions arise out of this instance as Veena Das (1990) has pointed out.

Such political pragmatism, aided by legal sophistry, has kept this issue dangling and even the opinion of progressive Muslims demanding reform in the personal laws (Shakir 1972, 1980; Dalwai 1969; Engineer 1984; etc.) has been ignored "for reasons of State".

The Shah Bano case refers to the events which followed from a criminal appeal by the appellant Modh. Ahmad Khan against the respondents Shah Bano Begum and others in the Supreme Court in 1985 (Engineer 1987). The appeal arose out of an application filed by a divorced Muslim woman, Shah Bano, for maintenance under section 125 of the Code of Criminal Procedure. The appellant who was an advocate was married to the respondent in 1932 and there were three sons and two daughters born of this marriage. According to the respondent, she was driven out of the matrimonial home in 1975. In April 1978, Shah Bano, filed an application against her husband under section 125, in the court of the judicial magistrate, Indore, asking for maintenance at the rate of Rs 500 p.m. On 6 November 1978, the appellant divorced the respondent by an irrevocable *talaq* (divorce) permitted under the personal law of the Muslims. His defence to Shah Bano's petition for maintenance was that she had ceased to be his wife after the divorce, that he had paid a maintenance allowance of two years and had deposited a sum of Rs 3,000 by way of dower during the period of *iddat*, which normally is three menstrual cycles or the passage of three lunar months for post-menopausal women.

The prehistory of the case need not concern us here. What is important for us is to note that the husband was in the Supreme Court by special leave and the court had to give its ruling on the question as to whether the provisions of Section 125 of the Code of Criminal Procedures were applicable to Muslims.

The judgement given on 25 April 1985, has a heterogeneous structure. The court decided that the provisions of the Code of Criminal Procedure were, indeed, applicable to the Muslims and therefore upheld the High Court decision as regards the provision of maintenance to Shah Bano. In the course of giving the judgement, however, the Chief Justice Chandrachud, also commented upon several other issues including the injustice done to women in all religions, on the desirability of evolving a common civil code as envisaged by the Constitution, and on the provisions in the Shariat regarding the obligations of a husband to provide maintenance to the divorced wife. In a way it was this very heterogeneity which allowed the judgement to become a signifier of issues that touched upon several dimensions, including the nature of secularism, the rights of minorities and on the use of law as an instrument of securing justice for the oppressed.

It is not that the judgement by itself created these issues; the Muslim community was clearly in the midst of debating these issues itself. The very fact that Mr Yunus Saleem had appeared as Counsel on behalf of Muslim Personal Law Board and not as Counsel for the defendant attests to this interpretation. The issue had become contentious at both the legislative and adjudicatory level. Baxi (1986) summarised this well when he stated that "What has caused this insecurity (among the Muslims)? Surely not the affirmation by the Supreme Court of India of an order raising the maintenance of Shah Bano from about Rs 70 to Rs 130 from a husband whose earnings as a lawyer were very substantial indeed? Ahmad Khan did not resort to the Supreme Court because maintenance amounts caused great financial hardship to him.

The real meaning of Shah Bano litigation was an attempt to secure reversal of two earlier decisions of the Court allowing maintenance to divorced Muslim wives under section 125 of the Criminal Procedure Code. The litigation was devised to reinstate the Shariat. And it succeeded in the first round when Justice Fazal Ali explicitly referred to a five judge bench the question "whether the earlier decisions were in consonance with the Shariat Act, 1937, which laid down that in all matters of family, including divorce and maintenance, courts will decide the questions in the light of the Shariat".

Following this judgement there was a great agitation as well as heated debates within the Muslim community — between 'progressives' and 'fundamentalists', between women's groups and Muslim leaders as well as argumentation in Parliament. The political debates, pressures and counter pressures finally led to the passing of The Muslim Women (Protection of Rights on Divorce) Bill, 1986. The Bill was hailed as a victory for fundamentalists by some and as a triumph for democracy by the others; it was alternately seen as a betrayal of women's rights and as a document which had vindicated the position of women in Islam, which, it was alleged, had been questioned in the Supreme Court judgement.

Veena Das (1990) has raised several questions on this issue. The first is the nature of the judgement itself. On the legal issues the judgement was quite clear. The judges stated quite categorically that earlier decisions of the Supreme Court had referred to the matter of whether Muslims were exempt from the application of section 125 of the Criminal Procedure Act. The judges stated that the particular section referred to the case in which a person of sufficient means refused to maintain a wife, including a divorced wife, who was unable to maintain herself. Incidentally, the provisions of the Act also applied to aged parents, children and also handicapped adult children. The purpose of the Act was to prevent destitute persons from becoming vagrants providing for their relatives to maintain them.

The judges quoted from speech of Sir James Fitz-James Stephen who piloted the Code of Criminal Procedure, 1872, as a Legal Member of the Viceroy's Council, to establish the purpose of the relevant sections of the Code. He had described this particular section as a 'mode of preventing vagrancy or at least of preventing its consequences'. Supporting this interpretation, the judgement stated that, "... the liability imposed by section 125 to maintain close relatives who are indigent is founded upon the individual's obligation to society to prevent vagrancy and destitution. That is the moral edict of the law and morality cannot be clubbed with religion".

Quite obviously, the colonial legislation was not concerned with individual rights but with 'prevention of vagrancy' as a threat to public order. That the judges should have invested this clause with such moral fervour without considering at any point the state's responsibility towards the maintenance of the indigent is another matter.

The judgement did not raise any questions that had the potential of becoming symbols of the contests that were to follow. The judges stated that Section 125 was part of the Code of Criminal Procedure and not of civil laws. They further stated that they were not concerned with the broad and general question of whether a Muslim husband is liable to maintain his wife, including a divorced wife, under all conditions. The correct subject matter of Section 125 related to a wife who was unable to maintain herself and their ruling was limited to these cases. Clearly given the fact that there is a uniform Criminal Code to which all Indian citizens are subject, the Court could not take into account the religion of the persons involved. Had the judgement stopped at this point the issue would only have been on the application of the criminal and penal codes to all citizens of India.

The judgement, however, went beyond this issue and considered questions relating to the interpretation of the Quran and of Islamic law on the issue of maintenance of divorced wives. The judges also made several comments upon the desirability of evolving a common civil code as a means of achieving national integration and gender justice.

It was stated in the opening paragraph of the judgement, that the appeal did not involve any questions of constitutional importance. However, the judges stated that it did raise issues of other kind that were important. "Some questions which arise under the ordinary civil and criminal law are of a far reaching significance to large segments of society which have been traditionally subjected to unjust treatment. Women are one such segment". The judges then quoted from Manu the famous line that acts like a signature for all discourses on Manu, viz., "na stree swatantryam arhati - a woman does not deserve autonomy." Having shown their critical capacity in relation to the Hindus they then criticised Islam taking for their authority a statement of Sir William Lane made in 1843, that the fatal point in Islam is the degradation of woman.

Veena Das (1990) holds that "the semeiotic function of this framing paragraph in the judgement was to establish the secular and learned credentials of the judges, for by a time honoured tradition in our political culture, one signals one's secular credentials by handing out in an even manner so to say, criticisms of the majority community and the minority community". The second purpose was to show the concern with gender justice. "This appeal ... raises a straightforward issue which is of common interest not only to Muslim women, not only to women generally, but to all those who, aspiring to create an equal society of men and women, lure themselves into the belief that mankind has achieved a remarkable degree of progress in that direction". Thus we have now two moral ends posited in the judgement: the first is the creation of a society of equals between men and women and the second is the moral duty of the individual to support destitute relatives in order that society does not have to bear the consequences of vagrancy. The two ends, however, clearly do not belong to the same moral plane."

The third set of observations that are relevant here are those on the importance of evolving a common civil code. "It is a mater of regret", state the judges that "Article 44 of our constitution has remained a dead letter". They deplore the absence of any official activity for framing a common civil code. "A common civil code will help the cause of national integration by removing disparate loyalties to laws which have conflicting ideologies."

Thus the case of Shah Bano became the occasion for an attack on the conflicting ideologies that rule family and marriage among the difference communities in India.

From the perspective of the secular and progressive opinion, the opposition to the judgement of the Supreme Court was led by 'fundamentalist', and 'communalists' and their rise to power was indicative of the 'regressive' threats to Indian society — a somewhat simplistic characterisation of the complex issues that were raised.

The first such issue was the relation between community and State. While no claim was ever made on behalf of any section of the community that Muslims should be ruled in accordance with Islamic laws in matters pertaining to crime and punishment, it was, however, aggressively asserted that in civil matters pertaining to family and marriage, the Muslim community recognised only the authority of the Shariat (Engineer 1987).

Veena Das (1990) feels that one way to interpret this claim of the community over its civil matters is to see it as part of a worldwide pattern which is connected with the decline of the idea of the nation state which pretends full ideological and political loyalty to its value. In challenging the state as the only giver to values, the community, from one point of view may be seen as claiming authority over its private life. Nevertheless, the all-pervading presence of the state was acknowledged in the very act of the new legislation and the wide-spread support it received from the 'fundamentalist' sections of the community. In giving their support to the new bill, such sections were paradoxically reiterating the authority of the state to legislate and the courts to interpret the Shariat, while simultaneously assert-ing their own obligation to give a direction to state law. The bill postulated that a divorced woman was to be supported by those relatives such as sons, or brothers who were in the category of heirs, and that if such relatives were unable to support a divorced, indigent woman, then it was the responsibility of the community to support such indigent relatives through its *waqf* boards. Thus although the category of relatives who were to support an indigent woman was altered, the right of a woman to have these provisions endorsed by courts of law of the modern state were not challenged. In effect, the forms of legal mediation instituted by the State were endorsed, even as the contents were being directed through the mobilisation of the Muslim community in a particular direction. The community, then, can be seen, not as claiming sovereignty in competition with the state, but informing the State on the direction of laws in the field of marriage and family (Veena Das 1990). It is the response of the secular State to the articulate and influential "community opinion" in this regard that is interesting in the context of the tussle between institutionalism and primordialism in shaping India.

Compared to the situation of Muslims in India, the issues confronting other religious minorities are of a different order alto-gether. Firstly, some of the religious minorities are quite small in number, appearing minuscular in the vast Indian population. Sec-ondly, some are ethnically identifiable; the best example of such people are the Zoroastrians who call themselves Parsees. Others, like neo-Buddhist, drawn mainly from among Scheduled Castes in Maharashtra, and older Buddhist communities among Himalayan tribes, are far less heterogeneous than Hindus or Muslims. Among the Christians too, there are two relatively homogenous segments: the Nagas and other tribals of North-Eastern India who belong to the Baptist Church and the Anglo-Indians. These aspects of the social existence of such religious minorities impart special dimensions to their specific problems.

The Parsees, many of whose small number are part of the Indian capitalist, cultural, scientific and other elite, are most concerned at present not because they face discrimination as a minority community but about the prospect of genetic extinction or socio-cultural absorption into the overwhelmingly large non-Parsee population. This concern of theirs being recognised as genuine in view of their decreasing numbers, is not antagonistic to the interest of other communities who, if they show interest in the affairs of the Parsees, do so, by and large, either to marvel at the achievements of this minuscular community or in terms of scientific interest in their endogamous social organisation and genetic processes. Still, it must be noted that, in spite of the small numbers, the Parsees can by no means be ignored in India as they continue to be prominent in many fields and, being a fairly coherent community, take some care of the relatively worse-off members of their group.

The picture of the Indian Jews is markedly different from that of the Parsees. This group, which is mainly located on the western coast of India and specially in Kerala, has dwindled to the point of not being noticed at all except for stray individuals who make a public mark. The Indian Jews who claim great antiquity, having come to India nearly two thousand years ago, have suffered from reverse, if delayed, migration to Israel. Apart from dwindling numbers, this community too does not suffer from religious or communal discrimination to any noticeable extent and the same is true of other minuscule communities like Armenians, Greeks and some Arabs who are settled in India for centuries. Among small and distinct communities in India, the case of ethnic Chinese is also not dissimilar. Apart from a period following India's war with China in 1962 which led to restraints being placed on the community at large, the ethnic Chinese continue to exist freely in India while maintaining their own customs and traditions. The economic forces, however, are affecting them too, making them change their traditional occupations.

In the case of the Anglo-Indians, not only economic but political factors too are important. Being Eurasian in terms of origin, they received relatively favoured treatment during the British rule and the change of regime in 1947 marked a sharp deterioration in their conditions. Many migrated at the time of Independence itself and subsequently there has been a slow but steady exodus to Britain and the colonies, i.e., Canada and Australia. Those who have remained behind have had to compete on equal terms with persons from other communities, a traumatic experience for the Anglo-Indians, many of whom proved unable to cope with the situation and slid to positions far below those to which they were accustomed. As a remarkable and unique gesture, however, the Constitution of India contained special provisions for this microscopic group which considers itself as identifiably a racial, religious and linguistic minority. The community is provided particular safeguards like two reserved, non-elective seats in the Lower House of Parliament — a benevolently ignored anomaly in a democratic system — and similarly one or two seats in several state Assemblies. The language of the community is English which, for reasons other than those concerning Anglo-Indians alone, has statutory recognition as an official language. Anglo-Indians get special grants for their educational and cultural institutions and, although there is no reservation for them in government jobs any longer — the special transitory safeguards in this regard having lapsed some years ago — they have been given, what is acknowledged by leaders of the community, "fair treatment" (Anthony 1969). If there are occasional stirrings in the community, they are in fact against the self-assumed leadership by some individuals rather than on any other issue. Indeed, as one such self-proclaimed but fairly widely accepted leader of the Anglo-Indians has remarked, "The post-Independence period was marked by an almost miraculous recognition to the community in the New India which was denied to much larger minorities" (Anthony 1969: viii).

A religious minority which was denied any such privileges comprises the Buddhists and, in particular, the group among them that are known as neo-Buddhists. At the time of Independence,

Buddhism in India was generally confined to the relatively remote areas in the sub-Himalayan tribal tracts which were backward and poor. Their situation largely continued unchanged and, apart from benefiting from such general developmental (and defence-oriented) efforts as have taken place in their areas, if those Buddhists have attracted affirmative action, it has been only if they belong to Scheduled Tribes for whom special protective provisions exist in law. On the other side are the new converts to Buddhism, mainly in Maharashtra and from among the Scheduled Castes. By virtue of having renounced Hinduism however, until recently these neo-Buddhists have been deprived of whatever benefits they might have derived from belonging to Scheduled Castes, though curiously, the protective provisions in this regard are still available to Scheduled Caste converts to Sikhism (Vijayendra et al. 1982). Among the religious minorities in India, the Buddhists therefore, suffer from both religious and secular handicaps.

The Christians in India are such a heterogeneous group that it would be absurd to call them a community at all, consisting as they do of people as different from each other as Protestant tribals in north-eastern India to Syrian Catholic plantation owners in Kerala. The Christians themselves distinguish among their numbers between different groups depending on relative antiquity on conversion, e.g., those claiming descent from ancestors supposedly converted by St. Thomas the Apostle and the early Christians, mainly in South India; those converted by the Portuguese, mainly Roman Catholics in Goa; and later converts brought into the fold by missionaries of different Christian orders. Some relatively old Christian communities have even the caste system with Brahman and other Christians.

On the whole, except for the Christian Nagas, whose social self-identification is more as Nagas rather than as Christians, who for some time resisted integration into India, the Indian Christians are fairly well integrated into the social, economic and cultural structure. There are of course some outstanding issues which are occasionally voiced, the major problem being the right to propagate religious and missionary activities. From time to time, orthodox Hindus resent these activities, especially as conversion to Christianity, Islam or Buddhism, attracts the most oppressed among the

Hindus. It is pertinent to recall that the Vishwa Hindu Parishad first arose as an organisation to counter conversions of *dalits* to Christianity and Islam as at Meenakshipuram in Tamil Nadu. Indeed, a few legislative attempts have also been made by Hindu parliamentarians to put curbs on conversions. However, neither have these attempts been successful to date nor have they meant a serious threat to Christians in India. In fact, in Kerala many Syrian Christians enjoy positions of dominance and their political representatives are often in a position to tilt the balance between competing legislative coalitions. However, as the Churches, and particularly the Roman Catholics and among them specially the Jesuits, change to adopt aspects of the Theology of Liberation, paying more attention to issues affecting the Christian and non-Christian exploited and oppressed people, the issues will surely be articulated in secular rather than religious terms.

One community in which secular and religious issues have got so finely mixed up that an explosive confrontation has been reached is the Sikhs. The issues are so complex and the developments in their resolution are so fast that any report on this community is bound to be both simplistic and outdated. Nevertheless, as the Sikh problem in many senses epitomises the problem of ethnic and religious minorities in general in Indian pluralism, the issue cannot be evaded either. The following is therefore, a brief and admittedly inadequate account of the Sikh problem, based on uncited newspaper and other reports.

To start with, it must be recorded that for many centuries there was no Hindu-Sikh problem. Indeed there was hardly any clear-cut divide between the two communities and there was free intermingling, even in religion between Hindus and Sikhs. In secular activities too there has been no restriction on the Sikhs. They are scattered throughout India in small numbers though their major concentration is in Punjab where Sikhism first originated and found ready adherents among artisans and cultivators. At first secular rent-based exploitation and then general persecution by the then State drove Sikhism, from being a peaceful, reformist, integrationist movement encompassing both Hindus and Muslims and drawing from both their religions, to greater militancy and distinctiveness. However, all the ten Gurus of the Sikhs preached the common spiritual brotherhood of man and the later Gurus of the Sikhs got involved in temporal affairs only because their followers were subjected to exploitation and persecution. They were practically goaded into periodic rebellion against the Mughal empire on both agrarian and religious issues.

During the processes of rebellion and its articulation however, religion and temporal affairs became intertwined and when, on the decline of the Mughal empire, an independent and strong State emerged in the Punjab under Maharaja Ranjit Singh, it was perceived as being Sikh rather than Punjabi. This conception was strengthened by the assaults launched by the British on that State after the demise of Ranjit Singh: the British called their wars Angle-Sikh Wars and in due course were able to conquer the Punjab just before the great revolt of 1857 broke out against the East India Company in different parts of India. The Punjab, having been just subdued, remained quiet during that revolt and in fact the British were able to use soldiers from there to suppress the revolt in other parts. Partly as reward for this and partly to ensure that the Punjab did not rise up against them, the British took up a number of measures there which benefited the local population to an extent. The most important of these measures were the renovation of the old irrigation canal network which existed in parts of the Punjab and its expansion, leading to substantial increases in agricultural production. This benefited the British Raj, the landlords (many of whom were Muslims), the traders (many of whom were Hindus), and even the Sikh (also Muslim and Hindu) peasantry. Thus, relative to many other parts of India, investment in agriculture and corresponding benefits were high in the Punjab.

With the intensification of the national movement in India in the twentieth century, the Punjab too got affected and several strands of political activity and organisation started there. The landed interests among Muslims got involved in legislative politics in the provincial assembly in undivided, pre-Partition Punjab. Many Hindus and Sikhs got involved in Congress and various radical movements. The population did begin to get divided politically but the division was more between Muslims on the one side and Hindus and Sikhs together on the other.

As time progressed, however, a religious reform movement

among the Sikhs, the Gurudwara agitation, directed towards cleansing and liberating Sikh places of worship from the corrupt religious heads who had got control over them, led to the formation of separate Sikh politico-religious organisations like the Shiromani Akali Dal. In this communalisation of politics, the voices of secular movements like the Ghadar Party, the Hindustan Socialist Republican Army, the Communists and even some Congress leaders became cries in the wilderness.

On the eve of Independence, there was a three-cornered political/communal organisation in the Punjab but the principal antagonism was still between Muslims and others. It was this factor which led to the Sikhs in general aligning with Hindus and, after some prevarication by their leaders, ultimately throwing in their lot with India. The country was partitioned and the Punjab was divided up between India and Pakistan. Large-scale exchange of population accompanied by barbarous massacres took place in both India and Pakistan. Millions of people on either side of the border have not yet been able to recover from the trauma of Partition and all that it brought in its wake. In post-Partition western India, the Sikhs and Hindus who were uprooted from the part of the Punjab which went to Pakistan crossed the Radcliff line which divided their province, came to India as refugees and, by and large, accepted the residual India as their homeland and began afresh the business of living.

The political and constitutional processes that were under way at the time of Partition, however, had to be revised to correspond to the changed situations. In due course, most Sikhs came to reluctantly accept that they had irretrievably lost major portions of their homelands which had gone to Pakistan and that there being no separate Sikh state, they had to settle in India. However, in the Constituent Assembly and its various committees, the representatives and leaders of the Sikhs put forth several demands. These included assertions like (1) that the Sikhs should have the right to elect representatives to the legislature through a purely communal electorate; (2) that 50% and 5% seats should be reserved for Sikhs in the residual (East) Punjab and Central Legislatures respectively; (3) that seats should be reserved for them in U.P. and Delhi; (4) that Scheduled Caste Sikhs should have the same privileges as other Scheduled Castes; and (5) that there should be statutory reservation of a certain proportion in the Indian army for Sikhs.

The Constituent Assembly and its various committees examined the demands of the Sikhs and found that many of these were a fundamental departure from the decisions taken by the Assembly in respect of every other community including Scheduled Castes. A conclusion was thus reached that "the Sikhs are a minority from the point of view of numbers, but they do not suffer from any other handicaps... They are a highly educated and virile community and with great gifts not merely as soldiers but as farmers and artisans, and with a most remarkable spirit of enterprise... With the talents they possess, they will soon reach a level of prosperity which will be the envy of other communities. Moreover, while, in the undivided Punjab, they were only 14% of the population, they form nearly 30% of the population in East Punjab, a strength which gives them, in the public life of the province, a position of considerable authority" (Constituent Assembly Debates, cited in Wadhwa 1975: 67).

The question of communal electorates or weightage in the legislature which was the main demand of the Sikh politico-religious organisation, the Shiromani Akali Dal, was rejected on the grounds that "the demands of the Dal are, in principle, precisely those which the Muslim League demanded for the Muslims and which led to tragic consequences with which the country is only too familiar" (ibid.). Hence, it was decided that "no special provisions should be provided for the Sikhs other than the general provisions already approved for certain other minorities" (ibid.). At this stage, this decision was widely welcomed and representatives of the Sikhs too declared that they were "happy that the undemocratic demands regarding special safeguards, reservations, weightage and protection have not been taken into account. The Sikhs are an enterprising, energetic and hard-working people who do not dread competition in the open market whether it is in spheres political, economic or administrative. We can rub shoulders with our countrymen in every walk of life" (ibid.).

Very soon after this however, some Sikhs started voicing discontent. For many years, the major cause of dissatisfaction was that their demand for a Punjabi Suba was not being conceded. Indeed, the politics of the Akali Dal virtually centred around this demand. In February 1948 itself, Master Tara Singh, the then acknowledged leader of the Dal, stated, "We want to have a province where we can safeguard our culture and own tradition (quoted in Wadhwa 1975: 63). The concept of the Suba was however, vague; it was not clarified if it would be constituted on religious, cultural or linguistic lines. The general agitational demands in initial years seemed to suggest that the Suba would essentially be a state, within the Indian Union, of Punjabi-speaking people. The manifesto of the Akali Dal released for the first general election stated, "The Shiromani Akali Dal is in favour of provinces on linguistic and cultural basis throughout India, but holds it as a question of life and death for the Sikhs for a new Punjab to be created immediately" (cited in Nayar 1966: 89). This statement too was obviously ambiguous and the first systematic presentation of the demand for a Punjab Suba was made before the States Reorganisation Commission appointed by the Government of India in 1953. In a memorandum to the Commission, the Akali Dal urged the formation of Punjabi Suba by putting together the so-called Punjabi-speaking areas of (East) Punjab, PEPSU (Patiala and Eastern Punjab States Union, a conglomerate of Native States in colonial India), and Rajasthan. It suggested that those areas in Punjab and PEPSU where, according to it, Punjabi was not spoken should be detached from these states and merged into Himachal Pradesh and Delhi. The Akali Dal argued that the demand for Punjabi Suba was in line with demands in other parts of India for the linguistic reorganisation of states (Nayar 1966: 32-33).

Unlike in the case of other movements for creation of linguistic states, however, the States Reorganisation Commission categorically rejected the demand for Punjabi Suba. In its report submitted in 1955, it declared in unequivocal terms, "The proposed State will solve neither the language problem nor the communal problem and, far from removing internal tension, which exists between communal and not linguistic and regional groups, it might further exacerbate the existing feelings" (India 1955: 140). The Commission further pointed out, "... even if a Punjabi-speaking State is formed, the entire area will still be bilingual, in the sense that instruction in Hindi will have to be arranged on an extensive scale, and for official purposes also Hindi will probably have to be given special recognition" (India 1955: 146).

According to the Census of 1961, the number of Punjabi-speaking people in India was 10,950,826 i.e. 2.5% of the total population of the country. They were largely concentrated in Punjab where their number was 8,343,264 forming 41% of the total population of the state. On the other side, the number of Hindi-speaking people was 11,298,855 i.e. 55.6% of the total population of the state. In addition, the linguistic issue was complicated by religious considerations, many Punjabi Hindus declaring themselves to be Hindi-speaking and Sikhs identifying themselves with the cause of Punjabi and the Gurmukhi script. The problem thus took a bitter communal turn with Sikhs, by and large, pressing for the creation of Punjabi Suba and large numbers of Hindus opposing it.

It is interesting to note however that the agitation for and against Punjabi Suba was primarily nursed and nurtured in two important Punjab dailies, *Prabhat* and *Pratap*, the former representing the Akali view and the latter that of the Hindus; both the newspapers were published in Urdu (Wadhwa 1975: 165). Thus, though much of the Hindi-Punjabi controversy was waged on both sides through the medium of a third language (Smith 1963: 450), the irony did not have the effect of reducing mutual antagonisms which kept getting sharpened and polarisation that occurred became increasingly communal.

The States Reorganisation Commission noted, "While other demands for separation from existing composite States have had the backing of an overwhelming majority of the people of the language group seeking such separation, the demand for a Punjabi-speaking state is strongly opposed by large sections of people speaking the Punjabi language and residing in the areas proposed to be constituted into a Punjabi-speaking state. The problem, therefore, is sui generis" (India 1955: 141). An unofficial observer was less coy than the Commission about using communal terms to describe the situation, "The basis of the demand for a separate Punjabi-speaking State or Punjabi Suba is the sense of grievance among the leaders and the rank and file of the Akali Dal that there is discrimination against the Sikh community. It is felt that only if there is a State in which the Sikhs are in an influential political position, an end can be put to this discrimination, and justice assured for the Sikh community" (Nayar 1966: 112).

In spite of the apprehensions and conclusions of the States Reorganisation Commission and others, such was the simmering discontent among the Sikhs and the level of their continued agitation on this account that in 1966, a full ten years after most other states were reorganised on linguistic basis, that the Government of India was forced to revise its earlier decision and divide Punjab more or less linguistically into Punjab and Haryana. The Sikhs just about became the majority community in Punjab and, for a while, it seemed the problem had been solved. Even Master Tara Singh stated in 1961, "The only discrimination against the Sikhs was about the non-formation of Punjabi Suba" (cited in Wadhwa 1975: 165). Thus with the acceptance of Punjabi Suba — which, however, continued to be called Punjab — the main cause of restlessness and the chief example of alleged discrimination against the Sikh community seemed to have been done away with.

In 1961, prior to the creation of the Punjabi Suba, the Government of India had appointed a Commission to enquire into the general question of discrimination against the Sikhs and examine any charges of alleged differential treatment or other grievances of the Sikhs in Punjab. After examining evidence presented to it, the Commission came to the conclusion that there was no case of discrimination against Sikhs in Punjab. It was pointed out to the Commission that although in Punjab at that time (1962), Sikhs were only 34% of the population, 41% of members of the state Legislative Assembly, 45% of Members of Parliament from the state and 44 to 55% of Cabinet Ministers in the state were Sikhs. In fact, one Sikh leader, Surjit Singh Majithia stated, "We have no grievances (of discrimination against Sikhs) and the only grievance can be that the Sikhs are over-represented" (cited in Wadhwa 1975: 167). An academic study observed, "The Akali Dal has also made charges about government interference in the religious affairs of the Sikhs, but has not presented any concrete evidence on the subject. Some years back, the allegation of discrimination was made in report (sic) to Sikh Harijans but this was taken care of by government extending to Sikh Harijans, the same privileges that had been given to Hindu Harijans even though Sikhism recognises no caste" (Nayar 1966: 115). It was therefore, concluded that particularly after the Sikh demand for Punjabi Suba was conceded, the Sikhs would have no cause for complaint.

Such hopes did not seem to be totally unjustified. As noted earlier, investment in agriculture had begun in Punjab even during British rule, and after Independence the process was intensified. Vast irrigation and power systems like the Bhakra Nangal were built. Package programmes to promote agricultural productivity were taken up and they culminated in taking the shape of what was known as the Green Revolution. Production increased; productivity increased; the gross domestic product took a quantum jump and even per capita income progressed by leaps and bounds. In addition to income generated from agriculture, a large number of small and medium industries began in parts of the state and other productive activities like dairying, poultry and horticulture, also contributed their share to the state's prosperity. Punjab's long tradition of out-migration was intensified in the 1960s and 1970s. To migration to Argentina, Canada, U.S.A., Britain, South-East Asia, East Africa, etc. was added migration to the West Asian countries in wake of the oil boom, and remittances from such migrants added to the income of the families back home. The army continued to be a major avenue of employment. Altogether, as Punjab became more and more prosperous in both absolute terms and relative to other states of India, it dramatically reached the top of tables of per capita income and many other economic indices.

Politically too, with the eventual acceptance of the demand for a Punjabi-speaking state and the coming into power of the most important segment of the Akali Dal, which, in the manner of most Indian political parties went through the process of splitting, things seemed to be for the best in the best of all possible worlds.

It was too good to be true. The canker of discontent festered. There were many issues, big and small, which kept the state in turmoil. Many non-Sikh Punjabis assertively identified themselves with the cause of Hindus and as Hindus comprised nearly half the population of the state, their very presence, as the States Reorganisation Commission had apprehended, was source of continuing tension which was intensified when the Hindu backlash took place in the form of aggressive communal assertion on their part subsequent to the Akalis coming into power in Sikh-majority Punjab.

Another irritant was Chandigarh. After Punjab lost its capital city of Lahore to Pakistan at the time of Partition, a new capital city, Chandigarh, designed by a French architect, Le Corbusier, was created for it but when Punjab was divided and Haryana came into existence, both states laid claim to it. A messy situation ensued and long agitations were carried out. Finally, in 1969, three years after the creation of the reorganised states of Punjab and Haryana, it was announced that Chandigarh would eventually go to Punjab; Haryana would get instead the Hindu-majority, cotton-growing and prosperous districts of Abohar and Fazilka; and till Haryana built its own capital city, Chandigarh would continue to be the administrative headquarters for both states but would itself be administered by the Central government as a union territory. Except in the last respect, even this messy solution to a messy problem was put off to an indefinite date in the future and, instead of solving anything, created another source of agitation.

Punjab also had other grievances relating to distribution of river waters with Haryana and Rajasthan. A similar problem of distribution of waters of the Indus and its tributaries which had existed between India and Pakistan had been solved fairly amicably but no quick solution was found among states in India itself and the problem grew. Further, Punjab felt that compared to other states of India, the proportion of central public sector investment in industry was small in Punjab and that it was not getting an adequate compensation for being the bread basket of India. There were grievances regarding prices of agricultural commodities and inputs and the Akali Dal government in Punjab had a point of view different from that of the Congress party which ruled at the Centre on questions of centre-state fiscal relations regarding devolution of resources and investments. These were secular issues affecting, one would suppose, Punjabi Hindus as well as Sikhs. But the Akali Dal had religious demands also, like permission to transmit recitations of the Guru Granth Saheb (holy text of the Sikhs) from the Golden Temple in Amritsar, declaration of Amritsar as holy city and, perhaps the most important of such demands, stopping of all interference by the Central government and the Congress party into affairs of Sikh gurudwaras.

This last demand was significant because the gurudwaras not

only controlled vast resources but for the Sikhs represented both spiritual and temporal authority. It was on the issue of liberation of the gurudwaras from corrupt priests (*mahants*) that the Sikhs as a body had first confronted the British and the Akali Dal had been born. After the gurudwaras were cleansed, their management had been entrusted to a statutory body known as the Shiromani Gurudwara Prabandhak Committee (SGPC) which was periodically elected by Sikhs in general. With the Akali Dal claiming support from the gurudwaras and their apex body, the SGPC, it had an impregnable position in Sikh politics and the Congress was for a period driven out of power as it had no similar base in the new state of Punjab. The Hindus on the other hand were divided between various parties and even when the Akali Dal did not gain an absolute majority in elections to the state legislature, it was possible for it to form a non-Congress coalition government.

In this context, some political commentators have suggested that, in order to damage the base of the Akali Dal and to redeem its own position, the Congress took certain short-sighted measures which aggravated the situation. For instance, neither were the secular demands of Punjab accepted nor were grounds for their non-acceptance advanced. At the same time, there was an on-going cat-and-mouse game regarding the religious demands, some of which were conceded under pressure and about others there were on-and-off discussions.

This process of according priority to solution of religious issues before secular problems was, to say the least, curious. Simultaneously, some local leaders of the Sikhs suddenly got importance. The one among them who became best-known was Sant Jarnail Singh Bhindranwale, religious head of one of the many Sikh congregations, who encountered passive acquiescence if not active encouragement from the Congress in his early extremist activities.

It would be too simple, however, to see only a Congress conspiracy in the rise of Sikh extremism. The Hindu revivalists led by the R.S.S., the Jan Sangh and later the Bharatiya Janata Party and the Hindu Suraksha Samiti (Hindu Self-Defence Committee) did their best to provoke reaction. Among the Sikhs themselves, the rise of fundamentalism led to militant assertion of orthodoxy and intolerance. The relative "autonomy" of terrorism cannot be discounted nor can the links between drug, crime and terrorism. And there is evidence of the involvement of foreign powers in fomenting trouble in this sensitive and vital border state. Notwithstanding all these factors, the role of the Congress in communalising Punjab politics and creating a climate in which the later tragic events occurred cannot be ignored either.

But be that as it may, the fact was that large-scale trouble first erupted when some Sikhs attacked a Nirankari gathering as the orthodox Sikhs thought the Nirankaris to be a blasphemous group. There were counter-attacks and several people died. Bhindranwale was arrested and then, mysteriously, not only released but allowed, without let or hindrance, to roam around Delhi fully armed. The Akalis got divided among moderates, still interested in negotiated settlement, and extremists who, with the active involvement of some emigre Sikhs started talking of an independent Sikh state of Khalistan (the land of the pure: shades of Pakistan which also literally means the land of the pure!). Provocative acts were indulged in by both Hindus and Sikhs and there were many killings. More and more militant postures were adopted and the language of confrontation started being used.

In the climate of hatred which grew in Punjab, many facts were neglected and a spectre of communal terror was created. It was not much noticed that both communities suffered in the process. Only a detailed perusal of official reports indicates that among people killed in terrorist acts in Punjab the numbers of Hindus and Sikhs are almost equal. At the same time, in the sanctuary of the Golden Temple itself, arms and ammunition were accumulated and extremism became the order of the day. Finally, on 3 June, 1984, the Indian army attacked the Golden Temple and after a bloody battle, the shrine was liberated from the extremists. This action of the Indian State traumatised large sections of the religious Sikh population and they were further divided from the Hindus. In October, 1984, the Prime Minister of India, Mrs Indira Gandhi was assassinated and for several days after that Sikhs in different parts of the country were subjected to brutal murder, loot and pillage. Civil liberty organisations found evidence of the involvement of Congressmen in the anti-Sikh riots but no judicial inquiry was ordered for a long time and even after it was finally instituted and submitted a report, practically no action was taken against the culprits.

In 1985, the Congress government in New Delhi signed an accord with a section of the moderate Akali leaders and the process of democratic government, rudely interrupted in Punjab, was once again resumed. However, the situation had changed so much that status quo ante could not be restored by mere agreement among top-level leaders. Shortly after the accord, the principal Sikh signatory, Sant Longowal, was shot dead by the terrorists who thereby struck a severe blow at the effort of restoring normalcy in Punjab. Subsequently, although a democratic government was installed in the state, it was dismissed on partisan considerations by the Central Congress government which thereby delivered the coup de grace to the accord process.

Meanwhile, the extremist groups in Punjab have gone through a series of splits and at least some elements among them are indistinguishable from common criminals dealing in drugs and weapons. Others are on the fringe of politics and dabble with a curious mixture of electoral democracy, religious populism and extra-territorial support. Simultaneously the moderates too have gone through a process of attrition. The other political parties and formations have their own agenda determined by this phenomenon to such an extent that a sense of political hopelessness prevails in Punjab even as bloodshed continues.

The curious part is that production activities in the state have remained largely undisturbed by all this. Not only does agriculture continue to prosper in Punjab but indeed the state is getting more closely integrated with the overall Indian product, credit and labour markets.

How this economic integration will confront social and political disintegration will be decided by a variety of factors, as events in the Soviet Union have demonstrated. Nevertheless, at the end of this sorry and sordid tale of the unfolding of ethnicity on the basis of religion, certain general points can be made even at this stage.

It is important to note that religious ethnicity and communalism in India are modern phenomena. In concluding this however it must be asserted that although this understanding may appear identical to that arrived at by nationalist historiography, there are also significant differences with that approach. Some aspects of such analyses have been criticised by Randhir Singh (1990) as being both method-ologically and politically faulty. However, an additional criticism that can be made is that such nationalist historiography, although claiming Marxist pedigree, is unduly informed by an idealisation of the anti-colonial movement and in particular a hagiography of Jawaharlal Nehru. As such, while it correctly notes that virulent communalism came into existence during colonial rule, it sees the earlier period as one of the flowering of a "composite culture" as discovered by Nehru and the post-colonial era as one of an irrevo-cable and one-way march towards modernity and hence secularism.

Now, while it cannot be denied that many elements of Indian culture, as discussed earlier, are indeed "composite" and dialectical relationships between Islam and what has been called Hinduism have had a major influence on music, art, languages, literature, and even religious practices, it would be unreal to think of pre-cólonial society as being a fully integrated one. Indeed, while the existence of "non-antagonistic contradictions" between different communi-ties may have characterised pre-colonial society, available historical evidence points largely to the persistence of communities living "back-to-back" rather than as one integrated unit. If there were no aggressive assertions of communal identities and hence no major sectarian conflicts, it is attributable to what has been described as the existence of "fuzzy identities".

The coming of colonialism, and indeed modernity, changed that. In particular, the very enumeration of people on the basis of communities created both a majority-minority sense as well as a process of homogenisation within communities. This process is still on and finds most dramatic expression in the simplified, pan-Indian Ram cult that is being nurtured among the Hindus. In turn, this reinforces numerical majoritarianism on the one side and insecuri-ties among communities which conceive of themselves as minori-ties.

Paradoxically, the very democratisation of the polity adds to the segmentation of society. A democracy which is inherently imper-fect, as it is premised on a social order which is both inegalitarian and hierarchical, leads to the flowering not of individuals but of primor-dial groups. These identities often constructed on the basis of myths find expression in the modernity of ethnicity, a phenomenon which has profoundly undemocratic implications. The Catch-22 is completed.

Something like this is happening in India. The assertions of religious ethnicities in the modern context have to be seen with this historical perspective and the languages of majority and minority have to be understood as expressions of an imperfect modernity.

These cases and many others make it clear that for the Indian State secularism is not combating communalism but establishing a compromise between various communalisms. This was best represented in the series of events leading up to and following the destruction of the Babri masjid in Ayodhya on 6 December 1992.

The act of vandalism signified much more than the mere demolition of a historical monument or even of a particular place of worship. Religious revanchism was in fact only one aspect of the demolition.

As already discussed, the structure at Ayodhya had only limited religious sanctity for both Hindus and Muslims for centuries and it was only in the last several years that it became the focal point of competitive communalism. Ayodhya had of course a religious significance for many Hindus for a long time and a civil property dispute over ownership and control of the mosque and its adjacent areas had gone on for a long time. However, it was only in 1949 that the surreptitious installation of idols of Ram inside the mosque — which, it was asserted, was the very birthplace of Ram — exacerbated religious feelings by linking them to political matters. In due course, the Babri masjid – Ram janmabhoomi dispute got caught in the welter of politics and politicking.

A section of militant Hindus saw the structure not only as a symbol of Mughal conquest of India and as a mark of "non-Indian" Islam but also as a sign of the alleged "appeasement" of Muslims by the secular Indian state even after Independence. As a counterpart of this intolerance, a section of militant Muslims projected the mosque as a testimony of their faith and premised its continued existence as a guarantee extended to Islam itself by the same secular state. The issue got more and more embroiled in other unrelated matters like the desirability or otherwise of having a uniform civil code, imaginary fears about changing demographic proportions of religious communities in India, extra-territorial and international concerns about global balances of power, etc. Cynical politicians seeking vote banks inevitably began fishing in the murky waters.

The RSS-BJP-VHP-Bajrang Dal, constituting the Sangh *parivar*, aided and abetted by a motley collection of mendicants who styled themselves the *Dharma Sansad* (religious parliament), attempted to increase the invented Hindu passion to a feverish pitch through a series of campaigns which used potent religious symbols. Repeated assembly of thousands of people at Ayodhya to perform *kar sewa* (religious duty) in order to construct a massive Ram temple — and in the process destroy the Babri masjid — had ripple effects throughout the country and served to both intensify communalism as well as to mobilise votes for the BJP.

In order to deprive the BJP from taking sole advantage of this process of raising Hindu fervour, the Congress indulged in an ambitious gamesmanship. Despite its professions of secularism and even as it attempted to woo the Muslim voters by making compromises with obscurantist community spokesmen (as in the Shah Bano case), the Congress adopted a "soft Hindu" approach. As already discussed, it allowed the gate of the Babri masjid, which had been locked following a court order ever since 1949 when the Ram idols had been installed there, to be unlocked during the period when Rajiv Gandhi was the Prime Minister. Further, he allowed the Sangh *parivar* to carry out the *shilanyas* (laying of the foundation stone) of the temple on a disputed site adjacent to the shrine. And, he began his re-election bid in 1989 from Ayodhya-Faizabad with a speech in which he invoked "Ram *rajya*" in a deliberately ambiguous manner.

The response of other avowedly secular parties to the competitive communalism of the Sangh *parivar* on the one side and the Congress on the other was politically inadequate. They were accused of conniving with and even deriving electoral advantage from the "appeasement" of Muslims and were projected as opportunistic "pseudo-secularists". In any event, their political reach was limited and their control over state power was uneven over time and space.

The net results of this political imbroglio were the following: (1) a BJP government took office in Uttar Pradesh in 1991; (2) the post-Rajiv Gandhi minority Congress government at the Centre became even more ambivalent regarding secularism and more inclined towards pursuing the politics of "soft Hinduism"; (3) the sadhus (mendicants, Hindu holy men) and other random political forces became far more important than earlier; (4) the directions of the Supreme Court, the National Integration Council and other paramount institutions of the State became ineffectual; (5) social polarisation on religious basis was intensified;   (6) communal passions and insecurities became more acute; and (7) on 6 December 1992, the Babri masjid was destroyed by a frenzied mob while the State remained a silent spectator; the idols of Ram were quickly installed in a makeshift temple where worship was speedily allowed and, in the shambles of constitutional order in India, communal conflagrations broke out as a prelude to the appearance of deadly high-tech terrorism.

Many questions about the actual destruction of the Babri masjid and its immediate aftermath still remain unanswered and the government's White Paper on these has concealed more than it has revealed. In any event, the citizens of India are justified in asking if the Gordian knot be tied again after being cut? Can the Rubicon be double-crossed? Can one walk back on the bridge that has been burnt after crossing a turbulent stream? Only the future will show if truth is real or merely metaphorical and it will become clear if the anti-communal fight, apparently intensified by the Ayodhya outrage, is substantial and not merely symbolic.

For the present, it appears that the "business as usual" situation has returned. Rioting has stopped; curfew has been lifted; life has become normal for those who survived; even the Rashtriya *sansad* (Parliament) is in working order and the *dharma sansad* (of sadhus) has been adjourned. If there is a difference, it is only in the skyline at Ayodhya where a historical edifice — older than the very histories of most nations of the world — no longer exists.

Even the judiciary is back at work and the political ball is once again in court. The Supreme Court itself is seized of at least three extremely significant matters which have been placed before it. It has to pronounce on whether there is evidence of complicity beyond the RSS-VHP-Bajrang Dal in destruction of the Babri masjid; whether action can be taken against officials for following orders of the government of the day and whether the dismissal of BJP governments is constitutionally valid. However, while the Court deliberates on these matters, the dust from the demolished Babri masjid has not settled either politically or administratively. There are various aspects which are still under a cloud.

First, the government has by no means made it clear as to how it proposes to implement the assurance the Prime Minister gave to the nation that the Babri masjid would be rebuilt. Quite obviously, it is a tricky situation and the over-blown religious susceptibilities of either one group or the other are bound to be hurt.

Second, there are large loopholes even in the administrative response to the post-Babri masjid scenario. The very charges against the arrested voodoo politicians and the banned communal organisations betray lack of seriousness about enforcing the secular will.

Third, the fire and brimstone rained through speeches in Parliament, the allegations and counter-allegations, the reference to secret information and surreptitious videos, the appeals for peace and harmony, the rhetoric and demagoguery have not succeeded in creating the impression that all these are something other than sheer dramatics indulged in by two-dimensional cardboard figures with little depth and less conviction.

Fourth, despite assertions within the Congress of rallying behind the leader and it being time for all good men to come to the aid of the party, it is by no means clear that hatchets have been buried and that, in actual fact, knives are not being sharpened for internecine conflicts.

Fifth, the course of action of the political Left and other secular elements is also open to doubt. While they make appropriate anti-communal noises, their determination to fight the forces of communalism on the ground level either electorally or otherwise is still to be demonstrated.

Sixth, there is a strange reluctance among the guardians of the Republic in facing the ultimate test of republicanism viz. elections. The spectre of electoral democracy looms large over the elected representatives of the people and all the powers of the old order appear to unite to exorcise that spectre.

Seventh, there is much calculation of the electoral impact of the vandalism at Ayodhya and, paradoxically, much of it is premised on judging the "hurt to the psyche of the majority community" as if it is that which has suffered religious trauma. This takes the community to be homogenous and monolithic and a discount is put on its own inherent contradictions. The whole argument is premised on a conundrum that Hindus cannot be secular when there is no evidence to support such a view.

Eighth, while there are some whispered references to the possibility of the exacerbation of extremisism among both major religious groups in India, there does not appear to be any serious concern about handling such an eventuality through pre-emptive political action. Instead, politics once again appears to be being subordinated to politicking. Even the series of bomb explosions in Bombay and the discovery of vast arsenals of terrorism have not galvanised serious political responses. Attention is instead focused on the links between the underworld and terrorists and the shadowy spectre of trans-national "Islamic extremism" lurks in the background as political leaders appear to be merely following a western geo-strategic approach rather than addressing concrete domestic realities.

Ninth, neither the philosophical basis of religious extremism nor its political-economic dimensions are being exposed in a consistent manner. Indeed, the discourse of a secular, constitutional republicanism tends to get trapped on the terrain of either a pseudo-religious discourse or the ground of cynical realpolitik.

Tenth, and most simplistically, even the apparent political logic is obscured by wishful thinking. If indeed the vandalism at Ayodhya and rampant communalism elsewhere have struck a grievous blow at the constitutional order, if the supreme institutions of the State — Parliament, Courts and the executive — have indeed been betrayed, if the very ethos of pluralist India has actually been wounded, then there is no going back on political and administrative democratic action against the perpetrators of the outrage. The logical consequence of this is a new political order, political restructuring, as it were.

If there is reluctance to acknowledge this, it only means a vindication of the logic of fait accompli: the government has been fooled, the courts have been betrayed, the National Integration Council has been ignored and, in the end, today there is no Babri masjid and government functionaries make arrangements for Hindu worship at the site. However, if fait accompli is not to become the supreme law, then the clock of history cannot be stopped at a particular time on the afternoon of 6 December 1992.

Eleventh, and finally, as was said in another context, analysts will analyse the situation in many ways, the point is to change it.

CHAPTER 5

'HARIJANS' INTO 'DALITS':
FROM CASTE TO CLASS

No discussion of class formation in India would be anywhere near satisfactory without considering the situation of what are variously called untouchables, scheduled castes, Harijans, but who are increasingly calling themselves *dalits* (oppressed), and who constitute a very large segment of the exploited and poor people in India which is set apart from the rest merely because they happened to be born in certain families. Notwithstanding the fact that the articulation of their being and becoming, like that of the tribals, is increasingly in secular terms, scholars and politicians tend to ignore the process of class formation in their case and prefer to regard them, on sociological considerations alone, as communities determined by ritual and religion, distinct from others and largely discriminated against on the grounds of accident of birth and non-secular notions of stations in social living.

Ironically, the caste system itself seems to have been brought about by secular factors (Klass 1980) although a great deal of religious and racist myth still obscures knowledge about its origin. The most predominant and widely popular theory traces it, as in the racist version of the history of the tribals, to the supposed Aryan 'racial' invasion of India and links it to the process by which the invaders could subordinate indigenous inhabitants who (unlike the food-gathering tribals pushed back into primitive isolated jungle existence) could be integrated as peasants and slaves within a stratified society. Thus it is widely believed that the "twice-born" *varnas* (caste conglomerates; literally colours), i.e. Brahmans, Kshatriyas and Vaisyas, progenitors of the multitude which constitutes today's upper or 'forward' castes, are descended primarily from the original Aryans or later invaders from outside, while the masses of Sudras and Atisudras (and of course, the tribal peoples), are descended primarily from the vanquished non-Aryan natives. In today's India, there are few castes recognised as "twice born" and even aristocratic landlords are often classified as Sudras, and the majority of the population is thought to be non-Aryans, Dravidians or even Adi-Dravid ('Original' Dravidians).

This "popular" theory was originated largely by racist European scholars and encouraged by colonial administrators (Inden 1990). Such scholars and bureaucrats argued that there were basic racial and physical differences among the various castes. The racist theory was quickly taken over by Indians, at first by Brahman intellectuals who sought to use it to prove their own superiority over the low castes and their racial affinity to the ruling "white men", but later it was adopted even by cultural radicals such as Jyotiba Phule and E.V.Ramaswamy Naicker and other leaders of the non-Brahman movement in Maharashtra, Tamil Nadu and elsewhere to stress moral superiority, by virtue of ancestral antiquity, of the original non-Aryans or Dravidians (Omvedt 1976). In fact, of all non-Brahman leaders and intellectuals, only B.R.Ambedkar, pre-eminent leader of the 'untouchables', really rejected the racial theory (Ambedkar 1946,1979).

This hocus-pocus theory indeed has been sought to be given all kinds of scientistic validity by elaborate anthropometric exercises and intricate sociological constructs. The latter are posited on definition of the caste system as constituted by rules of "purity and pollution" or systems of belief about "code and substance" and these beliefs are in turn identified with orthodox Hindu conceptions having their roots in Sanskritic Vedic literature and thus in the period of the assumed Indo-Aryan conquest and the society arising out of it (Dumont 1970;Marriot 1974,1977; etc.).

But the falsity of the "Aryan theory" is evident on many grounds. In the first place, there is no conclusive evidence of any massive invasion by racially distinct groups in the 2000 – 1000 B.C. period. Secondly, there is reasonable evidence that many of the Brahmans, the highest of the supposed Aryans, were in fact not Aryans (in the racial or any other sense) at all (Kosambi 1950,1975:85-101). Thirdly, even if the invasion did take place, the theory neither explains why the Indo-European Aryan invaders should have given rise to caste only in India and not elsewhere nor throws light on the strength of the caste system in the areas least affected by such invasions, i.e. South India (Omvedt 1982). Fourthly, a peculiarity of the caste system is that not only is it uniquely Indian but it cuts across religious communities with even Indian Muslims, Christians, etc. adopting the system to various extents (see, for example, Ahmed 1973); and that surely has nothing to do with Aryan Hindu invasions. Finally, there is growing historical evidence that elements of traits connected with caste existed in India even in the pre-Aryan Indus Valley civilisation (Kosambi 1975).

Indeed, the secular explanation for the origin of the caste system is that when first economic surplus arose in India, caste was the means by which the till-then egalitarian clans adjusted to the inequality generated by the surplus (Klass 1980). This would place the origin of caste at the very beginning of Indian class society, with the first development of settled rice and wheat agriculture leading to the rise of the Indus Valley cities. Undoubtedly, the system was modified and adjusted to subsequent social formations and became more and more complex with the passage of time. The phenomenon of caste has existed in several different modes of production and, though it has taken new forms, it is clearly far from vanishing (Omvedt 1982).

All in all, through its long and involved evolutionary process, caste has been and is a system in which a person's membership of society is mediated through the accident of birth in a particular group which is assigned a specific status within a broad social hierarchy of such groups; this group is supposed to have a particular accepted occupation or range of occupations and only within it can a person marry and carry on close social relations such as inter-dining. This social formation is a corporate group that has certain defined rules of behaviour for its members and exercises some degrees of authority over them. A person is born into such a group, is a lifelong member (unless expelled by the group) and is not able to legitimately join any other group.

As noted earlier, during its evolution, the caste system has acquired immense complexities with the development of strata and sub-strata and sub-sub-strata, etc. in the social hierarchy. In more simple social and production situations, castes had a concrete social existence as the basic unit of the social division of labour (so that *jati* or sub-caste) names were most commonly "occupational" names like barber, potter and blacksmith, but as several types of production systems existing simultaneously added dimensions of complexity to the social scene, *jatis* started getting grouped and today what exist are clusters of sub-castes passing off as *jatis* (Das 1984; Sengupta 1979). In turn these *jatis* claimed and still claim a certain broader status as Brahmans, Kshatriyas, Vaisyas or Sudras within the all-India hierarchical *varna* system. As *jati* was for a long time the basic unit of the social division of labour and even today caste generally continues to have definite economic connotations, only in a very formalistic sense can "caste" be distinguished from "class" by saying that the former is mainly a "social" and the latter is mainly an "economic" concept (Das 1984).

Particularly during the feudal period, caste and class were in fact interwoven, with both corresponding to the social division of labour. With the coming of capitalism, however, the situation changed because not only were new classes like the bourgeoisie and workers created but capitalism under colonial rule also began a process of separating out a caste system from the class structure. This meant redefining both caste and class in the Indian context and creation of a complex social existence and consciousness based on a mixed class-caste syndrome which was historically inherited and carefully nurtured.

The nurturing of the caste system within the context of class-based economic exploitation meant that the lower orders of the hierarchy started losing such mitigating aspects of feudal patronage-clientilism relations as existed, without gaining optimally from the democratic ideals of liberty, equality and fraternity. Caste became a more and more vicious instrument of both social oppression and economic exploitation. At the same time, it also became the mode of articulation of solidarity.

Two important aspects of Indian social existence are relevant in this regard. First, as many scholars have pointed out, along with the thousands of castes, there exist in different parts of India indigenous "class type" categories that divide the population, in particular the rural peoples into main socio- economic groups according to their position in the system of production. For instance, in Bengal there are zamindars (landlords), *jotedars* (most often big tenants during the period of the Permanent Settlement), *bargadars* or *bhagchashis* (sharecroppers) and *khetmajoors* (agricultural labourers), along with, of course, merchants and artisans (Beteille 1974:126). In Tamil Nadu, there are *mirasdars* or *kaniyachikarar* (landlords), *paykaria* (tenants), village functionaries and artisans, and *adimais* and *padiyals* who are bonded and field slaves (Sivakumar 1978; Gough 1977; Mencher 1978). In Bihar, *ashrafs* (landlords), *bakkal* (traders and shopkeepers), *pawania* (artisans) and *jotiyas* (direct cultivators, further divided into *khetihar grihasthas*— landed householders— and *bataidars* or sharecroppers) and "a class of low caste landless labourers usually known by the name of the most numerous labourer caste at the local level constitute the major element of the rural stratification" (Harcourt 1977: 243-45). The basic north Indian division is between *malik* (landlord), *kisan* (peasant) and *mazdoor* (labourers) as well as artisans and merchants (Thorner 1976). There are similar divisions in other regions also (Omvedt 1982:15-16).

The second aspect of Indian society relevant to understanding of caste, pointed out by many scholars (e.g. Neale 1975; Klass 1980, etc.) is that owing to the prevalence of the caste system, access to produce within the village was almost never on the basis of market exchange. Rather, free market exchange was vitiated by caste, a scale of the services supposed to be performed by different *jatis* determining the right to a share of the produce. Of course, this system did not work "automatically". In fact the allotment of shares of produce (as well as the means of production) was under control of the dominant sub-caste at the village level. These were the rulers and the others were ruled by them differentially.

As is evident from the above, in agrarian society, the three basic divisions were between generally non-cultivating landlords, cultivating tenants and agricultural workers. And, in most areas, these divisions broadly (the emphasis is deliberate) corresponded to the three major caste conglomerations: the upper castes i.e. the "twice-born" Brahmans, Kshatriyas and some Vaishyas; the intermediate middle castes now generally grouped together under the label of 'Other Bachward Castes' and the lowest, untouchable castes which are given the statutory appellation of 'Scheduled Castes' and are otherwise variously known either by given names like Harijans (children of God) or terms like *dalits* (oppressed) corresponding to their self-perception, or most commonly referred to as a body by the caste names of the locally most numerous of their groups like *Mang-Mahar* (in Maharashtra), *Chura-Chamar* (in north India) and Paryas (*Pariahs*, in Kerala).

It is with this last group that we shall concern ourselves here because in the caste hierarchy as well as in the socio- economic and political system they are at the very bottom and as such are parts of the labouring poor who are together constituting the working class. There have been different interpretations regarding them, varying from seeing them as integral parts of Hindu society to a separate 'ethnic' group altogether. Physically many of them were made to live at the fringes of Hindu settlements and were of course subjected to all kinds of exploitation, discrimination and oppression.

A view has been advanced that one reason why there was only weak resistance to Muslim invaders was that the invaders when attacking towns and villages first came into contact with these 'outcastes' and untouchables who were not particularly interested in laying down their lives in defence of orthodox Hinduism. That many of those who converted to Islam were among the people at the lowest strata of Hindu society is therefore not a surprising fact. Nor is it surprising that the various religious reform movements which took place during the twelfth to sixteenth centuries addressed themselves to the inequities of caste Hinduism and racist aspects of the Muslim aristocracy and found adherents among the poorest untouchables who were most oppressed under any religious rule. In spite of such sporadic attempts at reform however, the basic structure of caste-based social formation (corresponding, as pointed out above, to basic economic divisions) persisted and even influenced Muslims in India who, notwithstanding the relative egalitarian premises of Islam, adopted their own caste hierarchy.

In short, up to the twentieth century, the untouchables re-mained, by and large, in their given low position, inhumanly treated and brutally oppressed. Even the social reformers of the nineteenth century, who addressed themselves to various 'abuses' in Hindu and Muslim society and tried to 'modernise' their respective communi-ties, paid little or no attention to the issue of the untouchables. It was only with the intensification of the anti-colonial national movement that the relative non-participation in it of the untouchables on the one side and the emergence of serious anti-Brahman (Omvedt 1976;Ram 1979) and untouchables movement (Patankar and Omvedt 1979) in various parts of the country on the other attracted the attention of some national leaders towards this issue.

The pre-eminent leader of the untouchables was Dr. B.R.Ambedkar, who, in trying to get for them legal and constitutional safeguards, demanded the setting up of separate electorates for them. Against this position, Mahatma Mohandas Karamchand Gandhi, the supreme leader of the Congress-led national movement, voiced strong objection. He asserted that the untouchables were very much part of Hindu society, and in protest against the demand for separate electorates, went on a long fast. He also simultaneously started a campaign against untouchability and asked Hindus to allow the untouchables entry into temples and consider them as *Harijan*, children of God, a name which stuck to untouchables as whole. After negotiations with Gandhi, Ambedkar gave up his demand for separate electorates but went on carrying out relentless campaigns for the betterment of the condition of the untouchables (Keer 1974).

On the eve of Independence and immediately after it, when the Constitution of India was being prepared, Ambedkar, who drafted the Constitution, strongly pleaded for special provisions for the untouchables. Even earlier, in the Government of India Act of 1935, lists of untouchable castes were included for taking special measures for amelioration of their conditions. This process of listing such communities separately was carried on in the Constitution of India which legally abolished untouchability and included measures of positive discrimination for groups who were listed under special schedules of castes. As in the case of the tribals, these legislative and constitutional processes resulted in conglomeration of people being 'scheduled'. Scheduled castes is the label for people whose untouchability has been abolished (indeed, the caste system itself has been legally abolished through an exercise of Canutian legislation—Kosambi 1975) but who continue to remain at the bottom of the social and economic hierarchies.

The debate about whether they constitute a minority community in the religious sense was never satisfactorily resolved. Dr.

Ambedkar categorically stated, "The Scheduled Castes are really a religious minority. The Hindu religion by its dogma of untouchability has separated the Scheduled Castes from the main body of the Hindus in a manner which makes the separation far more real and far wider than the separation which exists either between Hindus and Muslims, or Hindus and Sikhs, or Hindus and Christians" (Ambedkar 1946:334). In fact, he led a large number of people from the Scheduled Castes in getting themselves converted to Buddhism to distinguish themselves from Hindus. However, Hindu society, while continuing to oppress and exploit the children of God, the Harijans, was not prepared to let them go and like Gandhi, many Hindu leaders like K.M. Munshi and Seth Govind Das who were members of the Constituent Assembly, asserted that the "Harijans, generally known as the Scheduled Castes, are neither a racial minority, nor a linguistic minority, nor certainly a religious minority... the Harijans are part and parcel of Hindu community" (cited in Wadhwa 1975:19). Others had different views. S. Nagappa, for instance, stated, "I do not claim that we (Scheduled Castes) are a religious minority or a racial minority. I claim that we are a political minority" (ibid.). In any event, in all this discussion, the Scheduled Castes were treated as a distinct and discrete entity and their role in class formation was, by and large, ignored.

Not that the Scheduled Castes are homogenous. There are regional, linguistic, religious and even economic differences among them. What is common in most parts of India among Scheduled Castes is that they are poor; they are at the bottom of the social scale; many of them are bonded or casual agricultural workers; most are landless; many of them perform functions which are considered "polluting"; and the overwhelming majority among them is exploited and oppressed. It is this aspect whose realisation has been slowly growing among the Scheduled Castes in various parts of the country and, from the 1970s particularly, a movement has started among some of them to get organised and to struggle for the rights which are due to them as human beings, many of which have been given to them by law but which are denied to them in reality. In this process, they have renounced patronising appellations for them like *Harijan* and have started perceiving themselves and referring to themselves as *dalits* (oppressed) (Omvedt 1982).

In the meanwhile, oppression of the *dalits* has started taking new forms. Provisions made for positive discrimination for Scheduled Castes (and Tribes) in terms of reservations in government jobs and educational facilities, etc. have only benefited a fringe of their population (Dushkin 1979) and, in Maharashtra, Gujarat and Madhya Pradesh in particular, even this has unleashed an upper caste Hindu backlash.

As earlier stated, most of the *dalits* remain poor agricultural labourers and it is the dynamic of agrarian society which has resulted in the particularly vicious forms of exploitation and oppression which have emerged in recent times. Even in the anti-feudal movements during colonial rule when large, powerful and radical peasant organisations emerged in various parts of India, their memberships and beneficiaries were restricted to landed small and medium tenants. The *dalits*, being overwhelmingly landless, were excluded and the few isolated attempts, as through the formation of the Bihar Khet Mazdoor Sabha by the Harijan leader Jagjiwan Ram in 1937, that were made to raise issues of agricultural labourers and to organise them were unsuccessful (Das 1983). The fruits of the anti-zamindari and other such measures brought about by peasant organisations through pressurising the government were at best reaped by the tenants belonging to the upper and intermediate castes who, in due course, aided and abetted by the various productivity-increasing steps of the State known as the Green Revolution package, have become the emergent capitalist peasantry whose major antagonism is with labourers. Thus the *dalits* who have been oppressed by the upper caste landlords for centuries are now being intensively exploited also by the middle caste kulaks.

The State has desultorily enacted a few measures providing minimum wages, homestead lands, etc. to benefit the agricultural labourers but the implementation of these measures could only be described as farcical if the conditions of the *dalits* (and other rural landless workers) were not so tragic. In very few cases have the agricultural workers, most of whom are *dalits*, started getting organised but wherever such attempts have been made they have been brutally repressed to the extent of being burnt alive as in many instances in Tamil Nadu, Bihar, Uttar Pradesh, etc. in recent years (Alexander 1976; Bhushan 1977; Ghosh 1979; Rao 1978; Narayan

1978; Sinha 1978,1978a; Srivastava 1978, 1980,1980a; etc.). Aptly have such incidents been described as not atrocities on Harijans but as class war (Sinha 1982). The class war is going on and wherever the *dalits* have managed to get some kind of organisation by themselves (Barnett 1970) or with others in similar positions, they have either won significant gains as agricultural labourers (as in Kerala—Jose 1977; Krishnaji 1979; etc.) or are struggling to better their social and economic position. Through this process of struggle, the Harijans are changing their self perception to *dalits* and as such, are participants in the secular process of class formation and class action.

CHAPTER 6

THE TOWER OF BABEL: MISUNDERSTANDINGS IN MANY LANGUAGES

India has not one language problem but a complex of language problems. According to the linguistic survey of India, there are 179 languages and 544 dialects, and philologists classify them into four distinct family groups —Indo-Aryan, Dravidian, Austro-Asiatic and Tibeto-Chinese. Mercifully, although the number of languages and dialects enlisted for census purposes runs into several hundreds, the principal languages to be reckoned with in the context of linguistic politics are only about a dozen, known as regional languages prevalent in fairly large areas of the country. However, the linguistic scene is complicated because a language group does not generally correspond to an identifiable and distinct religious community. For example, Bengali is the language of the Hindus, Muslims and Christians alike in Bengal. Generally, it has been said, these groups have identical linguistic interests in definite areas despite their religious differences (Wadhwa 1975: 10). That this is not universally true is brought out dramatically by the example of Punjabi which is increasingly identified with Sikhs and Punjabi Hindus are going to the extent of renouncing the language they have spoken for centuries. Similarly, Urdu is identified with Muslims and large numbers of Hindus who were using it earlier, and still speak a language which is difficult to distinguish from Urdu, claim to be Hindi-speaking people. Various local and regional political considerations and historical experiences also condition peoples' responses to the language issue and a great deal of bitterness exists, as for instance in Assam on the question of Bengali and in Belgaum in Karnataka on the use of Marathi.

The Constitution of India recognises 'fifteen' official regional languages and Hindi as the 'national official' language. In addition, English is used as a 'link' language for communication between Hindi and non-Hindi states. An aspect of the language problem in India is that no language is spoken by an absolute majority of the people and even Hindi, the most widely-spoken language—even if one disregards its various dialects—is used by only about 42% of the total population of India. Thus, at the national level, there is no linguistic majority or minority in the arithmetical sense. However, the picture is different in the various states. In almost each state, there are several islands of linguistic minorities, the political permutations and combinations emerging from which are immense.

Thus, to explain the term 'linguistic minorities', the Commissioner for Linguistic Minorities says, "Linguistic minorities are minorities residing in the territory of India, or any part thereof, having a distinct language or script of their own. The languages of the minority group need not be one of the (15 'official') languages... In other words, a 'linguistic minority' at the state level means any group of people whose mother-tongue is different from the principal language of the state, and at the district and taluka levels, different from the principal language of the district or the taluka" (cited in Wadhwa 1975: 10). That the problem is wide and complex is of course evident from this definitional officialese, but the actual degree of complexity is almost unimaginable.

The problem was sought to be simplified to an extent through the creation of linguistic states (administrative divisions which were supposed to constitute the federal structure of the polity of the Indian Union). The sub-divisions of British India had no rational cultural or linguistic basis but had been carved out by the military, political or administrative exigencies or conveniences of the moment. Thus, at the time of framing of the Constitution, practically every province was multilingual and an attempt was made to reorganise them in such a manner as to bring about a degree of linguistic and cultural homogeneity of the people in an area. This task was entrusted to the States Reorganisation Commission which was appointed in 1953 and which submitted its report in 1955. On the basis of its report, many boundaries were redrawn on linguistic basis and a number of unilingual states were carved out.

However, this operation could not solve the acuteness of the linguistic problem. It left practically the whole of north-eastern India untouched and it required bloody agitations and sometimes even warlike situations for the composite Assam to be divided up into no less than seven states and union territories. Even then, the fact that the Bengali-majority district of Cachar, still forms a part of Assam keeps the problem alive. Further, the problem was aggravated by the influx of large numbers of non-Assamese, particularly Bengali-speaking people into Assam from Bangladesh (formerly East Pakistan and before that East Bengal) and West Bengal. In the long-drawn out agitation in Assam, the term 'foreigner' (ostensibly referring to illegal immigrants from Bangladesh) is actually an euphemism for Bengalis in general. The failure of the States Reorganisation Commission to satisfactorily solve the Punjabi Suba issue, because of the complication created by the intermingling in Punjab of linguistic and religious/communal passions, has already been discussed. In the case of the undivided Bombay province, although the issues were much simpler, again an agitation had to be carried out to achieve the division of the province into Gujarat and Maharashtra on linguistic basis. Even there, the problem of a Marathi-speaking area, Belgaum, being left in Karnataka rather than being merged into Maharashtra still rankles. And in other parts of the country too, in spite of the efforts of the States Reorganisation Commission, there are still 'boundary' disputes and other problems relating to linguistic issues. Even the Commission acknowledged, "The scheme of redistribution of state territories which we have recommended will result in many cases in bringing together people speaking a common language. To that extent, it will reduce the number of linguistic minorities. It is, however, quite evident that even if the linguistic principle were applied very rigidly, the problem of linguistic minorities will, by no means, be solved" (India 1955: 205).

A major confrontation on the language issue, however, did not concern linguistic minorities within different states but the issue of the declaration of Hindi as the 'National'/'Official' language. This aroused emotion in various regions and particularly in Tamil Nadu and West Bengal, there were language agitations. In Madras, there was even violence till the assurance was given that Hindi would not be imposed on the state and that English would continue to be used as a 'link' language for an unspecified time in the future. An aspect of this anti-Hindi agitation in Tamil Nadu was that it was led by parties which claimed to represent the linguistically, culturally and ethnically distinct 'Dravidian' people and whatever be the scientific validity of their claims and premises, they gained such popularity that since 1967, one or the other of the Dravid Munnetra Kazghams (Dravidian People's Party) has continuously been voted to power in the state. In Bengal and other non-Hindi states, the anti-Hindi agitation was not as vehement as in Tamil Nadu but even there the perceived attempts to impose Hindi is strongly resented. The problem has not been solved as, in spite of the report of Official Language Commission (India 1956), the issue has been kept in abeyance and English rather than Hindi continues to be used for interstate official communication among non-Hindi states, between Hindi and non-Hindi states and between the union government and the states. Otherwise, particularly in what is known as the Hindi heartland, the use of Hindi for official work is being actively promoted.

However, the very question of what is Hindi has itself posed a problem and linguists and philologists have debated amongst themselves for long years. It is a tricky question and with it is tied the issue of another linguistic minority, the Urdu-users. Even if various dialects (some of which claim to be full-fledged languages) are not taken into consideration, the language which is mainly spoken in urban north India is descended from both Sanskrit and Arabic/Persian. Depending on the weightage placed on words from either source and depending on whether it is written in the Devnagri or Arabic script, the language becomes either Hindi or Urdu. Within Hindi itself there is a tendency to deliberately Sanskritise it, even to the extent of its losing its common, popular 'Hindustani' character and convert it into an exact, scientifically constructed artificial Bharati.

While this problem is still being debated by philologists and it seems that its only solution will be in the peoples' continuing usage of the more colloquial and simpler version, the issue of Hindi versus Urdu evokes passions. This is especially complicated by the factor that Urdu is identified with Muslims though, during the British rule,

it was official language for both communities and a large number of
Hindus continue to use it even now in daily unofficial communication. Indeed, in the early stages of the Constituent Assembly, the
sub-committee on Fundamental Rights, following Gandhiji's lead,
adapted the following formula: "Hindustani, written *either* in the
Devnagri or the Persian (Arabic) script at the option of the citizen,
shall, as the national language, be the first official language of the
Union. English shall be the second official language for such period
as the Union may by law determine. All official records of the Union
shall be kept in Hindustani in both the scripts and also in English
until the Union by law otherwise provided" (K.M. Munshi's papers
cited in Wadhwa 1975: 189). However, the Partition of the country
in 1947 on communal lines and the death of Mahatma Gandhi in
1948 influenced the members of the Constituent Assembly to
reverse this decision and the communal response to this question
was to adopt Hindi in the Devnagri script as the official language.
Since then the Muslims have had a grievance on this account as Urdu
ceased to have the status of the official language.

The present conflict on this issue is over the place to be accorded
to Urdu among the 15 regional languages. The constitutional position entitles Urdu to the same rights and privileges at the hands of
the government which all other recognised regional languages
receive but the actual position is different. Although Urdu is the
declared mother tongue of a very large number of people and is
widely used, it is not the majority language in any state or union
territory. It is, however, recognised as the state language in Jammu
and Kashmir. Recently, after much agitation on the issue and in
order to mollify the Muslim electorate, Urdu has been accorded the
status of secondary official language in Bihar and Uttar Pradesh. It
is recognised as a regional language in Andhra Pradesh also. In spite
of all this, it continues to be a minority language: "The Urdu
speaking Indian is in a minority everywhere. Even in Kashmir with
its Muslim majority, the dominant language is not Urdu but Kashmiri"
(Smith 1967: 430). There are two major problems which Urdu
continues to face: one is the fact that considerable numbers of Urdu
speakers are scattered over India and the other that it has got
identified with Muslims and Islam even though in Bengal, Tamil
Nadu and Kerala, the local Muslims have little to do with Urdu and

the language of Islamic texts is Arabic and not Urdu.

The linguistic problem is in essence the problem of 'minority languages', i.e., of languages fairly widely spoken in states where the majority of the population, however, speaks some other language. The very reorganisation of states on a linguistic basis, which was expected to solve the linguistic issue, aggravated this problem to an extent because as a result of states being identified with the language of the majority of their populations, the propagation of the language of the majority became aggressive. The whole issue became emotive and passions were let loose. In order to bring about some order in the resultant linguistic chaos, a 'three-language formula' was introduced. It envisaged the teaching of three languages at the secondary level in schools and it was particularly recommended that schools in northern India should take up the teaching of a modern South Indian language. It was of course presumed that Hindi would be one of the three languages taught in non-Hindi states.

However, even the introduction of the 'three language formula' has not brought about the desired linguistic integration. For one, in most Hindi-speaking states, the whole scheme has been subverted by teaching Sanskrit and, in some places, even Urdu instead of the recommended modern South Indian languages. Further, the third language is most often taught in an extremely desultory fashion. And finally, in some states the selection of the third language is often an exercise geared to settling political or communal scores. Thus, for instance, in Haryana, instead of Punjabi which is the language of the neighbouring and parent state and which should be the commonsense choice for the third language, a political point is sought to be made in the cultural and linguistic context by adopting Tamil or Telugu for formal teaching in rural schools. Tamil Nadu has adopted a two language formula (to try to keep Hindi out) and Punjab insists that it is a unilingual state.

Thus, the safeguard for linguistic minorities enshrined in the Constitution or other agreed principles have not been fully accepted by all the states. The use of minority languages for official purposes, another important demand of linguistic minorities, meets generally the same fate as the three-language formula in the educational field, significant exceptions notwithstanding. And, while this is the situation of the 15 recognised languages, the position of small minorities using the many other languages and dialects is even worse in regard to this linguistic aspect of cultural preservation. Official assistance is generally lacking though, in recent times, some popular attempts are being made to vitalise some languages, particularly those of the tribals 'from below'. And this alone might work.

For, language is primarily the business of the people and linguistic integration has to be achieved at the popular rather than official level. Indeed this is one of the significant findings of the monumental 'Peoples of India' study carried out by the Anthropological Survey of India. The study of nearly 4,000 'communities' that constitute India has found that, traditionally as well as now, a very large number of them is bilingual, using one language for internal communication and the other for interacting with neighbouring 'communities'. In fact, this could have been the only way of survival in the multi-ethnic plurality of India. And, as in the case of religious communities, it is only the modernity of enumeration that disrupted the back-to-back existence of communities by creating distinctions on the one side and homogenising specific linguistic groups on the other. The case of the growth of Hindi as a created Leviathan in the colonial and post-colonial era illustrates this proposition. The formalisation of cultural processes through the intervention by the State adds to this phenomenon.

However, in the linguistic context, as in the religious and overall cultural contexts, there is a dialectic between the organic and the institutional which conditions both. While the issues of 'official language' and 'minority/majority languages' are obviously determined by processes of the State, it is also necessary to note the evolution of languages themselves as parts of societal change. And, it is as important to see languages as modes of communication as to note that they are also systems of misunderstanding. Thus, the linguistic problem has to be addressed at various levels: intra-group, inter-group; as elements of discourse and as barriers in social-cultural interaction.

Abram de Swaan (1990) has made some significant observations in this regard. He begins by identifying languages as those primarily serving statal functions (e.g. English) and those with strong popular-level intermediary functions (e.g. Hindi). For both types of such languages, he says, "(They) came in the wake of soldiers, merchants and priests. And the dozen or so languages (in the world) that are spoken by more than a hundred million speakers are no exception. The spread of mandarin Chinese, Hindi, Arabic, Portuguese, Spanish, English, Russian or French went at a par with the expansion of the respective empires and the concomitant commercial and religious penetration. Only the... Chinese state still controls all of its imperial territory. Most often, once the conquerors were driven out again, their language disappeared with the last of the colonizers, as is borne out by the fate of Dutch, which after three centuries disappeared from Asia in the 1950s, or Japanese which in this century spread and contracted with the victory and defeat of the imperial armies. But sometimes languages remain, long after the conquerors have been ousted, and often in connection with a religion : Latin and Arabic are examples. (Sanskrit may be said to play a similar role in India). But a language need not fulfil religious functions in order to continue being spoken in the newly liberated territories. Its permanence depends very much on the total configuration of languages in the area. The spread and continuation of languages are not entirely determined by conquest, commerce and conversion; it exhibits a dynamics of its own. The language system is relatively autonomous. It is this intrinsic dynamism of language configurations that is of special interest here.

"Two concepts are pivotal in this context : mutual intelligibility and proficiency. Clearly, the significant difference between one form of speech and another is one that inhibits mutual understanding. And, equally clearly, once such a difference between forms of speech exists, the significant proficiency is the one that allows to overcome this unintelligibility between the two languages. Attempts to devise a measure for mutual (un)intelligibility, which would allow therefore to identify distinct languages, have failed consistently. The measurement of proficiency has also turned out to be much more difficult than initially expected. Not only does fluency vary with the domains in which the language is used, respondents are also notoriously unreliable in reporting their skills, since they may have an interest in minimizing their knowledge and usage of languages held in low regard or exaggerating their competence when it is considered desirable as in the case of Punjabi or Urdu discussed above. Ideology continually interferes in the discussion, since States and language groups have an interest in emphasizing some differences and glossing over others.

"The problem may well be unsolvable, as long as intelligibility is conceived of as an objective characteristic of a pair of languages and proficiency as a quality of an individual speaker. Obviously, the problem is one of interaction, of people trying to make themselves understood to one another; it is thus a problem of context, intention and dialogue. In some episodes, buying and selling in markets, for example, the situation may structure the interaction to such a degree that both parties understand without much recourse to language in the strict sense of the word, and both parties may well be strongly motivated to understand one another. Pointing, gesturing and finger counting may be all that is needed to complete the transaction, since the episode is understood without so many words by both parties from prior contextual knowledge, their interpretations corresponding almost completely. Other situations, political or legal negotiations for example, may be so opaque, so dependent on shared verbal definitions, and the motivations to reach understanding may be so complex and ambivalent, that even minor differences in language may keep quite proficient speakers apart."

It is interesting to note examples of both these types of languages, the common and the arcane, in India. It is also significant that the two types become similar in certain contexts through the introduction of evolved or invented symbolisms. For instance, the mode of commercial intercourse, a bazaar language which is characterised by its simplicity, accessibility and intelligibility becomes quite mysterious when practised in the context of the stock market where elaborate signs and gestures are understood only by the initiated. On the other side, within the grammar of the same language different levels of expression of the same concept can also exist. An example of this is the absolutely abstract 'OM' invocation in Sanskrit for God at one level, the 'Vishnusahasra-naam' (thousand names of God) at another and the extremely accessible, almost vernacular, Sanskrit of the 'Sri Ramchandra kripalu bhaju man' of Goswami Tulsidas.

In other words, languages may be ordered in a matrix from high mutual intelligibility to high unintelligibility, and a rough ordering of speakers as to their proficiency is also feasible. But the smaller the differences, the more contested the ordering and the more mutual understanding becomes a function of the interaction, determined by context, and by the intentions and the interplay of the parties involved.

Abram de Swaan (1990) constructs a 'floral figuration' to understand the relationships between different languages and different levels of languages in the context of national unification by State action. The model is of great relevance for India. He talks of a metropolitan or 'official' language at the centre of the floral formation. "On the whole the central language was spoken in the centre of the realm, in the capital city, at the court, by 'metropolitan elites' who had learned it as their mother tongue and often spoke no other language. These metropolitan elites, moreover, were predominantly literate.

"The regional or peripheral languages were current in more or less peripheral parts of the realm and each serves as the sole language of a local population, which as a rule was mostly illiterate. Mediation between these illiterate populations with their regional languages and the metropolitan elite literate in the central language was carried out by local or regional elites, literate as a rule, and, bilingual: fluent in both the regional and the central language.

"In other words, there existed one language, in which translation was available to every regional language, and that is the central language. The metropolitan elite spoke and wrote the central language and usually no other. The inhabitants of each region spoke different regional languages. For every regional language, there existed a group which specialised in translation with the central language and in decoding or encoding written communication for its illiterate, monolingual clientele: that was the regional elite, which in so doing monopolised as a group the mediation functions in this figuration of languages: a floral figuration, in which the petals of the flower stand for the regional languages, hardly overlapping with each other, and the central language is represented by the heart of the flower which overlaps with every regional language petal."

During the colonial epoch, the colonizers were in the position of a metropolitan elite, most of them speaking only their mother tongue, English, which then gradually became the central language of the territory. Indigenous elites consisting of *pandits, maulawis* and other native informants occupied the peripheral role of bilingual mediators between the colonial language and the language of their region. Nationalist rejection of the colonial language in many cases meant at the same time abandoning a nation-wide means of communication and undermining the position of bilingual elites with an ethnic or regional power base.

However, once India became independent, the monolingual metropolitans who by then included some 'brown sahibs' more or less disappeared and a coalition of bilingual regional elites took power. Group jealousy often kept each regional language group from supporting the language of another as the official medium. But each bilingual elite still also has an interest in preventing the general spread of the former colonial language in its region so as not to dilute its monopolistic mediation gains. The equilibrium solution is to maintain the former colonial language as the central and official State language, but not promulgate it as a language of mass instruction; the peripheral languages continue, each as the vernacular in its region. An alternative lingua franca is discouraged since it threatens the monopolistic mediation functions which mastery of the central language conveys upon the bilingual elites.

States, de Swaan (1990) notes, are the great protectors of languages in the modern world, but only of the officially adopted languages, of course. First of all, all laws and administrative regulations are written in the official language, and this alone requires standardisation of terminology and permanence of meaning over time. Second, all business within the administration and all contacts with citizens are transacted in this language of choice. Third, and most important in the long run, the official language becomes the language of instruction in the schools, usually from the first grade on, compelling all citizens to become proficient in it as they grow up. Fourth, private business must use the language in its dealings with central and local governments, forcing the middle and higher echelons to master it. Fifth, the language will be associated with the prestige of high office, extended education and economic wealth: for that reason alone it will be considered prestigious to be fluent in it. (But by the same token, others may consider it a mark of disloyalty to class, religious, ethnic or regional origins to affect the official speech. And equally, they may well believe that even if they master the language, they will still be excluded from the spoils by the elite for lack of connections.) The State language will be further preserved by a cabal of appointed guardians, academic scholars, linguists, lexicographers, educationists whose appointed task it is to describe and, as the case may be, prescribe standards and see to it that they are adhered to. In so far as the State controls, or more informally influences, the mass media, this too will contribute to the use of the standard version of the language in newspapers and on radio and television. This in turn goes far to shape the canons of usage in the population at large.

As States in the contemporary world are among the most demarcated and permanent institutions, under their protection languages become less fluent and shifting, and, parallel to the State's borders, the differences with other languages are emphasised and perpetuated, while the language is no longer taken for granted but increasingly becomes a symbol, a cherished national and historical treasure, sometimes the only common denominator of the State's citizenry and itself constitutive of a sense of national unity from which the State takes its legitimacy.

In short, languages partake in the robustness of the States that adopt them and contribute to it. Where, in the course of centuries a single language has spread throughout the territory of the State, growing from a court language into the language of a plurality, a majority next, and then becomes the language, native or acquired of all citizens, and finally the only language in the realm, all its rivals having been abandoned, language and citizenship have become conterminous. But this is by no means the general state of affairs in the contemporary world. And even in those States where at first sight it appears to be the case, and where it is unthinkingly accepted as the normal situation, a second look reveals many inconsistencies. In the case of India, this is particularly timely.

The language situation in India, as discussed above, only roughly resembles the floral figuration. There are many important exceptions which distort the pattern (Brass 1974; Annamalai 1979).

It is time that a central, metropolitan language developed in India through political domination, particularly in the medieval age, of Delhi. That language was Hindi-Urdu whose modern-day descendant, *khari boli*, prevails as an important medium of inter-regional communication. Its spread is assisted by its official status as well as its adoption by a major section of the hegemonistic culture-ideology-entertainment industry, the Hindi film world.

However, the dominant position of Hindi is limited by several factors. First, Sanskrit and Arabic continue to be very important languages of religion and as such, in a religious people, occupy significance greater than warranted by their use by trained clerics. Secondly, even in the medieval period when Hindi-Urdu evolved into the central language, because of the need for the perpetuation of an exclusive courtly elite, Pharsi (Persian) in the Arabic script continued at the centre of power. Third, with the coming of the British colonial rule, Hindi-Urdu was quickly displaced from the central position by English and even after the departure of the British, English continued to be the central, metropolitan language albeit along with Hindi. "Where Hindi and related languages encompassed a plurality of the population in India, but left out a large majority, especially in the South (and the East), English became the language for all-India communication. By the same dialectic of unification and liberation, the colonial language also was adopted as the link language among the anti-colonial opposition" (de Swaan 1990).

The fourth, and most important, factor which limits the centrality of Hindi is the fact of the staggering illiteracy in India. Since almost two-thirds of the population is unable to read and write, it implies that language use for a majority of Indians is "tied to the soil" (de Swaan 1990), although the penetration of electronic, one-way oral communication through radio and television has enhanced the reach of Hindi even in that segment. "But illiteracy does limit the rural population very much to a restricted code, one that is context-bound, as opposed to the elaborate codes of the literate elite which is fluent in one or more of the standard languages. Accordingly, for many purposes, the players in the language game do not include these vast masses of illiterates, even though history of mass protest movements on language issues may have suggested otherwise" (de Swaan 1990).

Among the literate sections however, Hindi and English do occupy the position of the cultural, metropolitan languages today. Although according to some counts 880 languages are spoken in

India, only 14 of them have an official status. Hindi accounted for nearly 150 million speakers and their number is even larger if Urdu speakers are included (Khubchandani *et al.* in Wurm 1979). The fact that Hindi and the other 13 languages have official recognition and as such are supported by the State apparatus adds contemporary robustness to their individual literary traditions. Nevertheless, Hindi and English pre-empt many of the functions of these regional languages in modern combination. They hardly play a role in higher education and science, whereas for Hindi at least an attempt is being made in these fields. In addition, popular cinema, national television network, audio media and in particular film songs are dominated by Hindi. All-India politics, administration, law, commerce, industry, transport and communications are also carried out through the medium of Hindi or English.

At the same time, a characteristic of Indian languages, Hindi as well as the regional ones, is that they are fluid, varying over time, differentiated according to social status, caste configurations as well as occupational and class variations. They are not only relatively easily penetrable by higher languages, like Sanskrit or English, but they also change gradually from one area to another. Hindi itself is the best example. From its *khari boli* pole at Allahabad, it goes through various mutations in every direction.

In effect, this means that the 'floral model' of languages needs modification in the Indian context. "The Indian language system assumes cosmic proportions: it may be conceived as a stellar system, with at its centre, and in the Union level, a double star of Hindi and English, and in the periphery the planets of the other scheduled languages connected to the respective states, each of which in turn has a number of more or less obscure moons around it, tribal languages, local dialects, occupational, caste and class idioms, minority languages (sometimes belonging to the scheduled repertoire in adjoining states) etc." (de Swaan 1990).

As linguistic tensions pull this stellar system in different directions, the finely balanced gravitational forces of nationhood may get disrupted. Since the framing of the Constitution, the centripetal force of institutionalism has more or less prevailed. This may lead to an unsustainable involution where the Centre acquires so much mass and hence gravity that it pulls the others into itself and explodes as a super nova. However, the decaying of the Centre and hence a greater centrifugal movement too cannot be dismissed out of hand.

CHAPTER 7

NATIONAL INTEGRATION IN A FRAGMENTED SOCIETY

The colonial view of India was that it was not, and could hardly ever become, a "nation" : "The first and the most essential thing to learn about India is that there is not and never was an India, possessing according to European ideas any sort of unity, physical, social and religious; no Indian nation, no people of India of which we hear so much" (Stratchey, cited in Dutt 1926: 7). The first, almost knee-jerk nativistic response to this was that not only did the Indian nation exist but indeed there was a monolithic unity in it epitomised by the centrality of the Brahmanical tradition with its language and litera-ture, its myths and symbols, its various systems and sub-systems (Mookerji 1954). This sweeping generalisation, which was essential for a section of the emerging Indian elite to create a respectable self-image and fortify its ego against the colonial denial, aggression and humiliation (Azam 1981: 29), when it intruded in the political idiom of colonial politics ended up ironically by paving the way for recognition of divergence that ultimately led to the partition of India.

It will be erroneous to assume, however, that the conception of unity in Brahmanical terms was a deliberate attempt to accentuate schism; on the contrary, it was hoped through this to usher in new forces of unity. It was its lack of correspondence to the reality of Indian social pluralistic complexity that proved the ideology of monolithic unity not only to be an expression of false consciousness but also led to the ghastly irony of the proponents of *Akhand Bharat* (Undivided India) becoming a factor of social disruption and con-flict in both colonial India and even after Independence.

The idea of the fundamental unity of India caused by the commonality of the Brahmanical tradition has dangerous divisive political implications and effects. In fact, it is not even borne out by critical examination of Indian history which shows that so-called Brahmanical tradition itself is not monolithic and homogenous and was certainly not evenly spread through the Indian people even before Islam came to India (Kosambi 1962, 1975, 1975a). The vast submerged groups, the masses of India including the Dalits, the Adivasis and other 'ethnic' and religious minorities, had only a peripheral contact with this tradition and even this peripheral contact was not free from perversions and distortions as it came to them from those who had ideologically rejected the Brahmanical tradition or from those who themselves had imbibed it only partially.

Further, instead of becoming a fact of integration, the Brahmanical tradition only tended to alienate segments of the Indian population. In the deep South, it aroused suspicion as an instrument of Brahman domination of non-Brahmans and was equated with 'Aryan' domination over Dravidians. Muslims, Christians and other minority religious groups view the emergence of the centrality of the Brahmanical tradition in purely survival terms: they are aware of its absorbing capacity and feel that their distinct identity may get lost in a highly diffused culture. And, the caste-based hierarchical distribution of the Brahmanical tradition leads to two contradictory trends inhibiting social and emotional integration: one of rejection leading to antagonism between upper caste Hindus and the 'outcastes' like *dalits*, and the other of assertion leading to a competition for acquiring caste symbols and status.

In recent times, an aggressive assertion of the great Brahmanical tradition has been observed among the lower castes and has been given the name of 'Sanskritisation' (Srinivas 1962, 1966), a process which is in fact one of further stratification and social differentiation. Thus, the proponents of monolithic unity, of the ideology of 'one culture, one language, one nation'— "Hindu, Hindi, Hindustan"— (Golwalkar 1947) in effect are the destroyers of unity among the people. It is not surprising that as early as 1937, the then greatest exponents of *hindutva* (Savarkar 1942) also upheld this uni-dimensional idea of India. Savarkar (1949) propounded that Muslims constituted a separate nation altogether and gladly accepted the separatist implications of this position.

Against this blatantly revivalistic and exclusivist concept of

Indian nationhood, there were several variants of humanistic and even modernistic Hindu nationalism. These were pre-eminently represented by Gandhi, who while advancing his own Vaishnav interpretation of Hinduism, tried to make it open enough to accommodate all minority groups or at least not to antagonise them. Others like Rabindranath Tagore drew from the Hindu tradition in advancing nationalism but tried to fashion Hinduism into almost non-sectarian, secular 'way of life'. Through this non-sectarian Hinduism they tried to promote the "underlying unity" of Indian culture.

Among secular protagonists of Indian nationalism perhaps the most important was Jawaharlal Nehru (1946) who found "unity in diversity" as the predominant aspect of the Indian historical legacy. However, his otherwise brilliant *tour de force* of Indian history in the search of the elusive 'India' contained "a curious attitude towards the much abused term 'race'"; denunciation of racialism and imperialism occurs on p. 386 f., but on p. 387 we read: "Psychology counts and racial memories are long". Just what racial memory means is not clear, particularly in the case of a country that had forgotten the splendid Mauryan and Gupta periods, including the very script of those times, that ascribes almost every cave of any date to the mythical Pandavas; and is capable of pointing out as Prince Pratap Sinha the status of Outram (a butcher of the 1857 revolt) on the Esplanade at Calcutta" (Kosambi 1957: 11).

The underlying weaknesses of the Nehruvian discovery of the Indian nation are that he too generalised from stray historical allusions and on the whole arrived at a constructed, instrumentalist interpretation of nationalism, following a 'grand scheme' of a 'great tradition'. In the end therefore even in his scheme he found it necessary to order Indian nationalism through constitutional and other formal mechanisms rather than rely on its inherent organic entity. It was in effect an Invention of India rather than its 'Discovery' that Nehru carried out. Further, Nehru did not pay enough attention to class as a force in the making of the Indian nation. As Kosambi (1957: 12-14) points out, "The author could have asked himself one question with the greatest advantage, namely *cui bono*: what is the class that called for or benefited by a certain change at a certain period of history", a question which would have illuminated the very search for Indian nationhood at the given time.

Still, Nehru's attempt does mark a phase of doing away with trying to find general processes of the making of the Indian nation within the narrow confines of a particular tradition. Following Nehru, among both non-Hindu as well as Hindu secular modernists, the search for Indian nationhood has led to emergence of the concept of 'composite culture'. They do not deny the continuity of the Indian tradition, but they emphasise the diversity and variety in it, rejecting its centrality. They even accept a vague paradigm of 'culture' (and some go so far as to equate it with even 'ethnicity') as central to Indian unity, but reject its Hindu monolithism. This 'culture' is seen as eclectic, absorbent and unitary and its sources are found in the realms of ideas rather than material processes.

Among the secular modernists, one group, however, tended to give up the search for the 'Indian nation' altogether and concluded that India was a composite but multinational entity (Dutt 1949: 438). In the 1940s the Communist Party of India (whom Kosambi [1957: 3] referred to as Indian 'Official Marxists' - OM), relying heavily on the mechanistic Stalinist pronouncements on 'nation' and 'nationality', concluded that given the concatenations of geography, language, religion and culture, there were many 'nations' within the Indian boundaries and even went to support the sectarian demand for Pakistan as legitimate since, according to them, it was based on the right of nations to self-determination (Adhikari 1944: 29). These 'vulgar Marxists' either concerned themselves with basic factors related to production at any given time or hung their analyses and politics entirely on superstructural pegs. The 'Official Marxists' rejected the cultural principle of unity on the national level, but by advocating first, Pakistan, as based on a distinct 'Muslim culture', and later linguistic nationalities in the post-Partition period adopted the same cultural principle on the regional level. While correctly rejecting the Hindu hocus-pocus of the great Brahmanical tradition being at the root of Indian nationhood on perfectly valid class analysis (Dutt 1949), the Official Marxists forgot to apply class analysis to the needs of the emergent Indian bourgeoisie not only for a united Indian State and market but, in the interest of stability, integration and progressive homogenisation, for an Indian nation itself (Kosambi 1957).

The national question in India was extremely complicated in the 1940s. The separatist Muslims led by Mohammed Ali Jinnah, staunch and exclusivist Hindus led by V.D. Savarkar and 'Official Marxists' directed from Moscow took mutually indistinguishable positions regarding Partition and Pakistan. The votaries of Indian unity like Gandhi tried desperately to keep India united with all its religious and other minorities incorporated under a broad banner of religiosity derived from the heterodox Hindu tradition. Secularists and anti-racists like Nehru invoked the long memory of the Indian 'race'. In that context of confusion, Ambedkar's opinion "that in believing that we are a nation, we are cherishing a great delusion" but that only post-colonial India would become "a nation in the making" (Ambedkar 1946a) does not only seem candid but, given a comprehensive analysis of social, cultural, political and also economic features of the time, remarkably accurate. And, there were three principal forces involved in this process of Indian "nation in the making": Constitutional and other Statist measures; the integrationist force of the capitalist market; and the unifying spirit of the masses in struggle. It is still these three forces which are of the essence in the context of national integration of India.

Finding the 'spirit' of the nation and 'Indian national ethos', etc. elusive, secularists like Nehru, Ambedkar and many others who came into positions of power in post-colonial India, decided to give up this search for vague concepts and to hammer out a constitutional cast within which they could politically mould the Indian nation into being. In this respect, their most tricky problem was the one concerning religious, linguistic, cultural, caste and ethnic-tribal minorities. The constitutionalisation of unity in diversity was no mean task and the framers of the Indian Constitution were aware of the many complexities they faced (India 1966). Through a very tortuous and legalistic process, a system was devised which contains the ambiguity of unitarism and federalism, of particularism and integration, of pluralism and the structuring of "a single people living in a single imperium derived from a single source" (Ambedkar in India 1966: VVI: 33). One aspect of this exercise was that while it tried to secondarise conflicts based on creed, caste and, to an extent even class, it institutionalised a secular tension expressed in Centre-state fiscal and other federal relations. Thus, the seeds of secular regionalism were sown in the very process of creation of India as a union of states. It was nourished with the *ad hoc* and partial reorganisation of states and nurtured with the arrogation of more and more powers by the central political configuration to itself. The time may come to reap the whirlwind.

However, the storm signals that are sounding at present are more on account of cynical reversal of the secular polity. While minorities of different sorts were given only conditional recognition at the time of framing the Constitution and that too with only benevolent protectionist intent, the actual working of the political-electoral system saw an attempt to turn them into secure vote banks. There was an increasing communalisation of public life with all kinds of compromises made by all manners of parties. At best, Indian secularism became not a negation of communalism but a *sum total* of different communalisms. And it appears that, professions of secularism notwithstanding, the State, various political parties and other vested interests have become adept at using one communalism or the other, given the needs of the specific situation, to consolidate their position. They are not even averse to giving encouragement to and conniving with rank Hindu chauvinism and, since there is increasing awareness of the power, political or otherwise of the Hindu majority, a cynical process of overall Hinduisation of the polity seems to be taking place.

This process was begun much earlier by leaders like Bal Gangadhar Tilak and Savarkar during the freedom struggle itself, and has been consciously promoted by the Rashtriya Swayamsevak Sangh (RSS) through its slogans of *Akhand Bharat* and *Hindu Rashtra* (nation) with an overt anti-Muslim, anti-minorities bias. While the RSS has been direct in its attempts, others too have contributed to create a general climate of Hindu revivalism. But while all parties involved in electoral politics play this game, pulling out the communal card here, doing caste calculations there, the irony is that the 'best' players seem to be those who lay claim to inheriting Nehru's secular tradition. The playing off of one section of the Indian people against another which has been carried on by both parties involved in the Punjab situation seems to have worked, for although the hydra-headed monster of terror and hate that was unleashed through this made a victim of the Prime Minister Mrs Indira Gandhi herself and thousands of innocent citizens, the Hindu backlash paid at least short-term political dividends. The question is of what these short-term gains mean for the vital matter of Indian unity and the welfare of its people.

It is paradoxical that both the processes of the Indian nation-in-the-making through political, social, economic and cultural integration and of nation-in-the-unmaking through accentuation of atavistic sectarianism should be the product of the type of democracy that exists in India. The former relationship is clear enough: India itself has found a clear definition through its Constitution and it is that institutionalist framework that has also determined the expression, as it were, of the 'general will' of the people of India. However, while democracy, like the capitalist market, unites peoples into a collective entity, it also in certain respects homogenises society. It is this that has paradoxical results in an essentially pluralistic configuration of peoples.

To take one example, the practice of electoral democracy does not only create the phenomena of vote banks but it also reinforces majoritarian tendencies which have their impact on general social and cultural affairs in addition, of course, on politics. An example of this is the Ram cult being propagated among Hindus as a direct outcome of the type of electoral politics that has evolved in India. The Ram cult has many significant characteristics. It is anti-Muslim in as overt a manner as is possible but, more than that, it is also against the many 'Little Traditions' that have existed within Hinduism itself. In its attempt to create a majoritarian Hinduism, it homogenises, being synthetic rather than syncretic. Its proponents are not bothered that they violate the Hindu precepts of sacred space, sacred time, sacred material and sacred iconography. The last is clear from their depiction of Ram in the *raudra* warrior posture in clear violation of the traditional *maryada purushottam* image. But that is of little concern to such militant Hindus because their efforts have little to do with religion and nothing to do with spirituality. Theirs is clearly a political campaign aimed at first consolidating and then encashing on the Hindu majoritarian vote bank.

The problem is that such an exercise goes against the very essence of democracy. While determination of majority and minority is the crux of democratic practice, the reason why democracy survives in a pluralistic context like India is because, as in a kaleidoscope, the majority-minority pattern keeps shifting constantly. The same person who can belong to a religious majority can be part of a linguistic minority; he can be a constituent of a caste majority but of a class minority. However, if the social psychology of majoritarianism is consolidated and reified through politics, the majority-minority is frozen and, in such a situation, democracy is inevitably displaced by fascism. Indeed, it is this which is the major political argument against communalism.

In the process of communalisation of politics, the justifiable anger among the Indian people at their continuing poverty, deprivation and exploitation, is turned inwards; instead of attempting to change antiquated social institutions, exploitative economic mechanisms and cynical political manipulations, the people discover enemies amongst themselves. Hindus versus Muslims, Backward Castes vs. 'Forward' (upper) Castes, Assamese vs. Bengalis, Hindus vs. Sikhs, Marathas vs. South Indians and almost everybody against Dalits and Adivasis represent not a pluralistic but a fragmented and self-destructive society. Given the communal patterns in society and consciousness, political and economic tensions express themselves in pseudo-religious and pseudo-ethnic ideologies and even ideas of bourgeois secularism based on the unity of the market are put at a discount.

The Indian bourgeoisie as a whole does have an interest in national integration. With all its diversities and pictures of combined and uneven economic situations, one commonality that can be easily discerned is the growth of capitalism. The Indian industrial bourgeoisie was one of the most developed in the colonial and semi-colonial context and by the 1940s had started devising blueprints for further growth in the post-colonial period. Its plans were obviously based on assumptions of a stable and large protected domestic market as it was neither strong enough to compete with foreign capital in India and outside nor was its degree of specialisation such that its different units could have operated within a very limited universe. Further, a specific feature of the Indian market was that although the available average purchasing power was small, this weakness was made up by the largeness of numbers. The geographic dispersion of industries and raw material sources moreover was such that political unity of what remained of India after Partition was essential not only to future growth but even for minimal conditions of its survival. Political unity of India, combined with degrees economic development and social modernisation, was therefore very dear to the Indian bourgeoisie.

However, even this statement needs to be qualified as the very nature of the bourgeoisie is neither uniform nor constant. There are regional and sectarial interests in the bourgeoisie and, depending on various factors, one segment of the other tends to mainly determine policy. Thus, even the market acquires different meanings in different contexts and, for the purposes of profit-maximisation in the short or long run, it is not considered unethical to fragment the people and, if necessary perhaps even the polity. The regional bourgeoisie, particularly the agrarian capitalists, have their own axes to grind and, in their case, local interests are often more important than the broad goals of national unity, though, on the whole, even for them, the logic is that the larger the market, the more their profits and prosperity.

The recent attempt at globalisation of the Indian economy through liberalisation of policy has drastically altered the national context in this regard. The opening up of the Indian market to foreign capital is bound to have many consequences, among the most important of which will be the turning of a significant segment of the bourgeoisie into compradore capitalists who will seek to derive profit through vending foreign goods and services rather than through manufacture and expansion and intensification of the domestic market. Such a class can hardly be conceived as having a national perspective and, if its influence grows, even this major factor of the market determining what is India will weaken.

Simultaneously, the collapse of the Soviet Union, a nation-State conceived and nurtured on an ideal, and its fragmentation into numerous organic entities, ethnicities and 'nationalities' have also had considerable impact on the conceputalisation of the unity of India 'from above' through constitutional or ideological means.

However, the people provide the counter-point in any argument concerning India's unity and it is their vital contribution that has been most neglected in analysing the issue. Social scientists, in the interest of their specific fields of inquiry, have been so busy in segmenting and categorising the Indian people that they have tended to miss out the vibrant and organic interconnections between different groups and their role in Indian cultural, social, economic and even political unity. Thus, anthropology in its obsession with 'primitive tribes', sociology with its overwhelming concern with 'caste and kinship', economics with its attention on commodities and commodity producers, etc., have all cut Indian people into different types, pushed them into methodologically determined pigeonholes and studied them as categories rather than as living entities. Even political scientists who have studied various aspects of 'power play' have concerned themselves with given conceptual segments. Most social scientists, in this process of academic specialisation, have ignored the fact which stares any observer of India in the face, i.e., of the immense intermingling, interaction, interdependence in every field which makes the identification of 'pure categories' almost impossible. It is both empirically impossible, for instance, as discussed above, to clearly separate many aspects of tribe and caste; to sharply distinguish between 'organised' and 'informal' sectors; and to draw a demarcating line between peasants and labourers.

A tribal in an inaccessible area, for instance, can quite easily be a Christian who also worships various 'Hindu' deities; he or she can be practising rudimentary hoe cultivation and receiving remittance from a relative who may be a migrant worker in the advanced sector of capital-intensive commercial agriculture or even high technology industry. A worker in the oldest organised industry, e.g. textiles, may revert to 'informal sector' occupations in exigency, as happened in the case of the 1981-83 Bombay textile strike, and may find equal spiritual solace from both Hindu gods and Muslim *pirs*.

The kaleidoscopic patterns are endless. And they are real. In political expression in India there are not many identifiable 'solidarity-actions'. However, at the level of organic linkages, in the business of day-to-day living, it is the interconnections, social, cultural, economic and political, which sustain the majority of the Indian people for whom survival itself is a struggle.

And, the threads of Indian unity lie in this struggle.

CHAPTER 8

INCONCLUSIVE CONCLUSIONS: SOME THEORETICAL AND PRACTICAL CONSIDERATIONS

There can really be no meaningful 'conclusions' drawn on as complex an issue as that of the emergent situation in India. Thus, our attempt is neither to construct academic theoretical models nor produce policy prescriptions. To conclude the present exercise, we will simply reopen some of the conceptual controversies which we briefly touched on elsewhere and outline the pragmatic tight-rope steps which have been taken towards understanding, dealing with and perhaps solving the tricky questions of 'ethnicity', 'minority-status' and 'nationalism' in the Indian context. Thus, instead of the linear presentation of logic preferred by most academic exercises, we go right back to the beginning, in keeping with the complex nature of the problem to which we have tried to address ourselves in the previous pages.

First, the very concept of 'ethnicity' in the Indian context is vague, imprecise and even misleading. 'Ethnic' is often used to denote any one of the following: racial, religious, linguistic, tribal, immigrant and native or a combination of more than one or all of these (Shah 1983: 3). It is broadly thought that an ethnic group shares a common culture, or, to be a little more precise, language, social system and/or religion, and real or legendary historical heritage. At the conscious or subconscious level, the members of such discrete groups feel themselves to be different culturally from members of other groups. Thus, culture itself is understood in context with other reference groups: its various aspects may concern language as against the languages of other linguistic groups, and so on. The members of an ethnic group would, often in practice and almost always in theory, claim a common ancestor or a common place of origin or a common religion which sustains or develops among them the sentiment of solidarity (Shah 1983).

However, societies are seldom segmented self-consciously and subjectively according to pure criteria of ethnicity by the concerned people themselves except in exigent political situations. More often this kind of fragmentation is carried out by 'outside' observers, analysts or agitators who use this imprecise but emotive concept. And, this usage in the interest of academic simplification, ordering, categorisation and classification, or political demarcation for constituency-building is almost reificatory and often creates perverse and vicarious divisive and destructive effects. Because the concept has neither scientific validity nor correspondence with existing relations of exploitation, it serves only to obscure material reality by creating a 'cultural' smokescreen. Even if ethnic groups exist as pure categories, which they do not, there is hardly ever either internal homogeneity within them or uniqueness vis-a-vis others. In class-divided society, because of their greater control over the means of production and cultural dominance of some over others, there are material differentiations within so-called ethnic groups and communities between their situation and that of 'others' (Shah 1984).

The best illustrative example of the imprecise and emotive concept of 'ethnicity' is with regard to so-called 'tribals' who are given scholarly and political recognition as belonging to discrete and distinct 'ethic' groups and are most commonly accepted as such. But rarely is it realised that this ethnic-tribal equation is an exercise in tautology.

Further, as discussed earlier, the 'tribals' have hardly ever conceived of themselves as such and even academics are not agreed on what constitutes a 'tribe'. Some scholars use the word 'tribe' in a very general sense to identify cognate social groups in a given territory; for instance, "In general anthropologists agree on the criteria by which a tribe may be identified (as a system of social organisation): common territory, a tradition of common descent, common language, common culture and a common name — all these joining of smaller groups such as villages, bands, districts or lineages" (Honigmann in Godelier 1977: 76). Apart from the fact that this is almost an identical definition of 'ethnicity' and adopting it would make the argument circular, in India these characteristics apply to the so-called non-tribals too.

Some scholars define a tribe as a 'kinship society' in which kinship denotes 'multifunctional' relationship — social, political as well as economic (Sahlins 1968). Again, as any sociologist will assertively point out, the multiple role of kinship is applicable to most of the *jatis*, the epitomal non-tribal social formation in India.

According to some Indian anthropologists, 'tribe' identifies the people who live in "a primitive or barbarous condition under a headman or chief"; thus, according to B.S. Guha (in Mamoria 1957), the scheduled tribes of India have a primitive way of living, habitation in remote areas, nomadic habits and love for drink and dancing! This indeed is the stereotype of 'tribe' adopted by the elite and projected through films, television and even Republic Day tableaux. For some other scholars, tribes are characterised by corporate social organisations and indicate the sense of belonging to 'closed moral communities' (Aurora 1972). Some of these characteristics are indicative of the economic situation of most of the people who are labelled 'tribal', but they are by no means universal. As early as the 1940s, D.N. Majumdar (1961) pointed out that several tribal groups were at the food-gathering stage whereas others were settled agriculturists just like most non-tribals. Moreover, as cultural characteristics undergo changes with changes in the mode of production, the definition remains imprecise.

Even worse are the attempts at racial identification of groups in India whether of tribals as aboriginal non-Aryans, *dalits* as 'Adi-Dravids', Muslims as Turko-Mongols and Sikhs as Aryans. The attempts at tracing racial features of any such group have not yielded any scientifically valid conclusions and have, on the contrary, contained elements of fascist mumbo-jumbo. For instance, about the 'tribals' themselves, the 'easiest' of such groups to identify racially, opinion has been advanced about their belonging to Kolid, Gondid, Negrito, Mongoloid, Dravidian, and various other 'racial' stocks depending on the predilections of the particular scholar who is studying them. Thus, Sir Herbert Risley includes Santhals in the Dravidian stock whereas Guiffrida Ruggari believes they are Australoid while Freiherr von Eickstedt opines that they are descendants of the Kolid race (Ghurye 1963; Vidyarthi and Rai 1977).

Then there is the further complication of some castes of today having been considered as tribal groups not so very long ago [thus, e.g. *Bareeyas* of Gujarat (Shah 1975) or *Kurmis* of Bihar (Das 1984)] and some features of caste stratification having been integrated in supposedly casteless religions like Islam (Ahmad 1973), Christianity and Sikhism in India.

It appears therefore, that the division of Indian society into 'ethnic' groupings has little scientific validity and has more political purpose. The term tribe, for instance, was first used by the British census officials-cum-anthropologists to differentiate certain social groups from caste Hindus essentially on political considerations.

The listing of castes was a similar exercise and had queer consequences of reification. James Kerr (cited in Ghurye 1932: 164) was quite explicit, "It may be doubted if the existence of caste is on the whole unfavourable to the preference of our rule. It may even be considered favourable to it, provided we act with prudence and forbearance. Its spirit is opposed to national union". Middleton, Superintendent of Census Operations in 1921 (cited in Ghurye 1932: 160), had stated, "We pigeonholed everyone by caste and if we could not find a true caste for them, labelled them with the name of hereditary occupation. We deplore the caste system and its effect on social and economic problems, but we are largely responsible for the system we deplore. Left to themselves such castes as Sonar and Lohar would rapidly disappear... Government's passion for labels and pigeonholes has led to crystallization of the caste systems".

Not only the British but the Indian elite too appreciated the utility of these divisive forces for preserving the status quo: for instance, the Maharajadhiraj of Darbhanga (who incidentally was not the inheritor of the title to an ancient kingdom but merely a large zamindar or landlord) is reported to have remarked that "Caste is the best and surest safeguard against the spirit of unrest, against the growing bitterness between the classes and the masses, between capital and labour, which is constantly menacing civilisation" (OMalley 1941: 373). While tribal and caste divisions were thus used, the attempt to keep the people divided on religious lines but subjected to the same polity had disastrous consequences in the case of the Hindu-Muslim polarisation and is even today growing to menacing proportions through communal segmentation and conflict-generation.

Almost all these divisions and sub-divisions of the Indian people had political, administrative and legal recognition during the colonial period. There were communal electorates organised on religious basis; 'Backward Tribes' and 'Scheduled Castes' were terms legitimised under the Government of India Act of 1935 and the myriads of castes listed in hierarchical order were included in the various census and other relevant official records. After Independence, the situation was sought to be simplified by withdrawing recognition to the caste system, by creating a secular polity under the Constitution and by retaining the concepts of 'Scheduled Tribes' and 'Scheduled Castes' merely for extending to them protective discrimination. The Constituent Assembly even replaced the term 'minorities' in the draft Constitution by 'certain classes' unanimously and without any discussion (Wadhwa 1975: 5). While this Canutian method of abolishing distinctions (Kosambi 1975: 15), trying to solve a social problem by statutory exercises, hardly succeeded in its avowed aim, it instead succeeded in 'fixing' issues. The attempt to define became not only part of a scientific quest but a legislative necessity. And the result was no more illuminating. In the case of the 'Scheduled Tribes', the Assam government characterised them as those who were "(a) descendants from the Mongoloid stock, (b) members of the Tibeto-Burman linguistic group, and (c) part of social organisations of the village class type". The Hyderabad government considered tribals as "those who resided in forests, observed animistic religion, used a local dialect, practised marriage by force and resorted to hunting, fishing and gathering of forest food as the main means of subsistence". And, in a classic piece of tautological officialese, according to the Madhya Pradesh government, tribals were "of 'tribal' origin, speaking a 'tribal' language and (were) resident in the forest areas" (Mamoria 1957; Shah 1984).

Having thus tied itself into various definitional knots, the Government proceeded to enact many measures for different social groups in India. The most momentous document in this regard is, of course, the Constitution of India. The Constitution does not mention any group explicitly as a minority: in neither of the two places that the term occurs in the Constitution is it used for definitional purposes. However, it does contain special provisions for groups which can be broadly classified as (1) linguistic minorities; (2) religious minorities; (3) scheduled castes and (4) schedules tribes. After the Constitution was drawn up, demands were raised for special provisions for a large, loose and vaguely constituted group, known as 'Other Backward Classes' corresponding roughly to the 'intermediate' groups in the caste hierarchy but with practically no internal homogeneity. In spite of Jawaharlal Nehru strongly and logically declaring as early as 1953 that "he disliked the term 'Backward Classes' and remarked that it was basically wrong to label any section of the people as backward even if they were so, particularly when 90 per cent of the people in the country were poor and backward" (Wadhwa 1975: 18), the pressure for special measures for these groups kept building up and has acquired powerful force in recent years particularly on the demand for reservations in government jobs. Some states like Bihar, Tamil Nadu, Madhya Pradesh and Gujarat have taken halting 'One Step Forward, Two Steps Back' measures in this regard and the result has been administrative chaos and caste conflict. Most recently, the issue has exploded in the context of the implementation of the report of the Mandal Commission.

In today's context, the crux of upward social mobility lies not in ritual Sanskritisation but in grasping economic opportunity (Frankel and Rao 1989, 1990). And, in spite of right-wing economic privatisers and liberalisers who would like to limit the scope of the State, the State continues to be the prime mover in this socio-economic change. Both B.R. Ambedkar and Jawaharlal Nehru realised this when they sought to use the State to force the pace of de-Sanskritisation which they recognised to be the process appropriate to their times. For, in the end, Sanskritisation stands for ritualisation of society and the reinforcement of the structures of *hindutva* which go against the fundamental premises of a secular nation. By announcing implementation of the Mandal Commission recommendations, V.P. Singh took a gigantic leap in the same direction.

He recognised that the modern India has little use for Manu's ancient caste hierarchy. He also realised that the essential element in society today is the State and control over organs of the State must in the end correspond to economic power. If the rural economy itself is increasingly under the thumbs of 'backwards', so must be the government of a country like India. Indeed, in today's situation when government jobs are the best sources of rapid private accumulation, accumulating classes can hardly be denied access to them.

Shortly after Manu outlined his Brahmanical scheme of things, his whole prescription was questioned and seriously upset by the middle-ranking *kshatriya* and *vaishya*-backed Buddhist and Jain orders. If the Sanskritising Brahmans managed to recoup their predominance, it was only by keeping control over the rituals of passage: birth, marriage and death ceremonies. In the expanding modern sector of Nehruvian India, after the passing of the Hindu Code Bill and Special Marriage Act and the functioning of electric crematoria, an Indian hardly needs a Brahman to order his life. The dominance of Brahmanical ideology, and the appeal of Sanskritisation, were also on account of their control over symbolic language, whether the ritual *mantras* (incantations) of the Vedas or the gobbledygook of Persian or English officialese, and discourses of sophistication. Today, however, language itself has been simplified and vulgarised; hence too it is an era of de-Sanskritisation.

Thus, there existed an opportunity for another Manu who would reorder society on the basis of economic realities rather than ritual prescriptions. And V.P. Singh decided to play that role.

The problem is that the reasons for V.P. Singh's actions were extremely narrow. His attempt to rise above politics, politicking and even the given boundaries of the existing social structure were primarily motivated by his individual need to project himself as a charismatic leader whose rhetoric carries him beyond his immediate circle that circumscribes him. His problem is that he has to project grandeur of vision in times which are sordid. And, when there is overall cultural degeneration, Manu can only go backward, as he did in his own time between the decline of Indus Valley and Vedic sophistication and the rise of the Magadhan civilisation. V.P. Singh's attempt to play a latter-day Manu was similarly foredoomed. It was pragmatic while pretending to be idealistic; its rhetoric did not match its substance.

And yet, in a time when symbolism overtakes substance, Indian politics, if not culture, was substantially Mandalised in the face of strenuous opposition by the upper castes. The most horrifying manifestations of the opposition were the self-immolations by scores of young upper caste students who sacrificed their lives protesting about the implementation of the Mandal report whereby the OBCs came of age in the Indian polity.

Even after much blood was spilled, the central point of the anti-Mandal agitation however was still not obvious to the unbiased observer. Was it about jobs? Or was it about caste? Was it about promoting an undifferentiated Hindudom? Or was it merely to bring about a change in the government? The mincing one-step-forward, two-steps-back jig performed by V.P. Singh on the Mandal issue indeed left little room for doubt that there was in fact an electoral vote bank calculation behind the announcement.

At the same time, the resistance to even such minor changes as may be brought about by Mandalisation was quite disproportionate. The active role being played in the anti-Mandal movement by anti-social elements, political operators with unsavoury pasts and the votaries of aggressive *hindutva*, whose *sine qua non* is caste, made it clear that the upsurge was directed towards the issue of jobs only to a very limited extent.

Without doubt many anti-Mandalites, particularly students, were extremely insecure about their career prospects and their intense insecurity was reflected in the obsessive anxiety which drove them towards dramatic gestures ending even in death. However, it is the very gestures and symbolisms of the less spontaneous forms of protest which gave away the protestations that the movement was primarily about jobs. The articulation of blatantly casteist slogans about the *dalit* minister, Ram Bilas Paswan and others, the demand of the confederation of Class I government officials to do away with reservations altogether, even those relating to scheduled castes and tribes (SC-STs), the insidious linking of efficiency and merit to upper castes, such as through pseudo-statistical assertions by the pro-*hindutva* as well as pro-Western journalists like Arun Shourie that railway accidents have increased on account of employment of SC-STs, etc., showed that the movement was at least as much about preservation of caste inequities as about cornering jobs in a limited job market.

The reinforcement of such ideas which go against the very bases of civilisation and modernity by ideologues and publicists who claim to stand for those very values, through repeated, articulate and powerful propaganda in the mass media, obviously inflamed the tinder in the minds of the youth. Apprehending their own defeat in the battle of numbers that democracy is, those who have enjoyed upper caste plutocracy were urging the youth to commit *jauhar* (self-sacrifice by burning) for a cause that was only thinly disguised as being noble: the protection of merit. Even the fact that dominant elements in the movement were rampaging lumpens, who have nothing to do with promotion of merit, and upper class-caste men, out to preserve their traditional class, caste and gender superiority, did nothing to make the ideologues drop their masks of merit. Such a manipulative 'meritocracy', a plutocracy of the privileged, is inherently hypocritical. The arguments of the anti-Mandalists who pretended to be promoting meritocracy would have been more consistent if they had the honesty to deny democracy altogether.

It is amazing how the Mandal move of V.P. Singh was able to make large numbers of the urban elite suddenly recall principles and values. Gurus of statecraft who spent years preaching the a-moral art of republican *realpolitik* suddenly woke up to deep societal concerns. They found themselves on the same side as those publicists who have no use for the hurly-burly of democratic politics and would be happiest in an elite-dominated plutocratic paradise which might appear fascistic to some but which has the apparent advantage of being aseptic. Analysts who for long propounded the importance of vote-banks and who made caste calculations a fine art abruptly discovered that they have all along felt caste to be evil. At the same time those free-market-*wallahas*, who abhorred Marxist class analysis, pleaded for taking class rather than caste as the basic unit of social transformation.

The one thing that V.P. Singh's dalliance with the Mandal Commission's recommendations did successfully was to throw the pet theories of simple-minded sociologists into disarray. The Parsonian pedants who for decades have sworn by the validity of caste, ritual and kinship were forced to assert that the intellectual wares that they peddled were spurious. Before Mandal was resurrected, the same sociologists and anthropologists who suddenly waxed eloquent on the merits of considering economic criteria laughed at the mention of class. They felt it was a concept which was misplaced in the Indian context and was imported by disgruntled and displaced Marxists who wanted to disturb the harmonious co-existence of *yajmani* groups based on traditional patron-client relationships and performing different social roles evolved through a uniquely Indian historical process.

The same academic elite which in the post-Mandal period proclaimed that there are only two valid categories into which Indians can be divided, i.e. the rich and the poor, was engaged for long in the exercise of casting finely meshed sociological nets into India's turbulent social waters and drawing out not class but the familiar fishes of 'tribe', 'sex' and above all 'caste'.

The hypocrisy of academic sophistry was matched by the inconsistency of the political practice of the Indian elite. It affirms that its quest for the modern El Dorado is premised on the outright rejection of the primordial social organisations like caste and that it seeks an order where the individual is the unit of society, economy and politics. It loudly inveighs against differentiation on the basis of social groups and reluctantly justifies its acceptance of positive discrimination in favour of scheduled castes and tribes (SC-STs) only because it says those groups suffer from historical disabilities.

While it admits this exception to its self-proclaimed rule of individual-as-unit, it opposed affirmative action by the State in favour of other backward castes (OBCs). It conveniently forgot however that while it expresses solicitous concern for SC-STs and aims its ire against the OBCs, even in January-February 1990 when reservations for SCs and STs were extended through a Constitu-tional amendment, its storm-troopers had indulged in widespread rioting against those very SC-STs.

But the Indian elite can hardly help its hypocrisy. Used for centuries to deriving disproportionate advantages from a society ideologically subjugated by it, it has lost the self-confidence to stand by its own profession of promotion of merit. That indeed was the crux of the anti-Mandal movement.

The Indian elite, which constitutes less than a quarter of its population, has the possibility, even when Mandal's scheme is implemented, of filling more than half of all Central Government and public sector jobs. In addition it has open to it the vast vistas of the private sector. But such is its moral and intellectual degeneration that it feels insecure. It raises the bogey of merit being swamped by the multitude because it is not sure of its own competence.

Indeed the lack of merit in the Indian elite is apparent to all except those who perversely avoid looking at the sordid state to which centuries of elite domination have reduced Indian society. Up to the announcement in 1990 regarding implementation of the Mandal commission recommendations neither have OBCs had reserved quotas nor have SC-STs been allowed to fill those set aside for them. And yet such a state of affairs was created that Indian society became dangerously fragmented, its economy nearly bankrupt and its polity characterised by venality and inefficiency.

This is not without reason. The Indian elite has frozen its mind in time, as it has lived by the self-serving social order ordained by Manu. Or, at best, it has moulded its thought according to hierarchical patterns imposed on it by elite-reinforcing ideas of colonial rule. While subaltern strands of Indian thought, whether of the Hindu *bhakti* or Islamic *sufi* tradition, rejected caste, the culturally alienated metropolitan elite, informed by colonial anthropology and Indology, saw idealised caste as the quintessential element of India. The colonial regime did not only deindustrialise India, it seriously de-intellectualised the elite too. And the de-intellectualisation reflected itself in rejection of the rich tradition of subaltern thought and a mechanistic adoption of social *idie fixe*. The humdrum secular existence of peasant and artisanal India was ignored as the British produced Risley to conveniently reinforce Manu's ritual hierarchy. A fresh ordering of society on the basis of caste comfortably conformed to the limited mental frame of even the westernised Indian elite which was bemused by its quaintness, intrigued by its complexity and, of course, benefited from its ordained nature.

The simplification of social ideas was further vulgarised by the promotion of borrowed metropolitan values. The urge for high living eminently suited the plain thinking of the middle class mass. In the last few years there has been much talk about the growing ranks of the Indian affluent who are supposed to number nearly three hundred million. The political-economic establishment has taken pride in doing its best to satisfy its import-oriented, consumerist urges. The State has been a prime player in this process. Even as it has allowed institutions of education and ideas to atrophy, it has encouraged mindless consumerism. While accumulation has been primitive, consumption tends to be ultra modern.

It has been possible to do this because the metropolitan elite, occasionally supported by its affluent country cousins, has maintained its stranglehold on institutions of governance. It is that control which today appears to be slipping. And, given the limited nature of resources available, the elite can continue to live in the style that it has got accustomed to only by maintaining an inordinate presence in the government. It is only in that manner that it can squeeze out the high rates of return on investment in government jobs by extraction of exorbitant 'rent' through corruption and provide for its extravagance. The talk of "small government" and liberalisation is as unreal as the elite's commitment to "equality of status and of opportunity" enshrined in the Constitution.

Implementation of the Mandal recommendations, even its invocation, has shown the Indian elite for what it is: self-serving, selfish and disingenuous. The fact that today it feels called upon to talk of "economic criteria" and yet is not satisfied when those criteria are provided for; the fact that it sheds crocodile tears for SC-STs while it continues to occupy seats reserved for them; the fact that it feels insecure in the face of the growing rural power of the OBCs and their consequent search for governmental avenues of faster accumulation; the fact that it uses merit as an euphemism for privilege: all these demonstrate that the metropolitan mind which dominates elite behaviour is both devious and desperate. It is capable of converting any progressive substance into a merely symbolic shell of itself.

Paradoxically, the most potent danger to India comes not from substantive matters but from symbolism. It is the revival and born-again sanctification of primitive and macabre ritualism that poses the gravest threat to India at the end of the twentieth century. The symbolism of a crude combination of casteist recalcitrance and religious ritualism was represented by the dramatic attempt of some upper caste men in Patna to cut off their necks and offer their severed heads to the goddess Durga. The logic seeking to endow legitimacy to self-immolation is similar to the revivalist arguments used to justify *sati* (the burning of widows, a practice that has been declared illegal but, under the influence of orthodox Hindus, instances of *sati* do occur occasionally even now; the latest instance was the burning of Rup Kanwar, a young widow, at Deorala in Rajasthan in 1987).

There are also other instances of bizarre and barbaric ritualism, for instance along the progress of the *hindutva* juggernaut which rolled from Somnath in Gujarat through much of central India till it was halted in Samastipur in Bihar. That Toyota-Hindu odyssey of the BJP leader, L.K. Advani left a trail of communal carnage in its wake. The present to Mr Advani, and his willing acceptance, of bowls full of human blood was gruesome. Also ominous was the "symbolic" offering of weapons which the BJP MP Pramod Mahajan gleefully accepted with the remarks that "If all the arms presented so far (the third day of the *yatra*) were used, the Ayodhya issue would be settled in a day." And, finally, the Babri masjid was destroyed with ritualistic frenzy as the State, with all its might, stood by and watched.

It is infiltration of ideology through ritual symbolism that represents the continuum between the Mandal and the Mandir issues. The inequities of caste and the obscurantism of irrational rituals are integrally connected in *sanatanist* (orthodox) Hinduism. The inherent and iniquitous hierarchy of caste has been maintained for centuries through Brahmanical control over rituals, in particular over rites of passage, over birth and death. Blood-letting and sacrifice, subservience and deprivation of life are essential ingredients of the hierarchical orthodox Hindu order which negates the egalitarian urges of modern civil society.

To the extent that the anti-Mandal agitation is a reflection of the attempt to perpetuate casteist plutocracy and the Mandir issue is one of irrational, socially divisive, aggressive and ritualistic *hindutva*, the two are in effect the backward movements of the so-called "forwards". If they succeed, they will only encourage primitivism in a modern age, a horrifying prospect for India which is desperately struggling to emerge out of its cultural-economic shackles. Curiously however, it is not the poor, oppressed and "ignorant" Indian who is standing in the way of progress but the more privileged, even superficially "modernised", metropolitan. And it creates so much confusion through sophistry in the matter of affirmative action by the State that the very project of nation-building gets obscured.

The reactions to the Mandal Commission's recommendations brought to the surface several features which had been papered over by the State prevailing over society. One was articulated through the arguments used by the anti-reservationists to contest extension of reservations in government jobs for backward castes. They contended that such a move went against the basic premise of promoting merit, deepened casteism and intensified social strife. Pro-reservationists defended the measures on the ground that they promoted equity and indeed promoted social integration by broadening participation in processes and institutions of the State. It is interesting to note that both arguments and counter-arguments were premised on the centrality of State action in determining society.

However, the Mandal imbroglio also revealed two other facets of Indian society. One was the entrenched social, political and economic position of the upper castes and the other was their insecurity arising out of the upward mobility of backward castes which threatened to erode their power base. Once again, the issue of changing power balances was posited on relative holds on the State in general and on government jobs in particular. This is an important commentary on the very nature of social existence in India, determined and ordered as it is by the instrumentalities of the State.

In this context, it is also significant that the Mandal controversy contained a vital throwback on colonial enumeration. As discussed earlier, while castes, religions and groups have existed as "fuzzy communities" from time immemorial, their congealing into distinct, discrete and mutually antagonistic communities was certainly aided to a great extent by the counting of heads. In the case of the division of societies among upper castes (euphemistically called 'Forwards') and 'Backwards', the reference point was the 1931 Census.

This is important because after Independence caste was abolished by statutory fiat and hence no enumeration of caste was carried out in post-colonial censal exercises. (The 1941 Census, the last before Independence, was an abbreviated exercise because of the then prevailing disturbed conditions created by the Second World War). Hence, the use by the Mandal Commission of 1931 data to extrapolate caste entities in the 1990s. Now, what is of immense importance is the fact that the statutory abolition had not restored the *status quo ante* colonialism with regard to self-perception of

communities and the explanation for this lies not only in the
inability of laws and institutions to turn the clock of history back but
also in the hegemony of the numerate (and literate) on even the a-
numerate and illiterate subaltern peoples. In any event, notwithstanding Canutian edicts abolishing caste, caste continued to be a
major social reality. Indeed, with changing circumstances, not only
did the caste structure get solidified within the mould of politics but
the phenomenon of politicised caste even acquired an English name:
"casteism".

The unchanging India that Hegel conceptualised is obviously
wrong. Empirical evidence and critical theory have demonstrated
that caste is neither static nor is it even peculiarly "Hindoo". Indeed,
perhaps the most valid evidence of the composite nature of Indian
society is in the incorporation of the caste system within non-Hindu
religions. Thus, the Muslims in India ordered themselves with Syeds
corresponding to Brahmans, Sheikhs to Kayasthas, Pathans to Rajputs,
Ansaris to Tantis, and so on. For all the imperfections of his report,
and there are many, even B.P. Mandal realised this: his understanding of caste is of a hierarchical order which is relative to given space
and time: the same caste is forward in one region and backward in
another and caste characterisations of forwardness and backwardness cut across boundaries of religion. Even in as pathetic an
intellectual exercise as indulged in by Mandal, the picture of caste
that emerges is not of a static and lifeless arrangement of social
building blocks but of an unruly, ever-growing, verdant social
jungle.

In the inherently disorderly Indian society, it is the Brahmans
and Brahmanism that laid down the kind of law that existed. And,
the Brahmans claimed legitimacy for their laws on grounds of a
moral superiority in society. Thus, even while kshatriyas may have
controlled government, Brahmanism hegemonised society and State.

The revolt against Brahmanism, of which the backward castes'
assertion is a part, is therefore a subaltern resistance of the elite.
Earlier in history this was articulated through various heterodox
shramamik traditions. It is this process of resistance that has been
sought to be idealised, institutionalised and perhaps even regulated
through the Constitution.

Apart from the confused policy regarding job reservations for

'Other Backward Castes', the constitutional and other legislative provisions with respect to minorities in India are essentially the following:

1. Affirmation of the Principle of Non-Discrimination and Common Citizenship
   - Equality before Law
   - Prohibition of Discrimination
   - Equality of Opportunity in Public Employment (with specific exemptions for Scheduled Castes and Tribes and, in some cases, for Other Backward Castes)
   - Equality of Educational Opportunities - Universal Adult Suffrage
   - Directive to evolve Uniform Civil Code.

2. Secularism
   - No State Religion
   - Individual's Freedom of Faith
   - Collective Freedom of Religion including religious instruction.

3. Cultural and Educational Rights
   - Right to Conserve Language, Script and Culture
   - Right to Freedom of Education — No discrimination in State Aid on basis of religion or language.

4. Special Provisions for Scheduled Castes and Tribes
   - Special safeguards for political representation
   - Reservation in public employment
   - Special measures for education
   - Ban on untouchability
   - Declaration of Scheduled Areas
   - Prohibition of forced labour.

In spite of wide-ranging legislation and even special machinery for implementation and monitoring, however, the constitutional intent has been only very partially put into effect. On the other hand, the very legitimisation of social divisions through the operation of statutory process has led to a degree of their intensification in actual social conditions of existence. And, special provisions for one group of people have led to other groups to vigorously, and sometimes violently, demanding similar provisions for themselves and yet others resenting such provisions. Thus, for instance, while cultural and economic needs may have fragmented society into myriad *varna* and *jati* groupings earlier, political and legislative measures have led to the creation and nurturing of three-fold caste conflict between 'Forward' or Upper Castes, 'Backward Castes' and 'Scheduled Castes and Tribes' particularly on the question of reservation in public employment in many parts of the country. Similarly, repeated use of religious and other divisions by cynical political operation have not only put secularism but also the very unity of India in danger.

This brings us right back to the question of nationalism and the Indian nation-in-the-making. Experience of different countries suggests that nation-building involves at least three prerequisites. First, economic development (in whatever way one may define it). The nature of production relations, the level of economic growth and the method of distribution of the product provide a base for socio-economic relations among the members of a society who may belong to different so-called 'ethnic' or even 'sub-national' groups (Davis 1978). Second, the scope for participation in the decision-making process and share in political power enables members of various groups to belong to a common political community and a vigorous democratic polity is essential in this respect. Third, alongside providing economic opportunities and scope for real political participation, the development of secular institutions (such as political parties, class-based organisations like trade unions and peasant associations, cultural and educational bodies and systems) and scientific temper facilitate members belonging to various groups to interact on equal terms. Such development is necessary for instilling a sense of security, particularly among members of minority groups in terms of life, livelihood and cultural, social and linguistic rights (Shah 1983: 4).

In the nineteenth century in Europe, nationalism went hand in hand with the development of capitalism. In the twentieth century too, the bourgeois model of development of nation-State is being followed in many parts of the world. The State-capitalist variant of this process also addresses itself to the national question. And all these examples are useful for India. But, in the late twentieth century, a socially and culturally fragmented society, largely of poor and exploited people, will have to search for other solutions to the problems of non-secular divisions among the people by first of all secularising the issue and looking for an answer in actuality of popular existence and in struggle to better it.

CHAPTER 9

EPILOGUE :
ANOTHER REPUBLIC FOR INDIA

History rarely repeats itself. Nevertheless, if we are to understand what is happening in the Indian polity today, it is useful to follow the changing patterns of democracy in a country where the republic went through drastic changes, sometimes even appeared to be liquidating itself.

In France, the Revolution in 1789 added the ingredient of politics to the structure of the State. It upset the old established order, the *ancien regime*, and sought to articulate the ever-changing will of the people. It put a discount on order and a premium on change.

The making of the French republic took a zigzag course. Only a few years after the storming of Bastille and the proclamation of the republic of the French, there was such intense disorder that France once again relapsed into monarchical rule. The first empire under Napoleon replaced the first republic. The republic had been revolutionary; the empire was reformist but both together changed France for ever. However, the change was insufficient and France plunged once again into social turmoil and Napoleon himself was exiled. An insecure and hesitant second republic, which dallied with monarchical forms, inherited the Revolution.

This arrangement too was found wanting and, in a farcical encore of the tragedy of the first empire, there emerged a second empire under Napoleon's nephew, the somewhat ridiculous and definitely unfortunate Louis Bonaparte who staged his own version of the Eighteenth Brumaire in 1848. The second revolution and the second counter-revolution were both pathetic caricatures of their historical precursors and yet 1848 did what 1789 had not been able to do : it turned the peasants of France, characterised till then by exploitation, social oppression, the culture of rural idiocy and political atomisation, into citizens. The second republic and the second empire thus vastly expanded as well as intensified democracy.

However, the weakness of France in the international context, particularly vis-a-vis its strong neighbour in Prussia, resulted in the collapse of the second republic and its replacement by a populist third republic which lasted until the World War II. The War itself, the devastation caused by it, the need for reconstruction and, most important, the changed social and political circumstances necessitated a different political arrangement, leading to the creation of the fourth republic. It represented a government by consensus, with the changing political permutations reflected in frequent changes of government. This did not detract from the process whereby France was once again seeking and obtaining an important place in the comity of modern industrial nations. It was only when this arrangement proved inadequate in coping with the impact of decolonisation, particularly in Algeria, and civil strife once more intensified to explosive proportions, that France again changed its polity and created the fifth republic under a charismatic and immensely powerful president who overshadowed his cabinet as well as parliament.

This rather lengthy prologue is necessary only to focus on the patterns of changes in Indian democracy and to understand that, even if only as a historical approximation, the experiences of France can enable us to comprehend the present situation in India which, otherwise, appears full of despair. Indeed, it is possible to argue that India has already had several versions of its polity in practice and that the analogy with France is not totally unreal.

Let us begin from the beginning of modern Indian democracy. It is possible to see the stable, hopeful, reconstructive Nehruvian democracy in the 1947 to 1962 period as India's first republic. That dawn of freedom, republicanism, secularism and political and economic consolidation came under a cloud in 1962 and a more uncertain but brash and populist second republic came into effective existence. That continued up to 1975 and was marked by the breakdown of national consensus and the maturing of political opposition. It was the inability to come to terms with the fact of an effective opposition which led Indira Gandhi to attempt authoritarian rule by declaring the Emergency. Post-Independence India saw its first empire.

The empire was, however, fragile and it was hamstrung by the existence of Indian social pluralities which could not be homogenised by political fiat. In 1977, the empire was dissolved and the third republic was born. It continued till 1982, during both the Janata regime and the first few years of Mrs Gandhi's second coming. It was characterised by a consolidation of the subaltern classes, in particular the peasantry that had benefited from the Green Revolution. The international as well as the domestic political-economic context, however, soon ended the third republic and the second imperium was inaugurated with the IMF loan and the Asian games in 1982.

The trappings of parliamentarism notwithstanding, the absolutist character of the regime was demonstrated by the massive presence of the ruling party in the 1984 Lok Sabha and the style of governance by imperial *firmans* which lasted up to 1987. The weakening of the political authority of the states, the rise of the affluent consumer class, the pandering to its tastes through profligate international borrowings, the deinstitutionalisation of the various checks and balances of democracy, even the opening of the gates of the Babri Masjid to appease majoritarian communalism were all reflections of this period.

However, the pluralities in India are too many to allow for the consolidation and perpetuation of an absolutist regime in modern times. Castes, classes, religions, institutions, factions, groupings, lobbies— all contend with each other in the exciting adventure of operating the world's largest democracy. Thus, inevitably, circa 1987 the second empire came to grief and the fourth republic was born.

It is in that uncertain fourth republic that we live now. Its ingredients as well as manifestations are political instability, short-lived governments, the imperatives of speedy and intensive economic growth and the coming of age of new political power groups.

On the one side, articulated best but perhaps prematurely and hence unrealistically by the Congress, is the incipient cry for institutionalising a stable fifth republic with a larger-than-life charismatic leader. On the other is the urge, represented by the BJP which is run by the profoundly undemocratic elements of the VHP and the RSS, to dump democracy altogether and institutionalise majoritarian primacy. On yet another plane is the rather pathetic and somewhat redundant effort by the Janata Dal to use the catchword of equity to give power to the backward rich peasants who have started grabbing power in any case. There is also the establishmentarian Left, tailing the Janata Dal, and confusing backwardness with poverty.

The context of India's fourth republic is marked by several special features. In the first place the country stands at once on the brink of financial disaster, industrial collapse but also of a vastly productive agriculture. The 1991 Census shows that the country is undergoing an immensely significant upgradation of its manpower resources through increased literacy, labour mobility and female participation. In short, it is both the worst of times and the best of times. Secondly, this is also the stage when both the minorities and the peasants are becoming effective Indian citizens, demanding a share in the polity of this republic. The collapse of pan-Islamism has made Indian Muslims more Indian than ever before and both their insecurities and loyalties are consequences of that. As citizens of India they demand equality under the law. The peasant, too, has come of age and wants his share of the political cake. Third, those who have enjoyed an oligopoly of power are scared of these new claimants to power. Hence the attempt to instil fears of "minoritarianism" through aggressive advertising on the one side and the unspoken dread of the backward-turning-forward on the other. Fourth, the fact that 30 per cent of India still groans below poverty is overshadowed by the razzle-dazzle of both the economic as well as political preponderance of the rest.

These constitute a political-economic context that is uncertain; a society that is transforming itself; a culture that is changing. And sociology has difficulty coming to grips with this fast-changing society.

Indian political sociology has always had something of the quality of pseudo-science. The explanations advanced by it have often been ex post facto and the imagery used by it seems to derive more from zoology than serious social investigation. Thus, if the nationalist movement at the beginning of the century was sought to be explained in terms of KOBRA (Konkanastha Brahman) domination of the Congress, today the AJGAR (Ahir-Jat-Gujjar-Rajput) formation is endowed with the characteristics of the boa constrictor in relation to Indian politics.

While these make for picturesque description, they miss the immense complexities of Indian social and political reality. Such comic strip intellectualism is inadequate in a serious analysis of those factors that are today fragmenting India.

Three recent events graphically illustrate this. First, the Bharatiya Janata Party (BJP) seeks to project itself as the viable political alternative today since the centrists, both Congress and Janata Dal, are in disarray. A subdued reference to *hindutva* and greater concern with secular international and domestic political matters, including butter versus guns economic issues, point to its effort to occupy the political centre-stage.

Second, in Gujarat, the government, led by the infamous Chimanbhai Patel, allows the saffron storm-troopers of the Vishwa Hindu Parishad (VHP) to run amok for days on end. The staged communal carnage is facilitated by the utter incompetence, if not worse, on part of the state government in maintaining law and order. This enables the VHP even to carry out census exercises to determine demographic relocation through ghettoisation of both Muslims and Hindus.

Third, through a judicious mix of political drama and strong administrative action, the chief minister of Bihar, Laloo Prasad Yadav, checks the outbreak of communal tension and thwarts the designs of VHP *agents provocateur*.

The three events are interlinked and need an explanation which is beyond the realm of instant AJGAR-MAJGAR type of theory. The fact is that whatever may be the pretension, the assertion of aggressive Hindu identity by the BJP and its cohorts in the VHP, Bajrang Dal, Shiv Sena, etc. is a force that is inevitably geared to the fragmentation not only of Indian politics but even of Hindu society. In this dangerous pursuit it is aided by matching Sikh and Muslim fundamentalism. On the other side it is confronted by real, live subaltern secularism. This is missed by formulation of political sociology on the basis of the trees of caste while missing the wood of class altogether.

The ambitions of the BJP are abundantly clear and in fairness to its leaders it must be admitted that they have made no attempt to hide them. The party is quite obviously engaged in the task of capturing

State power through creating a socio-ideological base shaped according to the contours of an invented Hinduism. Its religious pursuits have little to do with the immense heterogeneity and pluralism that have characterised Hinduism historically. Even the symbols of such neo-Hinduism can be constructed afresh and used opportunistically. This was demonstrated dramatically during the Ram Shila Pujan exercise when suddenly the worship of bricks was introduced into Hindu rituals as a part of a marketing strategy.

The commercialisation and attendant homogenisation of Hindu worship also entails a significant change in the sociology of such religious politics.

Up to now the leadership of religio-political Hindu organisations like the Hindu Mahasabha, RSS and even the BJP has largely consisted of Brahmans of the KOBRA variety or otherwise. These formations have represented the interests of other social segments too, in particular of the trading petty bourgeoisie, but that has not prevented the top offices in these organisations being almost an exclusive preserve of Brahmans. Indeed a few years ago when a non-Brahman, Professor Rajendra Singh, appeared to be inching towards the top slot in the RSS, there was considerable disquiet and the Brahman plutocracy closed ranks. In recent years however the picture has changed.

In sharp contrast today the leadership of the aggressive Hindu organisations like the VHP and the Shiv Sena is increasingly dominated not only by non-Brahmans but indeed by traders large and small. In the *shethji-bhattji* (Bania-Brahman) combination, the *bhattji* seems to be losing out.

This is by no means an insignificant development. One of the characterising features of the ideology of politics among Hindus in India has been the fact that it has been impregnated by the syncretic qualities of Brahman legitimacy. Thus even the Bania in Mohandas Karamchand Gandhi had to change and acquire the neo-Brahman mantle of the Mahatma and adopt the traditions of philosophical pluralism and syncretism before he became the paramount leader of the national movement. The ideological influence of the Brahman had to do with a long historical tradition of unifying society and politics even while accommodating diversity. This had its antecedents in the very origin of the Brahman *gotras* themselves which, according to the pioneering work of D.D. Kosambi (1975), can be traced back to the non-Aryan elements of ancient India.

Today, in the era of aggressive commercialisation, the legitimising features of ideology are at a discount and he who pays the piper not only calls the tune but indeed wants to play the pipe himself. If this transformation of Hindu practice continues, there may yet come a day when there will be no place for Brahmans in Hindu India!

The Bania-dominated neo-Hinduism is monotonous, monochromatic and simplistic. Neither the intricacies of Vedantic philosophy nor the liveliness of the Bhakti devotion is of much use to it. Its deities are shaped in images portrayed in the kitsch art of Raja Ravi Varma and sanctified by the electronic mythology marketed by Ramanand Sagar and B.R. Chopra. It has sharply demarcated boundaries and is self-limiting.

The politics of this type of Hindu religiosity first of all cuts itself off from the Dravidian traditions of South India and of the non-Aryan north-east. It then restricts itself vis-a-vis the various subaltern elements in Indian society even as it seeks to insinuate itself into the tribal frame of India through spurious devices. One such device is the Vananchal concept which it has presented patronisingly to the people it calls *vanvasis* (forest dwellers) in lieu of the *adivasi* demand for Jharkhand. It alienates itself from the numerically limited but nevertheless influential intelligentsia which stands by the secular and democratic values of the Indian State. Finally, the aggressive trader instincts of the protagonists of such neo-Hinduism put them into conflict with the working peasantry.

It is this last element which today stands in the way of the BJP. Laloo Yadav is not a historical accident. He represents the fundamental grass-roots secularism of the poor peasantry and he is historically and culturally bound to combat communalism. The AJGAR theorists who see politics only in terms of fortuitous combinations of caste configurations based on colonial census classifications miss that castes span a whole political-economic spectrum.

If today peasant castes, or even some sections of such castes, resist communalisation of politics, it is because they see traders as the "natural adversaries" of peasants. It is also because they feel uneasy with the unitary religion imposed from above when for centuries they have evolved their own indigenous, localised modes of worship in keeping with the peasant universe.

On the other side, the self-constraining *hindutva* of the BJP is aided by the similar self-restricting Sikh and Islamic fundamentalism. In the political arena this is reflected in violation of ideological pluralism and democratic practice. Booth capture in Bombay and violent lumpenism of the Shiv Sena are the obverse of terrorism in Punjab and Kashmir and the sword of Simranjit Singh Mann is complemented by the *trishul* of the Bajrang Dal.

Clearly, facile political sociology fails unless it is enriched by recourse to political economy. And, the political economy of India is such that its politics must of necessity be shaped by those engaged in production rather than those who live off distribution. Unfashionable as it might be today, the mode of understanding society in terms of production relations and ideological formations sustained by them, rather than through simplistic classification of ritual hierarchies, is still valid. A complex political reality cannot be captured by simplistic social analysis and action.

These are confused times the world over. In India too, the times are murky. They are the best of times as well as the worst of times. There have never been so many in this country who have had it so good. And there have never been so many for whom things are so dismally bad.

In this situation of cultural and economic contradiction there is need for sophisticated social analysis and complex conceptualisation. Instead, however, the Indian elite is marked by the complacence of simple-mindedness. It has discovered bliss in ignorance and solace in second-hand theorisation. Its smugness would elicit wonder if it did not cause profound disgust.

The characterising elements of the intellectual exertions of the Indian ruling elite in recent times have been obsessions with shopworn modernisation theories, discredited policies of privatisation and so-called liberalisation, recreation of packaged historical hype and assertion of an uninformed anti-Marxian idiom of banter popular in MaCarthite middle America of the 1950s. What started a few years ago as pragmatism has now become a sort of 'whateverism' which includes periodic professions couched in the familiar socialist rhetoric combined with denunciation of populism.

The contradictions within the actions and utterances of this group are obvious. In the Indian situation where neither growth nor distribution has been vigorous enough to engender hope among the hundreds of millions of the poor, it is precisely populism that has succeeded in providing some succour to them. It is also wrong to think either that populism has been the monopoly of non-Congress governments or even that it has necessarily stood in the way of production and productivity. Indeed, regarding the populist mid-day meal programme in Tamil Nadu in particular, its economic as well as electoral productive nature was realised by elite Congress-men almost as soon as they had made their blanket denunciation of populism.

It is clear that the acquaintance of today's precocious as well as gerentocratic politicians and of the dominant elite in general with the intricacies of the social philosophy and economic logic is limited. Smugness born of such ignorance can be counter-productive.

There are two serious aspects of a politics put in the care of this set of innocents and cynics. One is the need to map the lay of their mental make-up. The other is to examine the impact of this kind of political thinking on fundamental institutions in India.

The first task of establishing the geography of such imagination is not difficult. That much of this kind of political thinking has its cultural bearings in affluent America is obvious enough. It is the politics of personalised affluence, a politics of mental distancing from unpleasant realities. It is the politics of post-Vietnam, post-OPEC, resurgent America that sought prosperity in the Silicon Valley and glory in Grenada. In the Indian context, it is the politics of a set which sees the world through Cartier goggles and for whom the grass is greenest on the other side of the green card. In one sense it is not even the politics of the dominant class, but that of the dominant culture.

In India the determinants of this politics are not the considered self-interest of an enterprising capitalism basing the premise of its prosperity on the expansion of its markets. They are hardly premised on production and growth, far less on distribution. They devolve merely on short-sighted self-indulgence. The feudal order, such as it was, having been destroyed in India and capitalism not having been vigorous enough to create its own cultural mores, the determi-nants of the geography of the ruling political imagination lie in the mere assertion of power through pelf and of pelf through power. Edgar Allen Poe once wrote, "We have no aristocracy of blood, and having therefore as a natural, and indeed as an inevitable thing, fashioned for ourselves, an aristocracy of dollars, the *display of wealth* has here to take the place and perform the office of the heraldic display in monarchical countries". What this writer on the grotesque had to say on vigorous capitalist America is apt for today's India with the caveat that the aristocracy of the weakened rupee, flaunting walkie-talkies as heraldic devices, is a pathetic caricature rather than the natural and inevitable inheritor of the material culture of a capitalism unburdened by history.

It is interesting that unlike the intellectual influences that played on the predecessors of the present political set, the ideals which shape today's ruling processes of thought have little to do with concerns regarding the moral economy of Europe. Raja Rammohan Roy broke his leg scrambling up on the deck of his ship at Marseilles to salute the tricolour which symbolised the French Revolution's goals of liberty, equality and fraternity. Gandhi was influenced by the moral thinking of Tolstoy and Ruskin. Jawaharlal Nehru's dalliance with Fabianism was as important in his intellectual formation as the values of Soviet Russia which he experienced first-hand when he visited it ten years after the Russian revolution. In the case of all of them, the West mattered not in itself but in the throes of change. All of them were also rooted in India and their predominant concerns were native. For a part of their lives, they all lived outside India, but they did not become intellectual Non-Resident Indians.

In its quest of Vallahala today's ruling elite has gone beyond old, historical Europe to the not-so-New World. And its role model is the prosperous but philistine NRI.

The impact of this set on the obtaining political reality is a serious matter. It will disrupt what has existed without having the capacity to create something new. The post-colonial State has been based on a compromise, durable if uneasy. The composite nature of its culture is no cliche nor is the multiplicity of interests playing in its politics a mirage. All these are real, as real as the 150 to 200 million people today who are upwardly mobile and the remaining 500 million or more for whom time seems to have stopped.

The patchwork politics of this dualistic India has been made by various elements which have come together and stayed together through the accident of geography, the design of history and the practice of populist politics. The economic pattern of this patchwork has contained both the warp of capitalist modernisation and woof of peasant production. Its politics has had an essential, normal, even inevitable, element of populism which has reinforced such democracy as we have. The dominant political set-up today threatens to pull the populist thread which holds the Indian patchwork together.

This Indian patchwork has not been particularly beautiful. It has had definitely ugly patterns. But while its socialism has only been a weak pink, it has kept within its fold at least some elements of secularism and democracy. And populism of different varieties has provided the very seam by which the pattern has been provided its enduring quality. The new ruling elite is replacing the "real" content of that populism by mere cynical sloganeering.

The system that has obtained up to now has not been conducive to rapid change. To that extent there is certainly a rationale for treading a different track. The point is to determine which is the right direction to walk in. The movement from the twentieth to the twenty-first century is a temporal inevitability. What is not inevitable is who will reach it and in what condition.

Technology promoted by today's ruling set will by itself not produce miracles. In order to develop policies and a politics based on policies, it must be realised that in the end, it is the people who shape the world, bridging seas and moving mountains. And if in the calculations of the rulers, the people do not matter, if populism becomes a pejorative word, the whole geography of political imagination may undergo a change.

In today's India, politics in the narrow sense of concern with the instruments of governance and their use and misuse so obsesses the public mind that political economy, which in the ultimate analysis is the essence of politics, languishes among the cinders like a poor cousin. Scandals, kickbacks, pay-offs, defections, defamation, ships, shoes and sealing wax, cabbages and kings dominate public discussion and larger issues concerning the people of India go by default.

The responsibility for this state of affairs is by no means only that of politicians. They are naturally engrossed with matters which affect them and their power. However even others who should be concerned with progress are not looking forward in a consistent manner. And, nowhere is this obsession with the immediate so marked as in the case of discussion on political economy.

Gone are the days when furious debates would rage on the nature of the mixed economy, planning and industrial modernisation. Today, phrases like commanding heights, basic industries, socialistic pattern and so on have been robbed of their meaning and are mere cliches which can be temporarily resuscitated to only ephemeral recall of a bygone era. The occasional ramblings of "Neanderthal Nehruites" on the public sector provoke some tired rejoinders from the old faithfuls but for all practical purposes, the State sector industries have reached a venerable bovinity which makes them holy cows, but of the aging variety which have to scrounge their living off the streets.

Agrarian modernisation also seems to have gone the way of all flesh. Rigor mortis affected land reforms long ago but even the Green Revolution has started turning brown at the edges. Large irrigation and hydroelectric works have proved to have been not unmixed blessings from 'the temples of modern India' and poverty has become *passe*. Its mention is mandatory but only in the context of serving as a warning against political unrest if the "safety net" strategy proves too weak.

In terms of economic policy, planning and analysis, a certain ennui which has developed is the consequence of the souring of old dreams, the limited effects of cynical manipulation of popular urges and the limits reached by theory in analysing a largely stagnant situation. Among professional political economists in India, after the 'mode of production' debate wound its weary way to the intellectual cul de sac, there were only sparks of interest ignited by the friction with feminism and an occasional brush with monetarism. For the rest, economics got back to the grind of empirical investigation of well-known realities. Counting tube-wells might have replaced counting heads but neither is intellectually less soporific than counting sheep. As numbers and measurement became the principal preoccupation of such professionals, econometrics rather than political economy became the name of the game.

But it is not only professional economists who have got mired in the depths of computations and calculations whose net result seems merely to point the way to the moribund Yojana Bhawan and the self-important North Block where both physical and mental architecture has the sturdiness of granite. The policy-makers too are deep into a coma of economics of consensus where *swadeshi* is most definitely a foreign if not, a four-letter word. It is not that such ideas as manage to come out of the edifices of economic management are by any means xenophobic; indeed, they proudly strut about in the borrowed clothes of Thatcherism, liberalisation, privatisation, the information age and service economy, but in the offices of the financial mandarins there is no child innocent enough to point out that these clothes are tattered and their colours are false in the light of the Indian sun.

Yet such is the weight of the economic consensus that obtains in India today that the catchwords of the West are adopted unthinkingly as a newspeak whose political import is incomprehensible to those who use it and economic meaning is obscure for those on whom it is used. What is the essential character of this economic consensus? It does stand for liberalisation, but it is only liberalisation of imports and expansion of the scope of operation for those whose elbows are strong enough to edge out others. And, not only borrowed ideas but even borrowed money sustains this ideology of 'import-led growth' which is premised on the simple-minded belief that things will go better with Pepsi Cola.

The dominant economic consensus today stands for privatisation, but its thrust is only at the privatisation of relatively minor public services and not of significant production activities which continue under State or non-State monopolistic control. It tries to keep pace with the world as it strides into the age of information, but it does so with mincing little footsteps of discrete personal computers which are mere bureaucratic status symbols, like air-conditioners, than sharp-edged weapons with the capacity to slice through the red-tape government whose very existence is premised on control over information.

It proudly announces the immense growth of the service sector whose contribution to the national income now out-weighs that of agriculture, but it ignores the share in the third sector of the bureaucracy and defence, both gargantuan and unproductive enterprises in the Indian economic context. It does not take into account that in terms of impact on production, productivity and growth, the tertiary sector in India is a third-rate sector without the knack of the NICs (newly industrialised countries) to galvanise the economy through application, if not development of technology. Some years ago, Andre Gunder Frank spoke of the lumpen bourgeoisie in Latin America. The nature of emergent Indian capitalism based on smuggling and speculation, on primitive accumulation and conspicuous consumption would astound the most cynical observer of lumpen development.

Nevertheless, in spite of the obvious limitations and consequent instability of the system, there is a consensus on these courses of development and the consensus pervades diverse political groupings. There is no need for the Swatantra Party today for elements of its policy can be seen to operate even in the CPM.

Such is the overwhelming concern with providing efficient services which are assumed to be available only privately and the vision of "the good life" to the burgeoning bourgeoisie, petty or otherwise, that much effort is spent on calculating the numbers of this special client group. It has been estimated to be anything between 100 to 300 million, no mean demographic entity, and no effort is being spared to woo this class.

Expand the 'middle class'. Inflate the third sector. Separate the proletariat from the poor. Finance this enterprise if necessary with borrowings from abroad. Intensify consumerism. These are the elements of the prevailing economic consensus.

That the policy implications of this economic outlook are broadly shared is obvious by the very lack of the kind of critical examination that marked discussion on earlier plans and programmes. Dissent is only regarding the shares of the cakes baked by the IMF and the World Bank, not about the need to restructure the cake economy to one where bread is considered more important. Thus, the Tweedledum of the Congress and the Tweedledee of the opposition are clones in the sphere of economic policy and they are left to vocalise their differences only on the nebulous issues of morality, probity and grand political schema. Even populism, the life-blood of electoral democracy, it seems, is only for the south Indian movie-stars turned leaders.

All this would perhaps be very nice and comfortable had India been a country of only about 300 million. However, the fact is that there are another 500 million people peering into the grand feast of the growing middle class. The dominant economic paradigm does not take into account the fact that the Indian economy is not so provided as to live with the luxury of continuing under-utilisation of manpower and natural resources.

Most alarmingly, the realisation is still to grip the economic policy-makers that the chickens of import liberalisation hatched under the warmth of international credit are coming home to roost on the dangerous debt-trap. It is not that there are no ways out of falling into this economic death-trap. But in order to find those ways, the blinkers of pseudo-politics must be removed. If regaining old paradigms does not help, new ones must be built with political-economic imagination and concern for the Indian people, beyond the simplistic consensus that seems to so deeply cover India today.

And yet, if one looks closely, it is clear that the consensus is only a surface phenomenon. In fact the present phase of Indian politics is one in which the fundamental consensus that obtained has been badly fractured. It will not be easy for the body politic to recover from this trauma.

Despite changes in form, a basic continuity in post-colonial Indian parliamentary politics has been maintained through the strands of pluralism, populism, secularism and social democracy. Today, that fundamental feature is in danger. Even as there is a superficial attempt to evolve unified positions on major national issues, society itself has become dangerously fragmented.

The dangers to economic nationalism are compounded by the fissures that have appeared in society. The increasing communalisation is matched by the aggressive assertion of other types of group identity. The prospering Patels of Gujarat who have switched their mode of interaction with the Harijan and *adivasi* agricultural labourers from one of patronage and exploitation twenty-five years ago to one of sheer exploitation based on an unadulterated cash nexus can now scarcely be expected to abide by a social consensus. Similarly, the assertion of the rich peasants-intermediate castes in other parts of India can only revive the spectre of the 20-Point toll that marked the 'Harijan-hunting' season, beginning from Belchhi in Bihar, which was unleashed under Janata rule during

1977-79. This is surely an indicator of the serious whittling down of the populist content of politics, an essential element of the political consensus that has prevailed since Independence.

This populism is not something to be trifled with. In a country where hundreds of million people are poor and are being pushed to the margins of survival, it is populism that has served to prevent large-scale calamities. And it is a combination of populism with social democracy, the other important ingredient of the Indian political economy, that has not only given the poor an insurance against famines and mass starvation, as Amartya Kumar Sen has demonstrated, but has indeed strengthened the very basis of India itself. It is not for nothing that today when communist regimes have collapsed like ninepins in Europe, the social democratic practice of Indian communism enables it to withstand the blow and indeed consolidate its hold. In India, if the erstwhile feudal Western parts are turning saffron, the East continues to be, if not red, decidedly pink. And curiously it is there that the populist, pluralist consensus is being maintained.

At the same time, in the context of India's electoral democracy with its inevitable populist content, it is also necessary to note and contest the obtaining myths about block voting by identified minorities.

One of the myths which inform the hocus pocus practised by "poll pundits" under the cover of psephology is that Indian minorities vote as a block. So deeply has the myth taken root, not only among analysts but even among political establishments, that many electoral stratagems are premised on this assumption.

Indeed, the pernicious nature of this belief is at the heart of the sorry fact of Indian political life that the road to the polls is often paved with violent communal and caste incidents engineered with the intent of either garnering the supposedly homogeneous block vote of the minorities or consolidating the votes of the majority community. In either case, there is cynical play with the minority or the majority cards.

The problem with building electoral houses of cards, however, is that they are apt to collapse. Nevertheless, in the meanwhile, on account of the material force that even incorrect ideas acquire, they do immense damage to both innocent people and the nation at large.

Serious analysis requires the raising of many questions in this context. There are three which are most important. First, who instigates election-oriented communal conflagrations? Second, who is likely to reap electoral benefits, if any? And third, are the underlying assumptions of block voting, which such a cynical and cruel calculation implies, at all correct? In other words, is there evidence to suggest block voting by minorities?

A myth repeated many times seems to acquire the characteristics of a truism. However, not all "self-evident propositions" are necessarily true. The one related to minority block voting is one such. Anyone who is in the least familiar with election data should not make such an assumption.

Analysts of voting behaviour go wrong on block franchise and vote banks because they carry out political election analysis in isolation from an understanding of the historical sociological characteristics of different Indian communities.

It is simplistic in the extreme to see Indian Muslims, for instance, as one homogeneous group. A long time ago Daniel Thorner (1976) had divided the Indian population into three types: *malik, kisan, mazdoor*. The division is as applicable to Muslims as to Hindus. Only the naive or the disingenuous will ignore the differences between the peasant-type Muslims of rural western UP rooted in the soil, indistinguishable in many respects from their Hindu *Jat* and *Gujjar* brethren, and the relatively more urbanised *malik*-type sophisticates of Aligarh and Lucknow. As regard the former, since it is their *kisan* characteristic that is most significant in defining their social group personality, it is almost axiomatic that their political behaviour should follow peasant preferences rather than be determined by calls of religion. Some recent events like the Kisan agitation led by Chaudhry Mahendra Singh Tikait and the several Gujjar gatherings commandeered by Rajesh Pilot have made it clear that these are supra-religious occurrences. If that is true and if the idea of the AJGAR (*Ahir-Jat-Gujjar-Rajput*) vote block is also valid, then quite obviously, there is no such thing as a specifically Muslim vote bank.

The differences between the *kisan* Muslims of western UP, the urban *malik*-type Muslims of Aligarh, Lucknow, etc., and the predominantly *julaha*-Ansari impoverished handicraftsmen-turned-poor peasant *mazdoor*-type Muslims of eastern UP and Bihar are so deeply sociological and economic that they transcend relatively transient electoral concerns.

In any event, the myth of homogeneity and uniform political block voting is accepted only by those who wilfully close their eyes to facts like the disparate record of the voting by Muslims even in the relatively small electoral arena of West Bengal. There, while Malda Muslims vote one way, Murshidabad Muslims vote differently. In Greater Calcutta itself, there are constituencies with a substantial Muslim presence which have gone to the Congress or to the CPM quite against the prevailing *hawa* in the state and the country.

Evidence of contradictory patterns of Muslim voting, election after election, in Secunderbad and elsewhere in Andhra Pradesh, in Malabar and elsewhere in Kerala, in the Konkan and other parts of Maharashtra, should burst the psephological bubble of block voting. The fact is that whatever the extent of religious passions, one of the successes of Indian democracy is that elections are no longer apocalyptic events. They have become routine exercises in the day-to-day politics of India. As such, it is the concern with day-to-day issues that determines voting patterns. Elections are more an articulation of feelings about the price of sugar rather than of thoughts about pies in the sky.

The structure of everyday life of contemporary India has engendered its own temporality even to the point of diluting the country's much vaunted "spiritualism". In the process, it has also created its own living secularism which is not a reflection of a grand ideal but of mundane reality. A Muslim today approaches the edifices of power not as a religious being but as any other supplicant and, if in Kishanganj, he votes for Syed Shahabuddin, it is not because of edicts of the *shariat* but because of the price of jute. The political and in particular electoral expression of this is in terms of secular "class" or even "casteist" behaviour.

The pricking of the bubble of block voting by minorities, however, brings us back to the other questions we posed earlier. Who initiates pre-election communal violence and who is likely to gain from it?

The answers lie in the fragmented nature of Indian politics. Just as the fragmented nature of minority voting has been deliberately brushed under the carpet by electoral strategists, so the fragmented nature of the vicious communal politics of the country is often sought to be obscured by recourse to stereotypes.

In today's India, it is clear that playing the Hindu card is not the monopoly of the RSS or BJP alone, but indeed is prevalent among almost all parties, particularly those who style themselves 'centrist'. Neither the Congress nor the Janata Dal has given evidence of being able to resist the temptation of playing communal politics for short-term gains. Worse, the internally fragmented nature of these political formations has so personalised power centres that political strategy has passed beyond being a party matter to one determined by factions, groups and even individuals.

Who then instigates pre-election communal violence? For the moment, all that needs to be said is that the pattern of recent violence indicates a change in the old communal map of India. New centres of conflagration like Kota and Sasaram have emerged, along with "chronic sites" like Ahmedabad or Jamshedpur. Undoubtedly, the invocation of the symbolism of the old-new mobilisation, for example the passing around of bricks by resurgent Hindu groups, in a manner reminiscent of the circulation of *rotis* before the great revolt of 1857, is stoking communal fires. But the very pattern of communal violence affecting "new" areas indicates a certain decentralisation of communal electoral politicking by local-level "warlords" of both 'centrist' formations trying to consolidate their own positions by raising "we-them" dichotomies. These however tend to grow so monstrously that they negate democracy itself, for, after all, democracy—howsoever imperfect it might be—is governance by the *whole* people.

Bertolt Brecht, the German anti-fascist writer, once talked of the desire of faint-hearted democrats to abolish the people and elect another one instead. The events in India in the last few years make politicians seem as if they warrant the same lament. Leaders who swear by republican values have shown immense reluctance to face the people and seek a mandate from them. All kinds of schemes and stratagems, plots and permutations have been worked out merely to avert or subvert elections. That the people have not actually been abolished is no thanks to such leaders.

The fact is that democracy is the only viable system that can preserve the Indian entity, constitute its whole beyond the sum of the various fragments that go into its making and promote its invaluable genius of stumbling along towards a humane order. If democracy is done away with, India itself will sink in the morass of the various particularities that constitute it. Universal adult franchise and a periodic renewal of the popular mandate obtained by the government are the *sine qua non* of democracy and hence of India's integrity.

There is a tendency expressed once again in today's unipolar world that democracy is a drag on speedy growth and that susceptibilities of politicians to pander to popular sentiments in the less fortunate countries are, therefore, to be discouraged. The US, leader of what was formerly referred to with pride as the "free and democratic world" has, for instance, often supported non-democratic and even anti-democratic governments in the interest of its economy. In such a circumstance, the argument that has been advanced is that ideology is irrelevant when economic interests are involved. If ideology is accepted to be an extravagant indulgence, democracy too can become dispensable.

The unfortunate part is that, for reasons of their own, many Indian political leaders too are discounting democracy at home. Their own fears of the electorate make them appear as reluctant sacrificial goats being dragged to the altar of elections rather than representatives of the people eager to seek the legitimacy of a popular mandate. Such subversion of democracy and negation of republicanism acquire dangerous overtones in an international context where the call is to exchange values for the fruits of pragmatism.

Hard-headed "realists", who are constantly urging the abandonment of irritating "domestic compulsions" which might find electoral articulation, point to examples and instances of the costs of idealism in a world which is determined by the lure of the green card, the power of the greenback and the might of the green beret. They advance a cruel, but no doubt effectively realistic, expression of pragmatism by citing the behaviour of the UN secretary-general himself: the story goes that every time a flight of ideological fancy about equality of nations overtakes him, he looks at the portraits of his predecessors in his office and comes down to earth because the alternative, he recalls, is to be brought down like the unfortunate

Dag Hammerskjoeld.

The combination of domestic pusillanimity about elections and international pressure to ignore "domestic compulsions" regarding the popular will forebodes ill for democracy. And, as argued earlier, it also casts a long and ominous shadow over the very future of India as an integrated nation and polity.

There are pressures enough on India today. The economic crisis brought on by decades of profligacy, the political strains on account of centrifugal forces aided and abetted by interested outsiders, the domestic tensions of regional disparity and social heterogeneity expressed in ethnic and caste terms are all reflected in a class configuration in which one-third of Indians are below the poverty line, another one-third or so float above the consumerist Plimsoll mark and the rest provide the ballast to hold the Indian ship of State steady on turbulent waters. In this precarious situation, the pluralism of India is only transcended by the articulation of a national popular will. Now it is that popular will which its selfish politicians are seeking to suppress.

An argument used by such self-seeking advocates of surreptitious fascism is that elections do not necessarily clear the political air: the outcome of the Tenth General Election is once again a hung Parliament. Their logic is seriously flawed. They ignore that democracy and uncertainty in electoral verdict are not necessarily opposed to each other. Indeed, political fluidity is best expressed, and stabilised, only through democratic processes. The cases of the French third and fourth republics, of Italian democracy and remarkable economic growth, of the inherent fluidity of proportional representation in the deeply democratic and stable systems of north European countries are all forgotten by those who posit pragmatism against principles.

Most of all, the fallacies of those who fear democracy in their march towards the autocratic economic El Dorado arise out of not taking into account the experiences of those in South America and elsewhere who sacrified democracy for growth and ended up with neither. They turn a blind eye to the sorry pass that the former Soviet Union and other East European countries have been brought to by ignoring "domestic compulsions", dismantling existing structures, in a fit of absent-minded *perestroika*, without simultaneously being able to replace them with other viable systems based on the bedrock of democracy.

Finally, they also ignore that, regardless of their wishes and prescriptions, the fact is that India has already entered into a new republican phase.

By the time India went to the polls even in 1989, it was becoming clear that the political-economic scene itself was changing with many more regional, ethnic, caste, class formations finding electoral articulation. Veritably, the people created a "new republic", one with an uncertain mandate, with ample political fluidity, with novel checks and balances. It was not done with the deliberation with which the founding fathers of democratic India "adopted, enacted and gave to ourselves" a written Constitution on 26 November 1949. Indeed, the process was much more nebulous: the Constitution of the "new republic" evolved, as indeed all constitutions of all democracies must.

The differences between the fundamental aspects of Indian and European constitutional evolution are revealed by the archaeology of ideas. The former is still premised on the first-past-the-post voting system whereas the latter has the greater flexibility of proportional representation. Nevertheless, the similarity is also apparent: both provide for the accommodation of particularities and specificities within the edifice of democracy. Both also aim at growth with equity, adding the important caveat of "social" to their democracy. Neither can brush aside "domestic compulsions" whatever they may be, neither the Europeans who have to listen to even their inefficient farmers propped up by bloated subsidies nor the Indians who have to shape their policies and their nation in keeping with the inevitable but altogether desirable inefficiencies of democratic pluralism.

Democracy does carry a price but the price is not an extravagance as is implied by the recent ideologies of pragmatism.

One of the boasts of Mussolini and Ayub Khan was that when they did away with democracy, trains ran on time. The price of democracy can be more than the unpunctuality of the railways : it includes the costs of elections, the uncertainties of political fortunes, the fuzziness of policies, the compromises between contending interests and moderation of the State through the influence of various groups of the people. Such a system may not ensure strict adherence to the railway timetable. Nevertheless, it holds people together and provides them pride of cultural ancestry and hope of equitable prosperity.

If such a democracy is forsaken, the choice is in fact to elect another people. But then it will not be "We, the people of India".

Now when politics is again floundering between the Scylla of religious obscurantist fundamentalism and the Charybdis of pseudo-modernist imported marketist models, the need for the republican vision is more apparent than ever before.

Today, the country is objectively moving to the appropriate locus of its politics: the twilight zone between town and country, between the oppressiveness of the State and the anarchic inegalitarianism of uncivil society, between ideological fanaticism and unprincipled pragmatism. India itself is discovering that it is mofussil.

In this self-discovery, it is aided on the one side by the sanctimonious and yet stern pressure exerted by the imperialist West which has never been easy with Indian distinctiveness. The self-discovery of India is also assisted, on the other side, by the exposure of its own ugly underbelly of violence, strife, exploitation, philistinism and vulgarity.

Republican India today is confronted by the choice between liquidationists on the one side and disruptionists on the other. There are those who in the name of liberty undermine equality and there are others who have no use for fraternity. The first cave in when the slightest gust of the Westerly wind touches them. The second want to carry on governance by abolishing the people themselves.

There is a curious complementarity between the two. One would fragment India's geography. The other would tear apart its history. One would allow the redefinition of its boundaries on the lines of religion, as in 1947. The other wants to redraw its cultural boundaries, also on the basis of religion. The common thread between the two is manufactured and manipulated religiosity.

Fortunately for India, the secular paradigm is deeply rooted in the very psyche of its ordinary citizen and the humdrum structures of his everyday life. For all the ritualism he practises, religious bigotry is still artificial and alien to the ordinary Indian. His very existence is premised on syncretism and philosophical vagueness.

There is a delightful confusion that informs his being and sharp boundaries cause him discomfort.

It is on this basis and on the basis of an essential materialism of those who have to struggle for sheer survival that republicanism stands in India. However, since Indian society, economy and polity are all in the throes of change, the future itself is uncertain and unpredictable although the process of change itself has been evident for a long time.

It can be argued that the processes of change that shape India today had at least a symbolic start in May 1964 with the passing away from the political scene of Jawaharlal Nehru. With him also passed away pre-Independence nationalistic idealism and *realpolitik* came to reign supreme. Till then, barring the "unpleasantness" epitomised by the Telengana uprising, occasional communal conflagrations and the traumatic war with China, the country had basked in the glow of optimism. India had become free, and the great drive for modernisation had been launched. The first five-year plan had focused on agriculture, the second on building the great infrastructural and industrial temples of modern India. Production had increased dramatically, productivity had looked up after centuries and even per capita income had crawled forward. There was pride in the new-found sense of the nationhood and if the ugly scars of the Partition of India still festered, there was enough salve for the national ego in Bandung and Belgrade. In all, it seemed to be the best of times for India in the best of all possible worlds.

The complacence got rudely shattered in the mid-1960s. Even earlier, absolute shortage of food had started making itself felt and then, as now, imports had begun on the grounds of building up buffer stocks. It was the drought and famine in 1966-67 which made well-laid plans to go awry. Starvation in Bihar and food riots in Bengal marked the plan holiday from 1966-67 to 1968-69. A war with Pakistan made further dents on an economy seriously affected by the pressures of enhanced defence spending brought on after the conflict with China.

A finance minister, Sachin Chaudhry (not to be confused with the founder-editor of *Economic Weekly*) emerged from obscurity, was instrumental in devaluation of the rupee in June 1966, and disappeared into oblivion. Various syndicates, cabals and kitchen cabinets emerged during the period as parasitic growths on the body politic. Different policies pursued by them did not prevent the country from going into a phase of industrial recession which dealt a *coup de grace* on the relatively old engineering industry of eastern India and unleashed a turmoil in industrial relations epitomised by the *gherao* phenomenon.

It is interesting to note that the pedigree of the government's new economic policy includes the thoughts of former members of the Praja Socialist Party like Asoka Mehta who wanted India "to open her womb to foreign investments". At that time too there existed a strong lobby promoting the entry of foreign capital, import-led and export-oriented growth aided by devaluation of the rupee and drastic curtailment of public sector expenditure in the name of restoring macro-economic balance. Taking advantage of unsettled political conditions and a relatively weak government at the Centre, the lobby succeeded in some of its attempts. The rupee was drastically devalued. The public sector in general, and the railways in particular, cut expenditure. The result was an economic disaster.

The cut in public sector investment resulted in a sharp recession. The devaluation of the rupee did not substantially aid exports but it made imports immensely more costly. And it took the country years to recover from the technological and industrial stagnation that ensued.

In the mid-1970s too, the concept of export-led growth was revived during the Emergency, and the "Brazilian model" was touted vigorously. The "softness" of the Indian State was held responsible for the inability to take "hard decisions". Some hard decisions did in fact get taken and export-oriented industries, like garments and diamond-polishing, which meant cashing in on sweated Indian labour, came to constitute the bulk of India's exports. However, India was not able to attract foreign investment meaningful in terms of quality and quantity. The "soft state" could not become hard enough to suit the MNCs. Nevertheless, the plight of Brazil should in hindsight demonstrate the virtue of "softness" and cultivation of a vast domestic market through increasing the purchasing power of the people rather than chasing the mirage of the exporters' El Dorado. The familiarity of today's rhetoric is scaring.

Meanwhile the situation has grown much more serious on

account of the prominence of two relatively recent phenomena: the Non-Resident Indian (NRI) and the resident Indian yuppie. The value systems of both have put enormous strains on the polity and very identity of India. And yet, such is the cultural hegemony attached to them that much of India's economic policy has been geared to satisfy them and its political practice has been premised on a significant role to be played by them overtly or covertly.

As the economy has proceeded convulsively from one crisis to another, a myth has been built up that some day from across the seas will arrive India's prodigal sons, the Non-Resident Indians (NRIs), bearing unlimited quantities of dollars and pounds which will serve to infuse new life-blood into this country's aged arteries. Eager messengers in the shape of different chief ministers went abroad to extend cordial invitations to the NRIs. Finance minister after finance minister prepared policies and projects and launched schemes and bonds to lure them into the Indian industrial web. As in the parable of the prodigal son, the fattened calf was made ready for the one who had gone away.

The NRIs did respond to these inducements. They came but, taking only one element of the parable literally, they concerned themselves with the fattened calf alone and India was left crying for them again. In spite of all the incentives offered to the NRIs, direct investment by NRIs on both repatriable and non-repatriable basis was tiny; portfolio investment amounted to a negligible sum; invest-ment in national savings certificates added up to even less crores and company deposits remained miserably small. An overwhelmingly large part of the total inflow of funds on account of various NRI schemes was in the form of bank deposits. The fly had obviously declined the invitation to step into the spider's economic parlour through the door at which the welcome mat of legitimacy had been spread. At the same time, it was also demonstrated that these were "fair-weather deposits." As soon as the balance of payments crisis manifested itself in 1991, there was a run on NRI accounts. This intensified the balance of payments crisis.

And yet, the NRI is by no means absent in India's economic scenario. Corporate takeover, financial buccaneering, free flow of consumer items through legitimate and not so legitimate channels of import, the staggering volume of gold and guns brought into the country and now the remote-controlled street-warfare in Bombay are all evidence of the ubiquitous NRI. Indeed, it is this element of the NRI operations, adventurous but arrogant, fiscal but also parasitical, that has come to characterise the Non-Resident Indian. And while it is an image that does little to justify economic optimism regarding possibilities of net productive investments, in the social and cultural spheres it has an impact strong enough to set the role models for a whole generation of a particular class of Indians.

The desire to get the hell out of stagnating India has characterised a large segment of the educated and qualified Indians for some time now. After all, it was the lemming-like Westward rush of the alumni of the country's various medical, engineering and management institutions that brought in the term brain drain into the lexicon of the 1960s.

It is not that Indians had not migrated before that. Way back in the hoary past, when the very concept of India was still being shaped, waves of Indian colonisers rode the seas to South-east Asia and elsewhere. Later too, intrepid merchants, missionaries and even soldiers-of-fortune had made their weary way out of India. By and large, they had merged into the population of the countries they inhabited and their particular mark was in elements of a cultural tradition rather than racial memory. However, in the nineteenth century a qualitatively new type of out-migration took the Indian diaspora to distant lands where compulsions of economic status as well as political considerations forced them to retain some sort of an ethnic Indian identity (Tinker 1974). Nevertheless, for the indentured labour that was taken from India to the Caribbeans, Fiji, Mauritius and other parts of the world, links with India were so severed that what mattered for more than a century was only their immediate identity of toilers labouring for a capitalism whose by-then aroused liberalism had made it look for surrogates for slaves. From Guyana to Fiji, from Surinam to South Africa, there were ethnic Indians whose external identity as well as a substantial part of self-image was limited to *coolies*.

At the other end of the economic spectrum too there were migrants from India. In England, resident princes and maharajas provided ethnic colour. In different parts of Europe and North America too there was a scattering of other Indians. The most notable among the expatriate Indians were men like Dadabhai Naoroji and Shapurji Shaklatvala who even became members of the House of Commons, the latter as the first communist to enter the mother of parliaments. But none of these, nor for that matter the hundreds of others who played prominent roles in both India as well as the countries of their residence, considered themselves non-resident Indians. They were either full Indians, for good or bad, or at worst, like the latter-day Nirad Chaudhury westerners in terms of mental processes if not by birth, or like M.N. Roy, citizens of the world.

Mohandas Karamchand Gandhi was perhaps the first conscious NRI. During his sojourn in England, his autobiography makes it clear, he was so absorbed in his own concerns that he hardly noticed anything English. Later, in South Africa he blossomed as a political leader of the Indian community but his eye was on India and its preoccupation with colonialism rather than on the fight against apartheid. He was non-resident but he was, above all, Indian. And when he returned to India, he came back for good.

It was during the latter part of colonial rule and even more in the early post-colonial years that there was a large migration of sections of the Indian professional elite to the West. And for a long time the West meant Britain. Indian traders and merchants had gone to East Africa and farmers had migrated to North America but it was England which was still the Mecca for the English-speaking Indian elite. The decline of the British economy, growing insularity and vicious racism that raised its head proved to be some disincentives to potential migrants but for many in the Indian elite whose minds were shaped by images of the 'mother country', the lure of Britannia continued to be strong.

Meanwhile, in a changing world, other pastures opened up. Australia beckoned Anglo-Indians; U.S.A. was the land of opportunity for enterprising Indian professionals and businessmen and the gushing black gold in the Gulf in the seventies summoned Indian labourers as well as entrepreneurs. Lately, there has even been a move towards Japan, the land of the rising yen.

And it has been in this period, particularly in the last two decades, that the persona of the NRI has found shape. He is entrepreneurial, aggressive and upwardly mobile. He seeks oppor-

tunity and grasps initiative. He is bold but he is also a bit brash. He
has both style and sleaziness. For the Indian who is resident in the
old country, he is both a dream and a nightmare. The prodigal son
had gone and India pined for him; now he threatens to come back but
on his own terms and the Johnny-stay-at-home feels uneasy.

Indians, unlike the Chinese, never had a concept of extended
nationality. Indeed, nationality itself has been defined in India
juridically rather than culturally or ethnically. Thus, it is not easy to
come to terms with a whole set of relatively rich people who claim
the privileges of that nationality, and more, without the disadvan-
tages of residence within its boundaries. For the Indian, since
nationality is determined by law rather than by ethnicity, patriotism
seldom extends to identification with India's people, and is at best
determined by residence within its geographical boundaries. The
very social and cultural segmentation of Indian society fragments
patriotism and permanent residence outside its legally determined
boundary almost inevitably leads to a traumatic severing of the
politico-legal identity of being Indian. In many cases, the substance
of this trauma even takes a ritual form: the renunciation of the legal
symbol of Indianness — the passport.

To expect hard currency patriotism from such expatriates is
illogical, unreal and in fact a contradiction in terms. Since nationalism itself is a recent construct in the Indian context, unlike for the
overseas Chinese in whose case it is based on organic ethnicity, and
the compartmentalisation of Indian society into discrete segments
on the basis of ritual and other hierarchies prevents broad social
identities from taking shape, the search of the Indian, resident or
non-resident, for roots does not go very deep. And in such a case
when patriotism and profit are weighed against each other, it is the
latter which swings the scales.

What has impelled the assumption of the NRI identity by a
segment of the Indian elite is the search for maximisation of
opportunity, professional, cultural and, most of all, economic. It has
decided that the grass is greener on the other side of the green card.
And, if the logic that informs its principal action is that of maximisation
of opportunity, obviously outside the realm of possibility in India,
the same logic will motivate it to invest not in poor, bureaucratic,
hamstrung India but in areas and spheres where returns are higher.

Liechenstein and Luxembourg, the Channel Isles and Bahamas, even Panama and the Isle of Man hold much greater promise than India. The bulk of money will continue to be located there and only speculative capital will come to India for short-term gains. It is the logic of the very identity of the NRI that makes his capital predatory.

In the context of the NRI's relationship with India, matters are further complicated by the logic of the Indian economy itself as it has developed over the years. The extent of the black economy on the one side and the needs imposed by a regulatory mechanism determining economic activity for 'white money' on the other have given a particular position to the NRI in the present context. It is well-known that while on the aggregate India is a poor country, there are a very large number of rich Indians and a substantial number of very rich Indians. Quite naturally such Indians would like to get richer and also in the bargain acquire or enhance their social respectability. What stands in their way, however, is that in the India of lumpen capitalism and bureaucratic red tapism, their initial capital is often not clean enough to find legitimate avenues of growth. The laundry industry therefore, acquires an importance far greater than would be warranted by usual circumstances. And there the NRI plays the *dhobi* role by facilitating *hawala* transactions and becoming the intermediary in various currency and bullion-based amnesty schemes.

As early as 1987, Vasant Sathe, the then Union energy minister, mooted a proposal for tapping black funds from abroad for channelising into investments in the core sector of the economy. He calculated that at that time there was at least Rs.50,000 crores of black money in India and no less than Rs.20,000 crores abroad. So he proposed issue of bonds to NRIs to facilitate them to bring in the black cash into India. In 1988 and 1991 such bonds were indeed issued and got reasonable subscription. But even at the time of their issue, there was skepticism about the productive investment of such money; what economic analysts thought more likely was that they would merely serve as instruments for recycling black money transferred from India through *hawala*.

Earlier, before the introduction of the bonds, the largest amounts of NRI funds came into foreign currency non-resident deposits (FCNR) which are repayable virtually on demand in the currency of deposit. Given this factor, it was surmised, not without reason, that at least a large portion of such deposits could well be "hot money", coming in and going out according to changes in the developed market economies rather than in India. And, as such the role of such money would hardly be to bolster the Indian economy in the long run. Notwithstanding this realisation, such is the scramble for attracting NRI money into India that by 1989 itself NRI deposits in non-resident external (NRE) accounts and FCNR accounts added up to the equivalent of the country's total foreign exchange reserves. The net result of this was the virtual mortgaging of India to NRIs whose playing with "hot money" made for a very uncertain fiscal scenario.

The implications of such "hot money" operations for industry in India have become obvious enough. Such mobile money cannot be locked up in investments where returns require long gestation periods. Hence it is unlikely that substantial NRI funds will be invested in new industries. They are more likely to be used in the predatory takeover of existing industries and, on account of their implicit hit-and-run nature, serve to milk those industries for the greater good only of those who control the flow of such funds. This is precisely what seems to be happening in the spurt of corporate takeovers by NRIs cornering controlling blocks of shares on account of the vast and liquid funds at their disposal. In effect what the NRI phenomenon has created is a repeat of the managing agency system which had led to disastrous consequences for Indian industry.

However, grim forebodings about the economic role of the NRIs have not cast a shadow on their social and cultural image. Indeed, more and more people want to emulate the NRI strategy as a whole or in part. This is true even in the realm of economics and finance as illustrated by the cases of leading Indian industrialists seeking to acquire NRI status and others confining themselves to the corporate takeover game rather than making fresh industrial investments.

The role model aspect of the NRI is even more dramatically evident in the social and political spheres. Till the mid-1970s, the role models for the elite were "foreign returned"; now they have become the "foreign settled". Earlier the expatriate Indian was symbolised by Krishna Menon or Hargobind Khorana. In due course, the image changed to that of Ravi Tikkoo. Then came Swaraj Paul followed by the Hinduja brothers. The Chhabarias and the

Ajitabh Bachchans followed almost inevitably and today one of the best known NRIs is Dawood Ibrahim. It is the logic of money itself in the concrete conditions of capitalism in India and the world that has led to this change.

And yet, the image of the NRI is strong enough to attract many aspiring young upwardly mobile Indians. Irritants at home combined with visions of the good life abroad, the lure of consumerism and the inherent inability of the pampered and weak Indian elite to face adversely, the low sense of patriotism on account of various socio-cultural historical factors and most of all the urge to make quick money impel many Indians out of its frontiers. It is after they have found their pots of gold at the end of the rainbow that they try to retrace their steps but only to seek another pot of gold at the original end of the rainbow which they had left earlier.

In the meanwhile, they spawn the stereotypical "yuppie", a set which even while resident in India, distances itself from "Indianness." Indeed, the evolution of the Indian yuppie should be an interesting matter for investigation for all those who are concerned about the weakening of patriotism. The yuppie has demonstrated that for it the market is much more important than the nation, a view that has quickly become a major element of the currently fashionable economic orthodoxy. It is the speed with which the ideology of yuppiedom has captured hegemonistic positions that is astounding, for the very phenomenon of the Indian yuppie is very recent.

In the beginning, not many years ago, there was the word. Indeed, in India there was only the word. A stagnant society could hardly have professionals who were mobile. In a situation where stability was the credo and security was the watchword, there was little scope for movement upwards or, for that matter, horizontally. And, as in a stagnant pool, what floated up was only the scum. In such a society, there was little dynamism, less professionalism and youth was at a discount. "Yuppies" (young upwardly mobile professionals) were therefore a mere notion, a label imported, like many others, from abroad.

The 1980s changed it all. By then the economy got into such a mode that it became possible for a breed of home-grown yuppies to exist and prosper in India itself. Both the growth of the economy itself as well as the structural dualism within it created conditions for this.

It was not as if there were no rich, Westernised oriental gentlemen (WOGs) before the arrival of yuppiedom in India. They did exist, but the difference was that, by and large, they were tied either to the processes of industrial manufacture or feudal agrarian surplus extraction. In both cases their fortunes were linked to production activities *per se*. There were others in the upper echelons of the service sector too, the bureaucratic *pucca sahibs* and the commercial *boxwallahs*, whose Anglophilic orientation impelled them to find role models outside India. But their numbers were limited, while both the weight of traditional culture as well as the constraints of the economy itself limited their dominance.

The systematic and continuous growth of the parallel, non-producing economy, the burgeoning of speculation as a get-rich-quick method even at the expense of long-gestation productive investment, the need for palm-greasers to make the licence-permit-quota machinery move, the emergence of marketing as a commercial mode superior to manufacture and the proliferation of a large set of professional consumers are all features which now characterise the Indian economy. And this has laid the ground for the flowering of the Indian yuppie.

Although these processes were taking place steadily but slowly even earlier, they reached a sort of take-off point in the 1980s. Indeed, if a date has to be set for the coming of age of the Indian yuppie, it can very conveniently be placed on 19 November 1982, the opening day of the Asian Games in Delhi.

In economic terms, the massive proliferation of the Indian yuppie is marked by the enormous expansion of the service sector in the years since Independence. Even as the share of material production in the total national income has been shrinking, the share of services has been rising inexorably. In the period 1951-56, as much as 60.5 per cent of the national output originated in agriculture, 24.4 per cent in industry and only 15.1 per cent in services.

By 1989-90, the picture was radically different. Only 33.1 per cent of national income comes from farm output, industrial production as a share of national income also remains almost stagnant having grown to only 27 per cent from 24.4, but services today account for a massive 39.9 per cent of the national income. While this shift also covers a very large number of the poor and not-so-well-off people in service activities, it is also an indicator of the presence of a substantial middle and upper-middle class of consumers. And, it is the consumerist character of this segment that characterises the Indian yuppie.

The Indian yuppie, like most Indian phenomena, is a complex being. Its eyes are oriented towards the consumerist societies of the West, but its feet are tied to the dead-weight of the poverty and scarcity-ridden Indian economy. Its professional skills are geared to the post-industrial, information age but its existence is limited by the continuation in many respects of even pre-metallic food production.

As such, the Indian yuppie cannot develop its own independent personality and has to depend on following role models located outside its own milieu. Ideally the Indian yuppie would not like to be Indian at all, but since the contingency of birth has made that inevitable, the Indian yuppie would, as a second best, like to be at the very least an NRI. It is only as a third and last choice that the Indian yuppie resides in India.

However, the value system of the Indian yuppie is determined by the NRI role model. Its constituents are making good in life so as to be able to indulge in consumeristic hedonism. But, after that urge is satisfied, the desire is to do good to the country, to change the fate of the poor blighters who make India what it is. Thus, after looking after himself, the typical yuppie also looks for causes to address in the larger interests of the poor and suffering people. The causes can range from, doing good deeds through foreign-funded non-governmental organisations, arousing the liberal conscience through various other measures and even engaging in the task of finding radical solutions for the country's ills in sophisticated and largely polite gatherings.

The existence in India of a large segment of the well-off, numbering about 200 million, almost equivalent to the population of Europe, has created a situation where there is variety even in yuppiedom. There are the "right" yuppies engaged in predatory takeovers and there are also the "left" yuppies who are looking for conscience on the cheap. If speculation is the watchword of the first lot, do-gooding is the cry of the second. If elements among the first lot hold up the picture of the jeans-clad, scotch-sipping "Gandhians", the Tilonia leather-bag-carrying second lot have equally bizarre symbols.

But the caricaturisation of social symbols on both sides of the political divide is not unexpected. In an era of the withering away of ideology, both designer capitalism and designer populism are bound to flourish. For the first, production is *passe*; the substance is in selling. For the second, mobilisation and struggle are outdated; profit lies in propaganda.

The Indian yuppie is both self-indulgent as well as unscrupulous. And, given the realities of India, it has to be so. On the one side it is a pampered lot living off the fat of the land; on the other it realises that it is an island in itself surrounded by the harsh and even cruel sea of poverty and dehumanisation. As such, the social space available for the operation of the alienated yuppie is under threat. And as actual politics, the stuff of which both elections and revolutions are made, catches up, the self-indulgence of the yuppie becomes unviable. The time comes then to again take into account the hurly-burly of popular existence and take recourse to populist rhetoric.

At the non-political, social level however, the Indian yuppie or even the aspiring yuppie has enough moral room in which to play. For it cynicism is purely individual and using issues and using people is only a matter of adoption of postures. If a posture fails, another can be put on with equal ease. Lumpen development is bound to create a lumpen bourgeoisie.

But politics is a different matter altogether. Politics in India outside the island of the 200 million cannot afford the self-indulgent, self-seeking, cynical, manipulative politics of the petulant Indian yuppie. In India, both material production and the ideology of equity still have an important role to play and this is evident from examining the impact of just two political developments which in the late 1960s themselves, before the NRIs and yuppies, changed India for ever.

There occurred two major events in 1967 which would have a lasting impact on politics in general. The first, affecting the apex of the power pyramid, marked the emergence of a new political alliance which demolished Congress rule in several states and struck such a body blow to the party that its character changed for ever. The second concerned the base of the Indian political economy and represented itself in the two contradictory phenomena of growth of commercial agriculture through the green revolution on the one side and agrarian unrest epitomised by the naxalite movement on the other.

To take the Congress first, the erosion of its mass base among the rural poor and middle classes, which became apparent on a large scale in 1967, put its leadership under tremendous pressure. And that had its consequences. Conflicting elements within the party reached criticality in 1969 and, in a chain reaction process, set off fission in the prime political institution of the Indian State. Electoral insecurity gave the Congress politics a certain neurotic quality from which it never recovered. The Congress had epitomised a consensual framework of politics as a game of inter-elite accommodation along with some commitment to incremental permeation of the benefits of development to the poor in general. These were given up for a structure of mere governance by exclusion and populist appeal by exercise of personal charisma. Lately even populist rhetoric fails to carry conviction.

On the other side of the ideological and political divide, 1967 also marked the reassertion of mass politics. The hollowness of the positive State vis-a-vis the poor in general and the rural dispossessed in particular was demonstrated not only by the fading ability of the Congress but also by the limited roles played by the incongruous entity which is unique to India, "opposition governments". Even the united front government in West Bengal which included leftists could not quickly meet the agrarian challenge. And the upshot was a flaring up of agrarian conflict in Naxalbari, marking the beginning of a new phase of political assertion by the rural poor.

The first manifestation of this politics was suppressed. Apart from repression used against the movement, there were many other causes of its fading away, not the least of which was the fallacious strategic and tactical thinking on the part of its leaders who turned a raging agrarian politics into a "Manickean simplification of modern warfare into a moral struggle between good and evil". But the issues that that movement raised did not die.

Arun Sinha (1991) and others have demonstrated that in fact the pro-change movement of the poor has gathered within its folds so many elements and forms of protest that today it can be characterised as being ranged against only a few. The basic agrarian issues of payment of adequate wages, abolition of bondage, distribution of land, security of habitat, preservation of the ecology, protection of the rights of women, etc. have been articulated through one major slogan woven around the affirmation of the dignity of the dispossessed. The result is that a movement has grown "beyond the fragments" and although organisationally there is still no unity, the idea has pervaded across different sections involved with the rural masses.

At the same time, the long-dormant industrial workers too are stirring themselves. The biggest industrial actions by workers in the world—the Bombay textile strike of 1981-83—had become a turning point in working class action. The almost continuous turbulence on the industrial front from the *gherao* movements of the 1960s through railway workers' agitations in the 1970s and the struggles of engineering sector workers in the late 1970s culminated in the massive strike in India's oldest industry in the beginning of the 1980s. For a variety of reasons— including the very nature of the industry, its growing technological obsolescence in the face of competition from the powerloom sector, the desire of the industrialists to close textile mills in order to profiteer from real estate speculation, the patently iniquitous labour management systems and industrial relations mechanisms, the inability of the trade union movement to cope with the many dimensions of the strike—the workers lost out. Many thousands were retrenched in the name of rationalisation, a large number of mills were closed and the trade union movement suffered a serious setback. In fact, textile workers outside Bombay too, in Ahmedabad, Coimbatore and other parts of the country and jute workers in Calcutta, were also subjected to the effects of industrial sickness leading to large-scale unemployment.

These factors compounded the inherent weaknesses of the trade union movement in reacting effectively to the changing techno-economic and socio-political situation. The urban-rural, formal-informal, adult-child, male-female segmentations of the working class were reflected in the organised-unorganised sector dichotomies. While a real "labour aristocracy" did not arise in India, there is no denying that trade unions were badly afflicted by economism.

The situation changed suddenly in the summer of 1991. The new economic policy took little account of the interests of workers who were threatened with an "exit policy". The trade unions were rudely awakened from their economistic slumber as politics suddenly came to the fore. Prospects of wide-scale unemployment, galloping inflation and even the threat to the right of free association into trade unions became political, democratic issues. And, the working class inched centre-stage in the democratic processes of redefining India.

Other issues too have come to the fore. Ecological concerns, issues relating to gender equity, ethnic upsurges, regional assertions—all these became important in the context of not only deciding on sustainable development and social equity but also in determining the very shape of India. It is increasingly being recognised that an unbalanced federal structure does not provide even political stability and certainly does not promote social equity. The over-centralisation of fiscal powers, for instance, has contributed to lopsided growth, uneven regional development as well as vastly increased red-tapism. It is not only entrepreneurs who have suffered on account of the licence-permit system but even whole states. It is interesting for instance to note that planning by the Centre does not have specific statutory sanction: social and political planning was included in the Constitution in the Concurrent List. However, the Centre arrogated that function to itself and in due course the Planning Commission, set up merely as an advisory body by the Centre, effectively superseded the National Development Council. The latter became merely an institution to provide *ex post facto* sanction to the decisions of the Planning Commission.

In many other respects too the federal character of India was subverted over time. Fiscal control, screening of important pieces of legislation, discriminatory policies with regard to various governmental functions and even outright subversion of elected state governments by the Centre have created grave federal disequilibrium. This puts the very existence of India in jeopardy.

Given all these factors, it should be obvious that there are very few alternatives for India. It can either disintegrate like the erstwhile Soviet Union or it can go through a situation as in the United States of America which is marked by a "secession of the successful" from the general public order. The dangers of the first are obvious enough. The second is more insidious as has been outlined by observers of the American scene who see in it the emergence of a new "caste system with the implications of utter social separation". They are in fact trying to envision what happens when 10 or 20 per cent of the population has enough income to bypass the social institutions it does not like. A simple example is the way that the fax, modem and Federal Express have already made the US postal service nearly irrelevant to the way some segments of American society communicate. A more portentous example is the mass exodus from State schools among urban elites. The Left has been complaining for years that the rich have too much power. They a'int seen nothing yet.

This secession of the successful from social and public institutions and formation of a parallel state system have grave implications for the very concept of nationhood. In the American context it treats the underclass as an analogue of the native Indian reservations—the original owners are dispossessed, subjected to genocide and the survivors are herded into enclaves of poverty and cultural degradation.

At least in part this recent phenomenon is a result of the artificially high monetary value of cognitive skills, meaning a combination of ability and training for complex mental work. This indeed is one of the major attributes of the age of information. It is easy to predict that in the coming years, the price of cognitive skills will skyrocket for reasons involving changes in technology (constantly getting more complex); politics (constantly creating more complicated regulations with more complicated loopholes); economy (constantly more one-sided, iniquitous and reflecting the selfishness of the rich); and the size of stakes (when a percentage point of the market share is worth millions then the people who can help get that extra percentage through legal or illegal manipulation are worth very large incomes). Meanwhile, real incomes for actual producers will increase slowly if at all, and efforts to increase those incomes artificially (by enforcing legally prescribed minimum wages or providing social security) will be cynically derided as "leftism" or, even worse, "liberalism".

If an emergent caste system scares perceptive American "conservatives with souls", the implications of such a "secession of the successful" for India, with its ready-made caste system, are even more horrendous. As if fragmentation of the Indian people on the basis of religion and ritualism was not enough, now the nation is being torn asunder on a political-economic basis too.

In the recent past itself, first the NRIs voted with their feet against India: they physically seceded. Their protestations of residual patriotism too were proved false in the summer of 1991 when their run on money deposited in India made the mother country's balance of payments crisis even more acute than it had already been made by the profligacy of domestic yuppies and the deliberate drumming up of India's lowered credit rating by demonstrably fallacious agencies like Moody's. Now, emulating the NRIs in mentally if not physically seceding from India, are the new economic policy-makers whose efforts are geared to fragmenting the nation much more effectively than was achieved by Radcliffe when he drew lines on a map in 1947.

The contours of nations in today's world are determined by economic factors more than ever before. Indeed, it was realised nearly a century and a half ago that "the workers have no nation". The migration of the poor across regions, nations and even continents in search of livelihood was adequate testimony to that. In fact, the first lot of migrants from India too were pushed by poverty. It is only the more recent NRIs who, having taken advantage of expensive education substantially subsidised by the people of this country, were pulled by greed.

Now it can be said that it is not the worker who has no nation but the bourgeois and his mercenary ideologue. The patently deceitful ambiguity of the BJP between the call of a US-dominated globalisation and an atavistic nationalism testifies this. At the same time, the coyness of the Congress government in taking action against black money even as it applies itself to reforming the legitimate economy on lines laid out in its memorandum submitted to the IMF, is testimony of the preparedness of the privileged to secede from the national mainstream. For, as anyone even slightly familiar with Euclidean geometry knows, the characterising feature of parallels is that they can never meet on a flat plane. The same applies to parallel economies. Only when the nation is sufficiently rounded that parallel economies can be made to converge at the poles of growth.

Both the scenarios of disintegration and secession of the successful are pessimistic though not unrealistic. However, there does exist a third alternative for India, an alternative that is premised on hope, ideals and human values.

The alternative lies in the formation of an India based on equity—social, economic, political, federal and gender-based. It calls for a constitution of India on truly republican principles — deeper and more multidimensional than mere formal democracy, an India where even the poor matter as citizens of an autonomous republic. This requires a considered evaluation of India's past, a critical examination of its present and a vision of its future.

Such an India cannot be formed on the basis of borrowed blueprints. It has to be invented anew.

REFERENCES

Ahmad, Imtiaz (1973): *Caste and Social Stratification Among Muslims in India*, Delhi: Manohar.

Akbar, M.J. (1985): *India: The Siege Within*, Penguin Books.

Alam, J. (1990): "The Muslim Voice In Post-Independence India", Seminar on Hinduism, Tubingen.

Alexander, K.C. (1975): Agrarian Tension in Thanjavur, Hyderabad: National Institute of Community Development.

Ambedkar, B.R. (1946): *What Congress and Gandhi Have Done to the Untouchables*, Bombay: Thacker.

Ambedkar, B.R. (1946a): *Who Were the Shudras?*, Bombay: Thacker.

Ambedkar, B.R. (1979): "Castes in India: Their Mechanism, Genesis and Development", *Selected Writings*, Bombay: Government of Maharashtra.

Annamalai, E.(ed.) (1979): *Language Movements in India*, Mysore: Central Institute of Indian Languages.

Arrighi, G. (1982): "A Crisis of Hegemony" in Samir Amin *et al.* (eds.), *Dynamics of Global Crisis*, London: Macmillan.

Aurora, A.S. (1972): *Tribe, Caste, Class Encounters*, Hyderabad: Administrative Staff College.

Bailey, F.G. (1961): "Tribe and Caste in India", *Contributions to Indian Sociology*, No. V: 7-19.

Bailey, F.G. (1977): "The Definition of Tribe", in Romesh Thapar (ed.), *Tribe, Caste and Religion in India*, Delhi: Macmillan India Ltd., pp. 7-14.

Barnett, Margueritte Ross and Stephen (1970): "Contemporary Peasant and Post-Peasant Alternatives in Tamil Nadu: The Idea of a Militant Untouchable", *Annals of the New York Academy of Science*, 220.

Baxi, U. (1986): Cited in Veena Das (1990).

Beteille, Andre (1974): *Studies in Agrarian Social Structure*, Delhi: Oxford.

Beteille, Andre (1977): "The Definition of Tribe" in Romesh Thapar (ed.) *Tribe, Caste and Religion in India*, Delhi: Macmillan.

Bhowmick, P.K. (1982): "Approach to Tribal Welfare", in Buddadeb Chaudhury (ed.), *Tribal Development in India: Problems and Prospects*, Delhi: Inter-India Publications.

Bhushan, Shashi (1977): "Bihar: The Belchhi Killings", *Economic and Political Weekly*, 18 June.

Bose, P.K. (1981): "Stratification among Tribals in Gujarat", *Economic and Political Weekly*, 16(6): 191-96.

Brass, Paul R. (1974): *Language, Religion and Politics in North India*, New York: Cambridge.

Brass, Paul R. (1991): *Ethnicity and Nationalism: Theory and Comparison*, New Delhi: Sage.

Breman, Jan (1974): *Patronage and Exploitation: Changing Patterns of Agrarian Relations in South Gujarat*, Berkeley: University of California Press.

Breman, Jan (1976): "A Dualistic Labour System: A Critique of the Informal Sector", *Economic and Political Weekly*, (48,49,50).

Breman, Jan (1977): "Labour Relations in the Formal and Informal Sectors", *Journal of Peasant Studies*, 4(3 and 4).

Byres, T.J. (1979): "Of Neo-populist Pipe Dreams, Daedalus in the Third World and the Myth of Urban Bias", *Journal of Peasant Studies*, January.

Byres, T.J. (1981): "The New Technology, Class Formation and Class Action in the Indian Countryside", *Journal of Peasant Studies*, July.

Chakraborty, D. (1976): "Communal Riots and Labour", Calcutta: Centre for Studies in Social Sciences (Occasional Paper).

Chatterjee, Partha (1990): "A Religion of Urban Domesticity," Seminar on Hinduism, Tubingen.

Chattopadhyaya, D. (1968): *Lokayata*, New Delhi: Peoples Publishing House.

Chaube, S.K. (1982): "Nation-Building and Politics in the Northeast Indian Hills", in K.S. Singh (ed.), *Tribal Movements in India*, Vol. I, New Delhi: Manohar, pp. 27-37.

Choudhry, Mamata (1977): *Tribes of Ancient India*, Calcutta: Indian

Museum.

Dalwai, Hamid (1969): *Muslim Politics In India*, Bombay: Nachiketa.

Danda, A.K. (1973): *Tribal Economics and Their Transformations*, New Delhi: Indian Council for Social Science Research.

Das, Arvind N. (1983): *Agrarian Unrest and Socio-economic Change in Bihar 1900-1980*, Delhi: Manohar.

Das, Arvind N. (1984): "Class in Itself, Caste for Itself: Social Articulation in Bihar", *Economic and Political Weekly*, 19 (37), 15 September.

Das, Veena (1990): "Cultural Rights and the Definition of Community", IDPAD Seminar.

Das Gupta, Ranjit (1976): "Factory Labour in Eastern India: Sources of Supply, 1855-1946", *Indian Economic and Social History Review*, 13(3).

Das Gupta, Ranjit (1982): "Workers In the Jute Industry" in Arvind N. Das et al. (eds.), *The Worker And The Working Class*, PECCE, New Delhi.

David, Kumar and Kadirgamar, Santasilan (1989): *Ethnicity*, Hongkong: Arena.

Dena, Lal (1979): "Manipur Under Paramountcy of the British Crown: Some Anomalies of Colonial Rule 1891-1919", *Bengal Past and Present*, XCVIII (1): 64-79.

Desai, A.R. (1963): *The Scheduled Tribes*, Bombay: Popular Prakashan.

Desai, A.R. (1977): "Tribes in Transition" in Romesh Thapar (ed.), *Tribe, Caste and Religion in India*, Delhi: Macmillan.

Desai, A.R. (1977): "Introduction" in S.C. Dube (ed.), *Tribal Heritage of India*, Vol. 1, New Delhi: Vikas.

Desai, A.R. and Pillai, S.D. (1972): *A Profile of an Indian Slum*, Bombay: Popular Prakashan.

De Swaan, A. (1990): "Political and Linguistic Integration", IDPAD Seminar.

Dhanagare, D.N. (1974): *Peasant Movements In India*, New Delhi: Oxford.

Dos Santos, Theotonio (1970): "The Concept of Social Class", *Science and Society*, 34(2).

Dube, S.C. (1977): *Tribal Heritage of India*, New Delhi: Vikas.

Dumont, Louis (1970): *Homo Hierarchus*, Chicago: Chicago University.

Dushkin, Lelah (1979): "Backward Class, Benefits and Social Class in India", *Economic and Political Weekly*, 7 April.

Dutt, R.P. (1949): *India Today*, Bombay: Peoples Publishing House.

Dutt, Sukumar (1926): *Problem of Indian Nationality*, Calcutta: University of Calcutta.

Engineer, A.E. (1987): *The Shah Bano Controversy*, Delhi: Orient Longman.

Frankel, Francine and Rao, M.S.A. (1989, 1990): *Dominance and State Power in Modern India*, Delhi: Oxford.

Ghosh, Anjan (1979): "Caste Idiom for Class Conflict: The Case of Khanjhawala", *Economic and Political Weekly*, 3 February.

Ghurye, G.S. (1932): *Caste and Race in India*, London.

Ghurye, G.S. (1943): *The Aboriginals — So-called — And Their Future*, Pune: Gokhale Institute.

Ghurye, G.S. (1963): *The Scheduled Tribes*, Bombay: Popular.

Ghurye, G.S. (1977): "Colonial Economics in South India", *Economic and Political Weekly*, 26 March.

Godelier, Maurice (1977): *Perspectives in Marxist Anthropology*, Cambridge.

Golwalkar, M.S. (1947): *We or Our Nationhood Defined*, Nagpur: Bharat Prakashan.

Gough, Kathleen (1974): "Indian Peasant Uprisings", *Economic and Political Weekly*, IX: 1391-1412.

Gough, Kathleen (1977): "Indian Peasant Uprisings", *Economic and Political Weekly*, 26 March.

Guha, Amalendu (1967): "Ahom Migration: Its Impact on Rice Economy of Medieval Assam", *Artha Vijnana*, 2(9).

Gupta, Raghuraj (1976): *Hindu-Muslim Relations*, Lucknow: Ethnographic and Folk Culture Society.

Habib, Irfan (1963): *The Agrarian System of Moghul India: 1556-1707*, London: Oxford University Press.

Haimendorf, C. Von Furer (1948): *The Raj Gonds of Adilabad: A Peasant Culture of Deccan*, Macmillan and Co.

Halbfass, W. (1990): "Practical Vedanta", Seminar on Hinduism, Tubingen.

Harcourt, Max (1977): "Kisan Populism and Revolution in Rural India", in D.A. Low (ed.) *Congress and the Raj*, Columbia: South Asia Books.

Hardy, Friedham (1990): "A Radical Reassessment of the Vedic Heritage", Seminar on Hinduism, Tubingen.

Hobsbawm Eric and Terence Ranger (eds.) (1983): *The Invention of Tradition*, Cambridge: Cambridge University Press.

Holmstrom, M. (1984): *Industry and Inequality: The Social Anthropology of Indian Labour*, Cambridge: University Press.

Humphries, J. (1977): "The Working Class Family, Womens Liberation and Class Struggle: The Case of Nineteenth Century British History", *The Review of Radical Political Economy*, Fall.

Inden, Ronald (1990): *Imagining India*, London: Blackwell.

India, (1955): *Report of the States Reorganisation Commission*, Delhi.

India, (1956): *Report of the Official Language Commission*, New Delhi.

India, (1966): *The Constituent Assembly Debates*, Vols. I to XII, New Delhi.

India (1975): *Towards Equality: Report of the Status of Women in India*, New Delhi.

Jain, R.K. (1979): "Seasonal Migration of Tribal Labour", *Economic and Political Weekly*, XIV: 1727-32.

Jha, Vivekanand (1975): "Stages in the History of Untouchables, *Indian Historical Review*, 2 : 14-31.

Jose, A.V. (1977): "Origins of Trade Unionism Among Agricultural Labourers in Kerala", *Social Scientist*, July.

Kapadia, K.M. and Pillai, S.D. (1972): *Industrialisation and Rural Society*, Bombay: Popular Prakashan.

Keer, Dhananjay (1974): *Dr. Ambedkar: Life and Mission*, Bombay: Popular Prakashan.

Khubchandani, L.M. (1979): "A Demographic Typology for Hindi, Urdu, Punjabi Speakers in South Asia" in Stephen Wurm *et al.*, *Language and Society*, The Hague: Mouton.

Klass, Morton (1980): *Caste: The Emergence of the South Asian Social System*, Philadelphia: Institute for the Study of Human Issues.

Kosambi, D.D. (1950): "The Origin of Brahmin Gotras", *Journal of the Bombay Branch of the Royal Asiatic Society*, 26, pp. 21-80.

Kosambi, D.D. (1957): "The Bourgeoisie Comes of Age in India" in *Exasperating Essays: Exercises in the Dialectical Method*,

Poona: Mrs. Vijaya Bhagwat, C/o Peoples Book House.

Kosambi, D.D. (1962): *Myth and Reality: Studies in the Formation of Indian Culture*, Bombay: Popular Prakashan.

Kosambi, D.D. (1975): *An Introduction to the Study of Indian History*, Bombay: Popular Prakashan (Reprint).

Kosambi, D.D. (1975a): *The Culture and Civilisation of India in Historical Outline*, Delhi: Vikas (Reprint).

Kothari, Rajni (1970): *Politics In India*, Delhi: Orient Longman.

Krishnaji, N. (1979): "Agrarian Relations and the Left Movement in Kerala", *Economic and Political Weekly*, 3 March.

Laclau, E. (1977): *Politics and Ideology In Marxist Theory*, London: New Left Books.

Lambert, P.D. (1963): *Workers, Factories and Social Change*, Princeton University.

Lenin, V.I. (1972) *Collected Works*, Vols. 20, 29, Moscow: Progress Publishers.

Lenin, V.I. (1976): "What Is To Be Done?" in *Selected Works*, Moscow: Progress Publishers.

Lutt, Jurgen (1990): "From Krishna Leela to Ramraj," Seminar on Hinduism, Tubingen.

Luthera, V.P. (1964): *The Concept of the Secular State and India*, Oxford.

Mamoria, C.B. (1957): *Tribal Demography In India*, Allahabad: Kitab Mahal.

Mandal, B.B. (1975): "Are Tribal Cultivators in Bihar to be called Peasants?", *Man in India*, 55(4).

Mandal, B.P. (1981): *Report of the Backward Classes Commission*, New Delhi.

Mandelbaum, D.G. (1970): *Society In India*, Bombay: Popular.

Marriot, Mckum and Ronald Inden (1974): "Caste System", *Encyclopaedia Britannica*.

Marriot, Mckum and Ronald Inden (1977): "Towards an Ethnosociology of South Asian Caste Systems" in David Kenneth (ed.), *The New Wind*, The Hague: Mouton.

Marx, Karl (1941): *Letter to Kugelmann*, London: Lawrence and Wishart.

Marx, Karl (1951a): "A Contribution to the Critique of Political Economy", in Marx and Engels, *Selected Works*, Moscow:

Progress Publishers.

Marx, Karl (1951b): "The Eighteenth Brumaire of Louis Bonaparte" in *Selected Works*, Moscow: Progress Publishers.

Marx, Karl (1971): *Capital*, Vols. I, III, Moscow: Progress Publishers.

Marx, Karl (1973): *Grundrisse*, London: Penguin.

Marx, Karl (1974): *Capital*, Vol. III, Moscow: Progress Publishers.

Marx, Karl (1976): *Capital: A Critique of Political Economy*, London: Penguin.

Marx, Karl (1976b): "Manifesto of the Communist Party", in *Collected Works*, Moscow: Progress Publishers.

Marx, Karl and Engels, Fredrick (1942): *The German Ideology*, London.

Marx, Karl and Engels, Fredrick (1945): *The German Ideology*, Calcutta: Modern Publications.

Marx, Karl and Engels, F. (1979): *Pre-Capitalist Socio-Economic Formations*, Moscow: Progress Publishers.

Meillassoux, Claude (1972): "From Reproduction to Production: A Marxist Approach to Economic Anthropology", *Economy and Society*, I (1).

Mencher, Joan (1974): *Agriculture And Social Structure In South India*, Delhi: Oxford.

Mies, Maria (1979): "Consequences of Capitalist Development for Women in the Rural Subsistence Sector in India", Institute of Social Studies, The Hague, Mimeo.

Mintz, S. (1977): "The So-called World System", *Dialectical Anthropology*, II (4).

Misra, Bani Prasanna (1979): "Agrarian Relations in a Khasi State", *Economic and Political Weekly*, XIV: 888-92.

Misra, Bani Prasanna (1982): "Kirata Karyokinesis" in Arvind N. Das and V. Nilakant (eds.), *Agrarian Relations In India*, New Delhi: Manohar.

Mishra, B.G. (1979): "Language Movements In The High Region" in Annamalai (1979).

Mitra, Asok (1977): "The Tribal Habitat", *Frontier*, 9(24-26): 10-14.

Mookerji, R.K. (1954): *Fundamental Unity of India*, Bombay: Bharatiya Vidya Bhavan.

Morris, Morris D. (1965): *The Emergence of an Industrial Labour*

Force in India, Barkeley: University of California.

Mukherjee, Ramakrishna (1974): "The Sociologist and the Social Reality", *Sociological Bulletin*, 23(2).

Mukherjee, R.K. (1948): *The Indian Working Class*, Bombay: Allied Publishers.

Munck, R. (1986): *The Difficult Dialogue: Marxism and Nationalism*, London Zed Books.

Mundle, Sudipto (1978): Bonded Labour In India: The Case of Palamau, Mimeo, II PA, New Delhi.

Myrdal, Gunnar (1968): *Asian Drama: An Inquiry Into The Poverty of Nations*, New York: Pantheon.

Narayan, Hemendra (1978): "Bihar: The Pupri Killings", *Economic and Political Weekly*, 16 September.

Nayar, B.R. (1966): *Minority Politics in the Punjab*, Princeton.

Neale, Walter (1975): "Land is to Rule" in R.E. Frykenberg (ed.), *Land Control and Social Structure in Indian History*, Wisconsin: University of Wisconsin (Reprinted in 1979 by Manohar, Delhi).

Nehru, Jawaharlal (1946): *The Discovery of India*, Calcutta: Signet Press.

Niehoff, A. (1959): *Factory Workers In India*, Milwaukee: Public Museum.

Ollman, Bertell (1968): "Marx's Use of Class", *The American Journal of Sociology*, 73 (5), March.

OMalley, L.S.S. (1941): *Modern India and the West*, London.

OMalley, L.S.S. (1976): *Indias Social Heritage*, New Delhi: Vikas (First published in 1934).

Omvedt, Gail (1976): *Cultural Revolt in a Colonial Society: The Non-Brahman Movement in Western India, 1870-1930*, Pune: Scientific Socialist Education Trust.

Omvedt, Gail (1980): "Migration in Colonial India", *Journal of Peasant Studies*, 7(2).

Omvedt, Gail(ed.) (1982): *Land, Caste and Politics in Indian States*, Delhi: Authors Guild.

Pandey, Gyan (1990): "Hindus and others: The Militant Hindu Construction", Seminar on Hinduism, Tubingen.

Patankar, Bharat and Omvedt, Gail (1975): "Perspective for Administration and Development of the Scheduled Tribes", in

V.R.K. Paramahansa (ed.) *Perspectives on Tribal Development and Administration*, Hyderabad: National Institute of Community Development.

Patankar, Bharat and Gail Omvedt, (1977): "The Bourgeois State in Post-Colonial Social Formations", *Economic and Political Weekly*, 12 : 2165-77.

Patankar, Bharat and Gail Omvedt, (1979): "The Dalit Liberation Movement in Colonial India", *Economic and Political Weekly*, Annual Number, February.

Pathy, Jaganath (1976): "Political Economy of Kandhaland", *Man in India*, 56(1): 1-36.

Pathy, Jaganath (1982): "An Outline Of Modes of Production in Tribal India", in Buddhadeb Chaudhuri (ed.), *Tribal Development in India : Problems and Prospects*, New Delhi: Inter India Publications, pp. 23- 48.

Pathy, Jaganath, Suguna Paul, Manu Bhaskar and Jayaram Panda (1976): "Tribal Studies in India: An Appraisal", *Eastern Anthropologist*, 29(4): 399-417.

Patnaik, Utsa (1976): "Class Differentiation Within the Peasantry", *Economic and Political Weekly*, XI (39): A-82-101.

Poulantzas, N. (1978): *State, Power, Socialism*, London: New Left Books.

Ramaswami, E.A. (1977): *The Worker and His Union*, New Delhi: Allied Publishers.

Ram, Kalpana (1981): "The Indian Working Class: Critical Issue in the Study of Class Formation in the Third World", Thesis submitted to Macquarie University, Sydney.

Ram, N. (1979): "The Dravidian Movement in its Pre-Independence Phase", *Economic and Political Weekly,* Annual Number, February.

Rao, M.S.A. (ed.) (1978): *Social Movements in India*, Delhi: Manohar.

Roy, A.K. (1982): "Jharkhand Movement and the Question of Internal Colonialism" in RSU (1982).

Roy, S.C. (1982): "The Effects on the Aborigines of Chhotanagpur of the Contact with Western Civilization", *Man in India*, 62(1) : 65-102, Reprint.

Roy Burman, B.K. (1975): "Perspectives for Administration and Development of the Scheduled Tribes" in V.R.K. Paramhansa (ed.) *Perspectives on Tribal Development and Administration*, Hyderabad: NICD.

RSU. (1982): *Nationality Question In India*: Seminar Papers, Hyderabad.

Saberwal, S. (1976): *Mobile Men: Limits to Social Change in Urban Punjab*, New Delhi: Vikas.

Sachchidananda (1964): *Culture Change in Tribal Bihar : Munda and Oraon*, Calcutta : Firma K.L. Mukhopadhyay.

Sahlins, M.D. (1968): *Tribesmen*, New Jersey: Prentice Hall.

Savarkar, V.D. (1942): *Hindutva*, Poona: V.G. Ketkar.

Savarkar, V.D. (1949): *Hindu Rashtra Darshan*, Bombay: L.G. Khare.

Scott, C.D. (1976): "Peasants, Proletarianization and the Articulation of Modes of Production", *The Journal of Peasant Studies*, III(3) : 321- 41.

Sengupta, Nirmal (1980): "Class and Tribe in Jharkhand", *Economic and Political Weekly*, 5 April.

Sengupta, Nirmal (1982): *Fourth World Dynamics*, New Delhi.

Shah, Ghanshyam (1975): *Caste Association and Political Process in Gujarat*, Bombay: Popular Prakashan.

Shah, Ghanashyam (1976): "Stratification Among the STs in Bhrauch and Panchamahal Districts of Gujarat", Surat: Centre for Social Studies, Mimeo.

Shah, Ghanashyam (1979): "Tribal Identity and Class Differentiation", *Economic and Political Weekly*, 14: 459- 64.

Shah, Ghanshayam (1983): *Minorities and Nation-Building*, Varanasi: BHU.

Shah, Ghanshayam (1984): *Economic Differentiations and Tribal Identity*, Delhi: Ajanta.

Shanin, Tedodor, (1978): "Defining Peasants: Conceptualisations and De-Conceptualisations: Old and New in a Marxist Debate", Manchester University.

Shakir, Moin (1972): *Muslims In Free India*, New Delhi: Kalamkar.

Shakir, Moin (1980): *Politics of Minorities*, Delhi: Ajanta.

Sharma, Baldev R. (1970): "The Industrial Worker: Some Myths and Realities", *Economic and Political Weekly*, Bombay, 30 May.

Sharma, Baldev R. (1973): "The Indian Industrial Worker: His Origin, Experience and Destiny", *Economic and Political Weekly*, Bombay, Review of Management, June.

Sharma, R.S. (1965): *Indian Feudalism*, University of Calcutta.

Sharma, R.S. (1975): "Class Formation and Its Material Basis in Upper Gangetic Basin c. 1000-500 B.C.", *Indian Historical Review*, 2.

Sheth, N.R. (1968): *The Social Framework of an Indian Factory*, Manchester: University Press.

Shivkumar, S.S. (1978): "Transformation of the Agrarian Economy in Tondamandalam, 1760-1900", *Social Scientist*, 70.

Singh, K. Suresh (1969): "Tribal Land Organisation in Chhotanagpur and its Development", in *Trends of Socio- Economic Change in India 1871-1961*, Simla : Indian Institute of Advanced Study: Vol. 7.

Singh, K. Suresh (1971): "State Formation in Tribal Societies: Some Preliminary Observations", *Journal of Indian Anthropology*, VI : 161- 81.

Singh, K.S. (1977): "From Ethnicity To Regionalism: A Study in Tribal Politics and Movements in Chhotanagpur from 1900 to 1975" in S.C. Malik (ed.) Dissent, *Protest and Reform in Indian Civilisation*, Simla: IIAS.

Singh, K. Suresh (1982): "Transformation of Tribal Society: Integration vs. Assimilation", *Economic and Political Weekly*, 17(33): 1318-25; 17(34) : 1376-84.

Singh, K. Suresh (1985): *Indian Tribes In Transition*, Delhi: Manohar.

Singh, Randhir (1990): *Of Marxism and Indian Politics*, Delhi: Ajanta.

Sinha, Arun (1978): "Bajitpur: Landlords Violence", *Economic and Political Weekly*, 10 December.

Sinha, Arun (1978a): "Class War in Bhojpur", *Economic and Political Weekly*, 7 and 21 February.

Sinha, Arun (1982): "Class War, Not Atrocities Against Harijans" in Arvind N. Das (ed.), *Agrarian Movements in India: The Case of Bihar*, London: Frank Cass.

Sinha, Arun (1991): *Against The Few*, London: Zed Press.

Sinha, Surajit (1958): "Tribal Cultures of Peninsular India as a Dimension of Little Tradition in the Study of Indian Civilization: A Preliminary Statement", *Journal of American Folklore*, 71: 504-18.

Sinha, Surajit (1965): "Tribe-Caste and Tribe-Peasant Continua in Central India", *Man in India*, 45(1).

Smith, D.E. (1963): *India as a Secular State*, Princeton.

Sontheimer, G.D. (1990): "The Erosion of Folk Religion", Seminar on Hinduism, Tubingen.

Srinivas, M.N. (1962): *Caste in Modern India*, Bombay: Asia Publishing House.

Srinivas, M.N. (1965): "Tribe-Caste and Tribe-Peasant Continua in India", *Man in India*, 45 (1).

Srivastava, Arun (1978): "The Bishrampur Carnage", *Frontier*, 22 April.

Srivastava, Arun (1980): "Class and Caste in the Parasbigha Massacre", *Economic and Political Weekly*, 23 February.

Srivastava, Arun (1980a): "Behind Pipra", *Frontier*, 29 March.

Srivastava, Sushil (1991): *The Disputed Mosque: A Historial Inquiry*, New Delhi: Vistar.

Stavenhagen, Rodolfo (1975): *Social Classes in Agrarian Societies*, New York: Anchor Press.

Sundarayya, P. (1977): "Class Differentiation of the Peasantry", *Social Scientist*, 5(8): 51-83; 5(9): 45-60.

Thapar, Romila (1974): *A History of India*, Harmondsworth: Penguin.

Thapar, Romila (1975): *The Past and Prejudice*, New Delhi: National Book Trust.

Thompson, E.P. (1968): *The Making of the English Working Class*, London: Penguin.

Thorner, Daniel (1976): *The Agrarian Prospect in India*, Bombay: Allied.

Tinker, Hugh (1974): *A New System of Slavery : The Export of Indian Labour Overseas : 1830-1920*, Oxford University Press.

Upadhyaya, A.K. (1980): "Peasantisation of Adivasis in Thane District", *Economic and Political Weekly*, 15 (52): A134-A146.

Vanaik, Achin (1990): *The Painful Transition: Bourgeois Democracy In India*, London: Verso; Madras: BR Publishers.

Vidyarthi, L.P. and Rai, B.K. (1977): *The Tribal Culture of India*, Delhi: Concept.

Vijayendra, T., Mohan Mani, Prem Pradeep and Probal Roy (1982): "Reservation of Jobs for Scheduled Castes and Tribes", New Delhi: *Human Futures*.

Von Stietencron, H. (1990): "Posing Question and Finding Answers", Seminar on Hinduism, Tubingen.

Wadhwa, K.K. (1975): *Minority Safeguards in India*, Delhi: Thompson Press.

Westergaard, John and Resler, H. (1976): *Class In A Capitalist Society*, Harmondsworth.

INDEX